JUNGLE WIFE

JUNGLE WIFE

by Sasha and Edith Siemel

and Gordon Schendel

DOUBLEDAY & COMPANY, INC., GARDEN CITY, N.Y., 1949

A PATHFINDER BOOK REPRINT EDITION
Complete and Unabridged

Printed in the United States of America

ISBN: 979-8-8691-2064-9

ILLUSTRATIONS

BRAZIL
MATO GROSSO
Cuyaba
Xarayes
Descalvados
Corumbá
Miranda
Rio De Janeiro
South Pacific Ocean
South Atlantic Ocean
SOUTH AMERICA

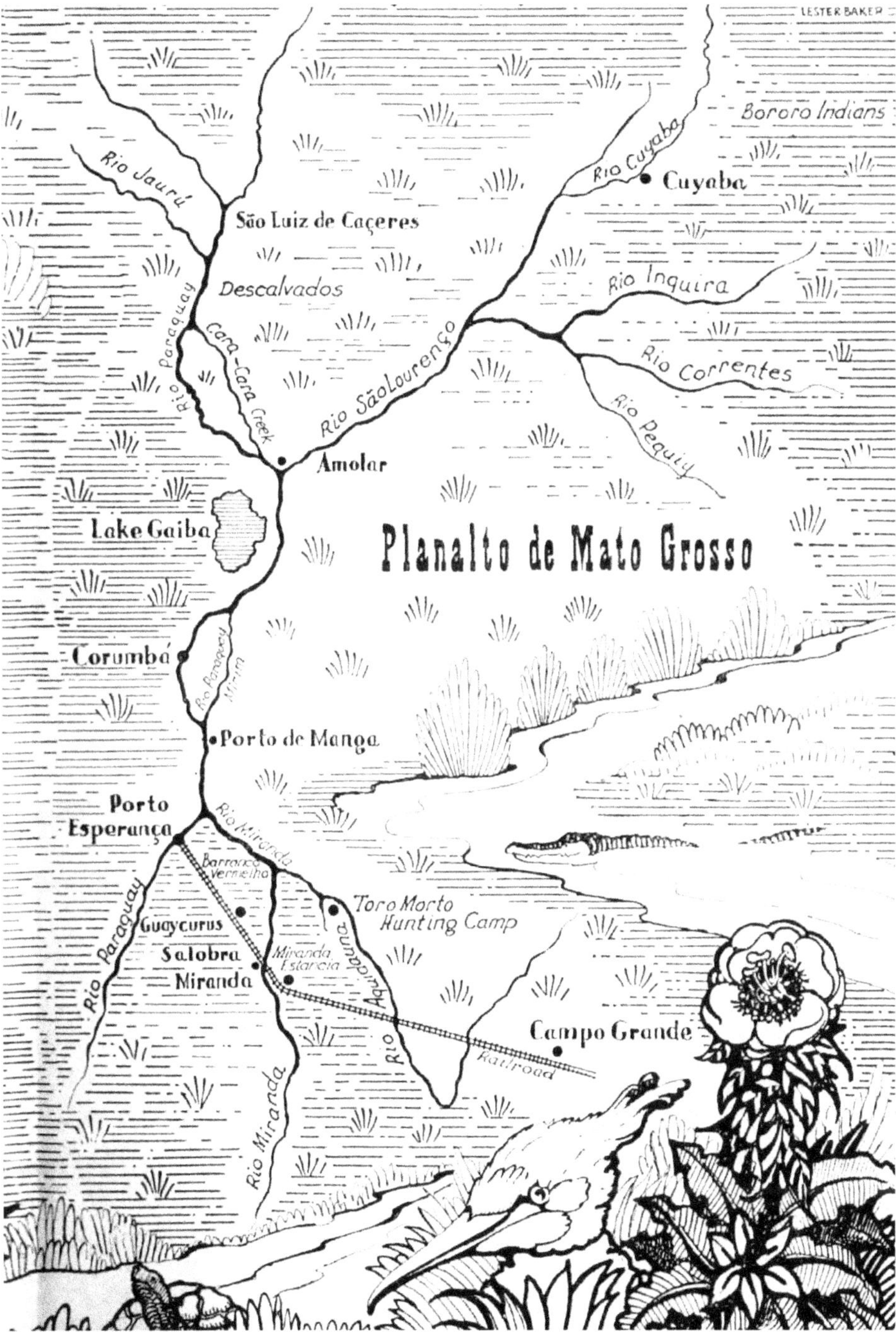

LESTER BAKER
Rio Jauru
São Luiz de Caçeres
Descalvados
Rio Paraguay
Cara-Cara Creek
Rio SãoLourenço
Bororo Indians
Rio Cuyaba
Cuyaba
Rio Inquira
Rio Correntes
Rio Pequiu
Amolar
Planalto de Mato Grosso
Lake Gaiba
Corumba
Rio Bonqueq Mirim
Porto de Manga
Porto
Esperança
Rio Miranda
Barranco
Vermelho
Rio Paraguay
Guaycurus
Salobra
Miranda
Miranda
Estancia
Toro Morto
Hunting Camp
Rio Aquidauna
Campo Grande
Railroad
Rio Miranda

THE BLAZING BRAZILIAN SUN STOOD HIGH OVERHEAD LIKE a white-hot magnet, sucking up the moisture that is the lifeblood of the jungle. Heat waves shuddered over the glittering Upper Paraguay River and blurred the dusty greens of its far shore. The drone of myriad insects steamed up from the rank, choked thickets in a monotony broken by the ragged cries of quarreling parrots, parakeets, and toucans. But despite these overtones of invisible activity, the entire Mato Grosso seemed to be in slow motion—lethargic and weighted down by the almost physical heaviness of the heat.

It was June 1940—and, south of the equator, a beautiful winter day.

"Damn you, Rupert dear! Do that once more, and I swear I'll hang a cowbell around your neck!"

I frowned in exasperation. Then I amended with a rueful smile, "I would, that is, if I had a cowbell—and if you had a neck."

Rupert was always underfoot; perhaps his habit of coming up noiselessly behind me wouldn't have been so annoying if he hadn't been an eight-foot boa constrictor.

Discounting Rupert, I was alone in our grass hut, rather lazily occupied in being domestic—straightening the mosquito netting over our woven-fiber hammocks and flicking a dustcloth across the row of books on the battered steamer trunk—doing this not in a little house dress and ruffled tea apron, but in a shirt, jodhpurs, and riding boots.

Whenever I wandered near the open side of the hut I paused to sniff appreciatively, for I fancied I could detect an alien, incongruous note among the jungle's fecund vegetable odors: the fresh, spicy smell of newly cut lumber. From beyond the tangled undergrowth at the river's edge there sounded recurrently the rasp of a hand saw, the sharp clatter of sawed board ends falling on a plank deck, and a running fire of conversation in hearty male voices.

"Edith, it's finished!" Sasha shouted abruptly. "Come and be impressed!"

"Kwa-a-a-wk! Kwa-a-a-wk!" our pet macaws, Rainy and J. Pluvius, squawked insolently back; they began critical, sotto-voce cluckings to each other. They were perched on the sloping roof above me; their yard-long, iridescent blue-and-green tail feathers dangled below the palm thatch and, as they moved about, from time to time obstructed my view of the river.

"Hurry, you sluggard!" Sasha's voice urged teasingly.

All day, except at siesta time, Sasha had been busy with his two native helpers on the deck of our half-finished houseboat. He had been extremely secretive at breakfast about what they were working on, save to say it wasn't the houseboat itself. The current project would prove a masterpiece, he had asserted with a grin; I'd agree when I saw it.

"Yes, my dear Mr. Siemel!" I said with exaggerated meekness. "I'm coming!"

I walked around the live *acuri* palm that supported a corner of the roof, then brushed through a cloud of gaudy butterflies eddying in the sunshine, and started down the incline to the water's edge.

"You're not running? Such a deplorable lack of enthusiasm, my sweet!"

Sasha stood with his arms folded, waiting for me on the lumber-strewn deck of the houseboat. His mocking smile was belied by the eager impatience in his blue eyes, so oddly light against his suntanned face. In his nondescript attire—the old trousers and

2

the shirt that hung limply on his six-foot frame—he somehow looked as distinguished as he did in formal dress. The beard helped, of course: neatly trimmed, brown like his thick wavy hair, and touched with the same faint traces of gray.

His helpers were standing beside him, smiling broadly. Both were mestizos of mixed Negro and Indian blood; the diminutive, cocky Lauro was nearly black, but the larger, phlegmatic Rosando was brown-skinned and of mainly Indian extraction.

"Well, where is this masterpiece?" I demanded.

"Oh, when we finished it we chucked it into the river," Sasha said carelessly. "However, that's where it belongs."

He looked mysterious and highly pleased with himself. Flinging his arm around my shoulders, he led me to the rear deck, to which several of our spare dugouts were tied, and indicated his achievement with a vigorous sweep of his hand.

"Milady," he said flamboyantly, "we have created for you a palatial Hollywood pool, guaranteed against alligators, piranhas, and all other hazards to life and limb—complete with a perpetual supply of running water! Or, to be more prosaic, Edith," he concluded, "here is your bathtub. No more must you bathe in the water bucket. Luxury," he grinned, "has come to the jungle!"

I stared. A boxlike affair—about six feet long, five feet wide, and four feet deep—rested low in the water, suspended by a wooden framework between two dugouts attached to the houseboat. A neat plank walk led to it. The box held water to the same level as the surface of the river, and I could see that the river was flowing through it—through scores of holes bored in its ends. Sasha pointed out that while the holes let the water in, they were small enough to keep piranhas out.

"Clever, eh?" He looked almost insufferably smug.

"You mean you invented it all by yourself?" I parried. "You didn't see a blueprint in *Popular Science?*"

Sasha looked crestfallen and slightly perplexed, and I added hastily, "No, I guess I can't accuse you of that since you weren't brought up in the U.S. You're a genius, then, Sasha." I smiled and said emphatically, "You really are!"

And I really was delighted.

"In fact, Sasha," I went on slowly, suddenly conscious of the overwhelming heat and my shirt sticking wetly to my back, "in fact, broad daylight and all, I think I'd like to try it out right now!"

"Why not?" Sasha shrugged. "Launch yourself and dedicate it."

There was a scuffling of feet and a clearing of throats behind us; I'd forgotten about Lauro and Rosando. Lauro, the more forward and spokesman for the two, smiled politely.

"*Patrão,* if the senhora and you will excuse us, please"—he smiled again, diffidently—"Rosando and I will go after more firewood now."

"Yes?" Sasha cocked an eyebrow at the ample pile of cordwood on the bank. Then, biting his lip to hide his amusement, he said agreeably, "Go ahead, Lauro—go ahead!"

The men self-consciously hurried ashore, scrambled up the bank, and disappeared.

I looked at Sasha.

"Heavens," I said, "do you suppose they thought I was going to undress right here in front of them?"

Sasha chuckled. "Possibly. But more probably they were just being gallant, so you really could bathe at once if you wished. They heard you say you wanted to." He laughed. "After all, if you insist on speaking Portuguese with me for practice, don't forget they understand you too."

"Well—I might as well take them up on it," I concluded. I glanced about a little uneasily—a hang-over from my more civilized days—but except for a few alligators sunning themselves on a mud flat and several big storks fishing downstream, there were no possible observers. I began to unbutton the shirt I wore; even though they were much too large for me, I practically lived in Sasha's shirts.

"Well, Senhor Siemel——" I paused significantly. "Are you less chivalrous than your helpers?"

Sasha grinned.

After giving me a kiss he strode down the gangplank. Halfway up the bank, he turned to call back flippantly:

"Don't drown now! Women are scarce in the jungle."

When he, too, had vanished, I leisurely resumed undressing, idly walking about the broad deck of the houseboat. So far, our floating home-to-be, which we'd already named *The River Gypsy,* was no more than a plank deck built on top of five thirty-six-foot dugouts. The superstructure, the "house" part of the houseboat, remained to be built. Although Sasha had been working on it for two months, he expected it would be several more before the houseboat was finished. The dugouts alone had represented weeks of backbreaking labor. Sasha and his helpers had felled several large *araputanga,* or mahogany, trees a couple of miles upriver and had dragged the logs by ox team to the bank, where with axes and adzes they had carved them out. The houseboat also was being built of mahogany, and it was an enormous job; every bit of lumber was sawed out from logs with a small kerosene-powered portable saw.

In spite of his helpers, Sasha was doing a great deal of the construction work himself, and he would have to do all of the finer finishing. Like most Mato Grosso men, Lauro and Rosando were excellent cowboys but not carpenters; God help them when they picked up any tool but the ax. In addition, they were temperamentally unsuited for long-term projects such as this; their interest lagged, and for them *amanhã* was always the busiest day of the week. In the meantime Sasha and I were living in the grass hut on the bank. Lauro and Rosando, with their wives and children—one had six kids; one had three—occupied similar huts a short distance away.

A sudden splash startled me; then I saw it was merely an alligator sliding into the water.

It certainly was going to be a treat to bathe in a full-sized tub. The last time I'd been able to was in the hotel in Rio de Janeiro on our honeymoon, five months ago. It seemed ironic that we should suffer from a lack of bathing facilities now, with a mile-wide river at our front door. But after being married in January, we had come here, to Sasha's old headquarters on the Upper Paraguay River, at the height of the rainy season when the river was bristling with piranhas. And although these little cannibal fish had decreased considerably with the end of the wet months, they were still too numerous for safety. After witnessing a swimmer being eaten alive —being reduced to a skeleton in only five minutes by a ravenous horde of the fighting, churning, razor-toothed fish—I didn't need any warnings from Sasha about piranhas.

Only three weeks ago we had had an unhappy demonstration

that the piranhas still were around. Cenaria, Lauro's wife, had been doing our laundry in the shallow water while her four-year-old daughter, Carlotta, sat on the bank idly watching. The mother was unmolested, but when the little girl playfully held her bare foot over the water a piranha leaped up and bit off her big toe!

Now undressed, I stepped out on the plank walk leading from the deck to our new built-in bathtub. The unclouded water rippling through the small holes made the straight lines of the new mahogany boards waver and curve. I swung myself in, and the water was deliciously cool.

I splashed about furiously for a minute, then stood still and watched the flowing, sunlit water warp my legs and thighs. No Hollywood star ever got such a thrill from her first marble pool. I leaned forward presently to study my reflected, flickering face. My bangs and long bob shot off at crazy angles.

So here I was, not Edith Bray now but Edith Siemel, in the heart of the wild Mato Grosso, five hundred miles upriver from Corumbá, the nearest frontier town; two thousand miles inland from Rio—and God knew how far from Philadelphia and my girlhood! Actually, though, my girlhood wasn't so far away as Philadelphia; I was just twenty-two. And because of this I'd had a heck of a time persuading Sasha his fifty years didn't necessitate a paternal attitude. I'd had to propose several times to convince him he wasn't too old for me—and I'd had to seize a writhing snake in my hands to change his idea that "the jungle is no place for a white woman."

I had first met Sasha at the University Club in Philadelphia when I was eighteen. He had been in the States to interest wealthy sportsmen in coming down to the Mato Grosso to hunt "tigers"—the South American *tigre,* or jaguar—for Sasha was a professional tiger hunter and earned his living by killing the huge cats that preyed on cattlemen's herds and by conducting sportsmen's expeditions. He had been born in Latvia but had run away from home as a boy and had knocked halfway around the world looking for adventure; he had found it in Brazil, finally, and had stayed there.

I had been so impressed by Sasha at that first meeting that I had gone home starry-eyed, so determined that I did the impossible—

6

I talked Mother into letting me go down to the Mato Grosso to hunt tigers!

And I had gone the next summer; not alone, of course, but with an older woman, a friend of Sasha's, Helen Post, acting as chaperone. We had stayed two months and each shot a tiger. Then, while Sasha was spear-fighting a third tiger, his revolver had accidentally gone off and discharged a bullet into his leg; we had managed, with his native helpers, to get him out of the jungle only after two weeks of travel by packhorse, oxcart, and dugout; according to the doctor at the hospital in Corumbá, in one more day gangrene would have set in. Sasha had gratefully said we "female tenderfeet" certainly had proved our mettle.

There was just room enough in the tub to stretch out and float. I lay back and stared dreamily up at the sky; high above a white heron was flapping its way across the river. . . .

I had returned to the States far from satisfied with one tiger hunt. Back in Philadelphia, I had spent my time writing innumerable letters to Sasha and waiting for the postman. And finally— I still don't know how I persuaded Mother—it had been agreed that I would again join Sasha in Rio the following July and spend several months in the jungle, serving as official photographer when he took parties of sportsmen tiger hunting. Then I had taken a quick course in photography.

Thus, in July 1939, I found myself once more in the Mato Grosso—and I had never left it since. As Sasha's girl photographer, I had always been well chaperoned by several sportsmen, to say nothing of Lauro and Rosando, but still I had been with Sasha constantly. And when I had realized his interest in me could hardly be based on my photographic skill, I had taken every opportunity to start breaking down his resistance.

I had been infuriated by Sasha's quixotic insistence that the difference in our ages was too great; that it wouldn't be fair to "bury" me in the jungle for the rest of my life. Our stormy sessions continued for months, over hundreds of miles of the Mato Grosso —in camp at dawn, riding over the grassy *largos* during the day, and, after the others had taken to their hammocks, around the fire at night. I had used every argument from "pish-tosh" and "piffle" to the one that completely outraged him: "Darling, won't you *ever* make an honest woman of me?"

Then, when I had almost given up, I finally succeeded one moonlit night as we sat on a log at the edge of a swamp, watching the fireflies glimmering over the water and listening to the hoarse bellowings of alligators. We had been quarreling over the usual subject—and abruptly I had seen a deadly coral snake weaving toward me through the swamp grass! I had had a horror of snakes, and screamed. Sasha had decapitated the snake with his machete and tossed its body into the underbrush; then he had turned to me and said with a maddening smile, "So you're the little girl who imagines she'd like to spend her life in the jungle with neighbors like that! I think this incident proves my point, dear."

I had sat without a comeback, silently raging at my stupid panic. And then fate had provided me with a second chance—another snake, presumably the first one's mate, slithered toward me. Gritting my teeth, I had drawn my machete and approached it stiffly, intending to chop off its head—or my own foot in the attempt. But I had almost screamed again when I neared it and realized that this snake was headless! It had been the same one, of course, propelled by spasmodic muscular contractions. Somehow, in a do-or-die attempt, I had forced myself to reach down, pick it up with its dreadful coils writhing against my wrist, and fling it back into the underbrush.

Shivering uncontrollably, I had stood there staring after it—and then I realized that Sasha's arms were around me and he was looking at me in a queer, admiring way and murmuring something that sounded like, "You win, dear; I surrender!" into my ear. . . .

A large fish jumped out of the river less than twenty feet away, and I watched the widening circle of ripples approaching the tub.

Why hadn't I thought to get soap from our hut? Well, I'd remember next time. This bath would have to be soapless. I wondered what Sasha was doing at the moment and why he hadn't returned to talk to me while I bathed. He probably was examining his guns; he hadn't been on a tiger hunt for a long time, and I knew he was anxious to go out again; he was always going over his guns.

Abruptly there was the sound of galloping horses. And a few seconds later I heard the warning by which all friendly travelers in the jungle announce their approach, a shouted:

"O de casa!"

"O de casa!" The call came again; I could hear horses whinny-ing as they were reined up.

"Amigos, approach!" It was Sasha's deep voice answering.

Then there was a babble of male voices exchanging greetings in Portuguese—sallies and laughter—and I could hear the jingle of spurs as the men alighted. Apparently they were just above me on the riverbank. A riderless horse poked his head into sight as he cropped leaves from the head-high bushes.

Ye Gods! I suddenly realized the predicament I was in.

If the men moved only a few feet nearer they could look right down on me—naked in my open-air bath! And my clothes were in a heap on the houseboat, fifteen feet away. I didn't dare leave the water to get them, for at that very moment someone would be bound to pop out.

Until now I had been lazily and sensuously enjoying every facet of my bath—the hot sun and the contrasting sharp coolness of the water, the luxury of a tub with a scenic view—but the realization that I was trapped immediately spoiled it all. The sun became too hot on my tender, untanned shoulders; the water became too cold. And this was particularly unpleasant because there was nothing I could do about it.

What was wrong with Sasha? Why didn't he get his visitors away from the river?

At that moment there was another burst of laughter from above, then louder words, as if the men were coming nearer. And I un-mistakably heard Sasha saying, *"The River Gypsy . . ."*

My God! Was Sasha going to show them the houseboat? Didn't he remember he had left me about to take a bath? What was the matter with him that he couldn't remember I was here? Surely he didn't think I had finished and dressed and gone? Or did he?

Indignant at being put in such a position, and beginning to shiver from being too long in the cold water, I became very angry with Sasha.

The voices came still closer, and there was the sound of several men crashing through the underbrush. I heard the word "house-boat." I remained indecisive only a fraction of a second longer, then angrily called out:

"Sasha! *Sasha!* Stop where you are! Don't you dare come a step nearer!"

There was an abrupt silence above me. Then I heard Sasha saying something to the men, and a second later he alone was looking down at me from the top of the bank. He peered at me motionlessly a moment, then began to grin.

"All right, laugh, darn you!" I shouted up furiously in English. "What were you planning on doing? Making me a sideshow for your visitors? Don't you have *any* respect for your wife?"

Sasha erased his grin and came silently down the bank a few feet.

"I'm sorry, my dear," he said soberly. "I apologize. I completely forgot you were here. We have some visitors. Four cowboys from the Descalvados Ranch. They just stopped to leave me a roll of copper screening that the Descalvados manager brought up from Corumbá."

I snorted indignantly.

"Well, take them away from here!" I demanded wrathfully. "I want to get out and get dressed."

Sasha continued to gaze down at me silently, and finally said, "Edith dear, no damage was done. They haven't seen you—and, in fact, don't even know why I held them back."

"I don't care," I shouted unreasonably. "Just *take them away!*"

"Certainly, my dear," he replied meekly. "I'll lead them far away—immediately."

Then he grinned wickedly, blew me a kiss—and disappeared in the underbrush.

Later, when I had retired unseen and fully clothed to our hut and brushed my hair—hard and angrily—my rage evaporated. I felt clean and polished and relaxed from my long soaking. And so what if my spouse was absent-minded? He was still Sasha. While I was smiling to myself over this Sasha walked into the hut. He gave me a conciliatory kiss on the top of my head and persuaded me to come out and meet his visitors.

They were talking volubly with Lauro, who, of course, had been a cowboy himself before he joined Sasha. One, who was introduced to me simply as Pedro, was extremely fat and almost toothless; the other three were younger and less remarkable. Each doffed his flat-brimmed felt sombrero and made an elaborate bow when he was presented to me—and thereafter pointedly avoided meeting my eyes, as custom decreed with another man's wife.

"The senhor has a handsome establishment," Pedro said, addressing Sasha after a somewhat awkward silence. He added, "Very handsome!" with a wave which took in our airy grass hut, the small corral of milch cows and saddle horses, and, farther down, the few cages in which Sasha kept his wild-animal pets.

Sasha smiled and thanked him.

"*Sim*, the senhor has made a fortunate choice of a site," the youngest-looking cowboy corroborated, in the manner of a veteran of the jungle generously complimenting one who possessed considerably less knowledge of the region. He added knowingly, "It is the only high ground along the river in thirty leagues. Here the floods will never touch one."

"Sim." Sasha smiled and forbore making the obvious retort—that it *should* be a fine site, for he had spent a week traveling up and down the river before selecting it. (And the wisdom of his choice had been borne out during the height of the past rainy season, when the headwaters of the Upper Paraguay for a length of six hundred miles surged over their banks and transformed the surrounding jungle into an island-studded lake two hundred miles wide, leaving us marooned but secure on our high site for nearly three months.)

Sasha then suggested to Lauro that our visitors might take pleasure in a drink of rum. And Lauro set off for our hut with a grin.

While we waited Sasha and the men discussed tigers and the relative scarcity of tiger signs in the neighborhood during the past few months. Absently listening, I studied the costumes of the cowboys, which always fascinated me.

The Mato Grosso's cowboys, or *vaqueiros,* are certainly colorful, and the outfits of these men from the Descalvados *Estancia* were typical. Each wore a silver-trimmed sombrero, a gaudy shirt, khaki trousers, and hip-high deerskin or calfskin leggings. And each had a hand-woven bright red poncho carelessly slung over his shoulder.

Seeing these waterproof wool blankets with the hole in the center gave me a sudden idea. Ponchos were used at night on the grassy largos as blankets, or in wet weather as raincoats, but they had a variety of other uses too. And I was going to invent a new use, starting tomorrow.

I knew that after my disconcerting experience just past I'd never be able to take another bath without some protection for modesty's sake. I'd get a bright red poncho and drape it over the tub! Sasha would roar at the idea, but let him.

Still discussing tigers, Sasha mentioned a spear fight, and as the vaqueiros were interested in seeing his spears, we moved off to our hut. I lagged behind, fascinated with the men's huge noisy spurs and their peculiar gait.

They wore enormous spurs with roweled rosettes six inches in diameter. And, like all vaqueiros, they were barefoot—which, combined with the size of their spurs, made walking quite difficult. The four of them rocking along behind Sasha walked not only pigeon-toed but also on tiptoe, for otherwise their oversized spurs would have enmeshed and tripped them.

Their spurs were made of iron, but hammered silver decorated their sombreros, saddles, reins, machetes, and six-shooters. Two of them even had their *tiradors* fastened about their waists with clasps of silver-mounted tiger teeth. (A tirador is a fringed little leather apron worn over the right hip to protect the trousers.)

We arrived at the hut and seated ourselves on several empty ammunition boxes. Lauro was there, very busily filling a quart bottle from the barrel and getting out a couple of tumblers; as he'd had plenty of time to rejoin us, he'd obviously been sampling the rum.

Lauro spoke hurriedly: "Would the patrão care to pour the drinks himself?"

But Sasha, an amused glint in his eyes, indicated with a wave that Lauro should do so.

Lauro filled one glass a third full of the colorless *cachaça,* or native sugar-cane rum (it is made by ranchers in small distilleries, and a fifty-gallon barrel costs twenty-five dollars; Sasha had put one by to last through the year), and then he filled the second glass to the brim. He handed the first to me and the second to the fat vaqueiro, as he was the oldest of our guests. (We had plenty of glasses, but Mato Grosso hospitality decrees that one is passed

12

around instead; Lauro had supplied me with a separate glass only in deference to my oft-expressed objections, within our own circle, to this practice; Sasha, of course, had long ago become habituated to the customs of the country.)

Pedro raised his brimming glass to Sasha and me.

"May the lives of the senhor y senhora be long and happy!" he said, tipping it; he halted for breath when he had it half emptied.

"Very fine cachaça," he grunted appreciatively. He passed the glass on reluctantly.

The others, in turn, each drank deeply and smacked their lips. And then Sasha had half a glassful, and the quart of rum was emptied.

The second quart was consumed more leisurely, for Sasha displayed one of his tiger spears—a twelve-inch, bayonetlike steel blade topped by a three-inch crosspiece on a six-foot hardwood shaft—and then the talk shifted to firearms. The men obviously were awed by Sasha's fairly large collection of guns.

Pedro proudly exhibited his .38 Smith & Wesson six-shooter with its handsome chased-silver mounting. He rubbed his thumb over it caressingly, and it was obvious that he considered it his most valuable possession.

"This was stolen from me once," he said almost dreamily. "While I was asleep. We were out on the largos. I woke up just as the thief galloped out of camp. When I reached for my gun it was gone, and I jumped on my horse and took after the dog. I caught him, too."

"And you recovered the gun, obviously." Sasha smiled. "Did you have difficulty?"

"Oh—no difficulty," said Pedro with a crooked grin. He gulped more cachaça and reached into his back pocket. "And the thief steals no more guns."

He brought his hand out of his pocket suddenly and opened it to display a couple of small objects. "Regard!"

I leaned forward for a closer look at the brown shriveled-looking things on his extended palm. Then I gasped with horror, for I saw that they were unmistakably human ears!

Pedro grinned, tossed them into the air, and caught them non-chalantly. "I took my receipt!"

There was a silence, which Pedro took as proper tribute to his feat. Then he shrugged modestly and stood up, returning the grisly objects carefully to his pocket.

"We are grateful to the senhor for his hospitality," he said politely. "But the sun is descending. We still have six leagues to ride to our camp site."

The other vaqueiros got to their feet rather unenthusiastically. They were all on their way to a jungle camp where they would make their headquarters for the next two weeks while hunting down stray cattle in the marsh.

We walked with them to their horses. They mounted, then sat for a couple of minutes, saying their farewells. I noticed that each man had in his saddle holster a .44 Winchester carbine, an old-time "Buffalo Bill gun." They were traveling light, each with only one small *garupa,* or saddlebag; the remainder of their camping supplies was loaded on two pack horses.

Pedro assured Sasha that if they ran across any fresh tiger signs, anywhere at all, they would let him know.

"One of us will ride to inform the senhor directly," he promised emphatically. "He will ride as with the devil behind him!"

Then, touching their spurs to their horses, the men were off with farewell waves and shouts, their pack animals trotting behind on lead ropes.

We stood watching as they cantered along the edge of the jungle, until they disappeared in a thick growth of brush.

I turned to Sasha. "Pedro really shocked me! And he seemed to be such a polite, easygoing person, too."

"Well," Sasha mused, "of course he had a real grievance if his gun was stolen. Guns are fairly essential equipment in the Mato Grosso. And you must remember that this is a country where thieving is considered a worse crime than murder."

"Well—perhaps so," I agreed unwillingly. "But to carry those ears around as trophies! That seems pretty callous, to say the least."

Sasha rubbed his elbow before replying. "To be perfectly fair" —he was always perfectly fair; too much so at times, I thought— "to be perfectly fair, even *that* is only an old 'thief-taker's' custom."

I knew about thief-takers, of course. Since there were no law officers in the jungle, a thief-taker—a man about one step above a professional gunman—was often hired to track down a fleeing criminal by a victim or a victim's relatives. And when he caught up with his quarry, he seldom brought him back alive. It would, naturally, be difficult, singlehanded, to guard a desperate criminal night and day through hundreds of miles of jungle, and in any event it was much simpler to bring back just the ears as proof of a successful mission. Sasha had told me that he once knew a thief-taker who had taken fifty pairs of ears. For that matter, John T. Ramsay, the former owner of the Descalvados Ranch (and an ex-Texas sheriff), who never was a thief-taker at all, at one time had twenty-eight human ears nailed on his ranch-house doorjamb: trophies of his skirmishes with various Mato Grosso bad men.

"True, patrão." Lauro spoke in a scornful tone. "True, patrão, if that were all. But that Pedro—I know him. I know other things he has done—and said." He spat contemptuously. "That one is no good. He is a big bag of air."

Sasha rubbed his chin thoughtfully. "Is he, Lauro?"

Lauro sneered.

"He brags he is so fast with his gun. He tells everybody he is one very tough *caboclo!*" Lauro spat again. "The only people he shoots are people who have no guns! Remember, I told you how a vaqueiro met an old Indian on the trail and shot him dead, and when the other vaqueiros asked why, he just laughed and said, 'That Indian was too ugly to live!' Remember, patrão?"

Sasha and I both nodded. I'd found that story hard to believe.

"That vaqueiro was Pedro!"

Sasha looked thoughtful. And having seen Pedro with those dried-up ears, I now could believe that the Indian story was perfectly true.

"But I still can't understand *how* he could do it." I shook my head.

Sasha laughed shortly. "Well, people in the Mato Grosso need less reason to use their guns than people do in Philadelphia."

Not that I didn't realize this by now, nor know the Mato Grosso pretty well.

The Mato Grosso today is very like the North American Wild West of a hundred years ago—and its melodrama frequently surpasses the most lurid Hollywood Western. It is located in the very heart of the South American continent (whose civilization still hugs the coasts), and large parts of it still are barred from settlement or even exploration by tribes of hostile Indians. Virtually the only officers of the law are the semi-official thief-takers, and frontiersmen frequently take the law into their own hands.

In fact, the .44 and the .38 Smith & Wesson revolvers, carried by nearly every vaqueiro, hunter, and prospector, are known respectively as "The Sheriff of the Mato Grosso" and "The Deputy."

And as in the North American Wild West, pioneering cattlemen represent the only real inroads of civilization. The isolated ranches, many owned by foreign capital, chiefly English, often occupy enormous land grants. (The Descalvados Estancia, within the boundaries of which we were living, covers five thousand square miles, an area nearly half the size of Belgium.) But the ranches are widely separated, for they occupy land only on the largos, the stretches of flat, unforested ground bordering the impenetrable jungle.

And the vaqueiros—almost all of mixed Negro, Indian, and Portuguese blood—who work the huge herds are a wild and lawless sort. The typical vaqueiro will shoot at the drop of a sombrero—Pedro was no exception. The Mato Grosso, in fact, for many years has been a refuge for desperate criminals wanted by the law in other parts of the world.

So, knowing this, I shouldn't have been so surprised at Pedro. As a matter of fact, Sasha had told me long ago a very similar tale. While hunting he had run across a vaqueiro who related, as a funny story, an encounter he had had that week with an oxcart driver on a lonely jungle trail. The driver had asked first for a match, then for tobacco, and finally for paper to roll a cigarette. The annoyed vaqueiro had asked whether he liked to smoke, and the man admitted he did. Then the vaqueiro said, "So you like to smoke but you don't have sense enough to bring your own smoking things." The oxcart driver sheepishly guessed that that was right.

"Well," retorted the vaqueiro, "if you haven't got that much brains, you don't deserve to live."

And he shot him dead on the spot.

There was our own Lauro, too, who had been with Sasha for several years. He had twenty notches on his gun. Yet he was a capable, intensely loyal little man, and Sasha trusted him implicitly. Many of Lauro's notches represented men killed in the outgrowth of a feud which began over a trivial incident years earlier.

Then a vain young vaqueiro, Lauro had slicked himself up and ridden into a little town near the Bolivian border to see his sweetheart. Deciding on a haircut as a finishing touch, he rode down the main street toward the barbershop. A town dandy scornfully looked him up and down. (Lauro is stunted-looking, black, and bandy-legged, no Adonis.)

"Well, well," the townsman sneered. "Look at the little monkey all dressed up!"

Lauro smarted but held his temper.

All during his haircut, however, his resentment smoldered. And when an hour later he chanced to meet the smart aleck again, it was unfortunate that the man was inspired once more to apply the term of "little monkey."

Lauro whipped out his six-shooter. The other drew, too, but his gun caught in his sash.

As the man had plenty of relatives, Lauro left town abruptly and began a flight which took him deeper and deeper into the jungles, until he eventually met Sasha and decided to become a tiger hunter's assistant. But during his flight, and over a period of years, he was several times forced to shoot revenge-seeking relatives of his original victim who were trailing him. At least that's the way he explained it to Sasha.

Lauro now had a wife who was nearly white and six children, four of them his own. But he had to make a widow of the lady first. He happened to come upon her when her husband was giving her a beating. Lauro gallantly berated him for being so unchivalrous, and the man turned on Lauro. Which was a mistake.

I was abruptly aroused from my thoughts when Sasha playfully whacked me on the rear.

"Wake up," he said. "I'm hungry!"

"Already?" I said without too much enthusiasm. And immediately I realized how like a typical housewife I sounded—always surprised and slightly annoyed at the shortness of time between meals and the eternal necessity to prepare another.

"Well, I suppose I'll have to keep feeding you regularly if I ever expect to move into that houseboat," I said reluctantly. I sighed with pretended great weariness. "A woman's work is never done!"

Sasha grinned and deliberately misunderstood the cliché.

"It isn't? Is that so?" he asked very politely. "But I shouldn't think that you, being a woman, would admit it."

Five minutes later Sasha had a roaring wood fire going in my outdoor kitchen "stove" on the riverbank. And while I started dinner he busied himself nearby so that we could carry on a random conversation over the sound of pots and pans.

My cooking facilities were more than adequate and represented real luxury in the jungle. Sasha had constructed the "stove" simply by digging a shallow hole in the rusty red earth and piling a low wall of rocks around it. This was the fire pit, and above it he had set a four-legged iron grill, a portable one he had taken along on all his hunting trips. The grill was large enough to hold a frying pan and two kettles.

My prize, however, was my oven. It was nothing more than a vacated anthill which an ant colony fortunately had erected within a short distance of our hut. I say "erected" with due respect, because a Mato Grosso anthill frequently is an architectural achievement. I have seen some four feet in diameter at the base which rose up out of the high grass on the flat largos like obelisks to a height higher than the head of a man on horseback. An ant colony begins building a new home during the dry season, using the earth brought up in their subterranean tunneling and cementing it with an excretion from their bodies; the result, when baked in the hot tropic sun, is almost as hard as concrete. When the rainy season begins and the swollen river starts flooding the largos, the ants repeatedly are forced to heighten the thick walls of their chimneylike home to keep from being drowned.

The anthill which Sasha appropriated for my oven was of a slightly different kind—only about six feet high, since it was located on high ground that seldom became flooded. It was six feet in diameter, like an overturned big bowl, and ideal for our purpose. Sasha simply chopped an oven-door hole in the base and enlarged the ants' exit in the top for a chimney, then used a shovel to scoop out the honeycombed interior.

"Well, I think we can start our baked potatoes now," Sasha announced after glancing at the wood fire which had been burning in the oven for about fifteen minutes. "If you'll throw me some, I'll take over."

"Coming right up, boss," I retorted breezily, and began pelting him with imaginary potatoes.

"A half dozen are *quite* enough," he protested, dodging. Then he squatted before the anthill and began raking out the hot coals.

I made a short trip to a sack suspended from the limb of a nearby tree and returned with six small cassava roots. Sasha rolled them into the oven and then placed a piece of sheet iron before the door opening to hold the heat in.

In about twenty minutes the cassava roots would be baked, and then they would taste just like baked potatoes.

Cassava roots, incidentally, are a staple food in the Mato Grosso jungles, taking the place of both wheat flour and potatoes. They grow wild and in their raw state are poisonous, containing prussic acid. However, cooking eliminates the poison. The raw root, when grated into fine particles, soaked in water, and roasted, makes a coarse, kernel-like flour somewhat like wheat flour and similarly usable. (I had even learned to make a jellylike relish to serve with fish by boiling cassava flour with fat and water.) And the large coarse kernels, roasted, became a breakfast cereal, or a dessert, when served with wild honey and milk.

Once I had made a cake with this flour. Previously I had baked bread in my anthill oven, but I had never had any eggs, and I knew of no recipe for an eggless cake. But then one day while riding over the largos, Sasha had run across an ostrich nest. He had brought the huge egg home triumphantly, for an ostrich nest is not easy to find. The female ostrich is of a dull gray color, and when she sits on her nest she pulls down her long neck and is difficult to see in the high grass; even if seen, she is often mistaken for a rock. One egg that size, I decided, surely equaled a dozen chicken eggs, so I wouldn't settle for anything less than a cake. We had no sugar, so I used honey. And, greatly to my surprise, the cake was a success!

While the cassava roots were baking I turned my attention to the grill. One pot held water heating for our maté; in the large frying pan I was frying breasts of *arancuão,* a large pheasantlike bird; and I was ready to broil over the flames a couple of thick steaks from a peccary, or wild pig, which Sasha had shot that morning.

We ate a lot of meat, like most people in the Mato Grosso. One reason was that we had few vegetables, for the millions of bugs made raising a garden in the jungle virtually impossible. And the other reason was that meat was so plentiful. The manager of the Descalvados Estancia allowed Sasha to kill one beef animal a week from among the thousands of strays roaming the marshes and the fringes of jungle as payment for Sasha's efforts in reducing the number of tigers which preyed on the herds. And this beef plus river fish and wild game—deer, tapirs, peccaries, wild turkeys, and dozens of kinds of wild ducks, the latter so numerous in the marshes that they blackened the sun at times—provided us with more than enough meat for ourselves, for Lauro's and Rosando's families, and for Sasha's eighteen tiger-hunting dogs and our caged wild pets.

Our only difficulty was that we lacked refrigeration, and meat spoils quickly in the tropics. However, Sasha and his two helpers followed the native custom of converting part of each beef animal into *charqui,* or dried beef, which remains edible for as long as a year. (Charqui was simply made. They merely cut the beef into long thin strips and spread it on a wooden platform on the river-bank to dry in the hot sun—meanwhile guarding it from vultures, of course.)

As everything was nearly ready, I hastily began placing our heavy native pottery and silverware on our outdoor dining table, which Sasha had dragged close to the fire, so that when it became dark we would be within the circle of firelight. The table, which Sasha had made from mahogany, was the first piece to be completed of the furniture planned for our houseboat. We still used empty boxes for chairs.

Just then a familiar voice shouted: "O de casa!"—the warning of approaching strangers.

"Amigo—approach!" Sasha replied lustily.

A moment later Lauro, grinning widely at his little joke, appeared around a clump of bushes; behind him was Rosando; a half dozen of Sasha's tiger dogs trailed at their heels. Rosando had his arms loaded.

"Patrão y senhora, we bring you food." Lauro managed to say it as though the whole of the credit really belonged to himself. He quickly took the armload of palm hearts from the overburdened Rosando and placed them on the table with a flourish—many more than we could use. Palm hearts, carved from the center of the acuri palm's leafy crest, made a tasty dish somewhat like both lettuce and cabbage, which we ate in lieu of salad and vegetables.

Lauro grinned disarmingly. "I climbed so many trees, I feel like a monkey. But for the patrão, it was a pleasure."

"Why, thank you, Lauro," I said, smiling. It was always a slight surprise to me when the men did these little things. Although Sasha had instructed them to keep me supplied daily with palm hearts and whatever fruits were available, it was surprising how often they could find other more necessary jobs that interfered with this duty. And when they did undertake it, they perversely brought such quantities that inevitably the greater part spoiled.

The dogs were crowding close, stretching their necks and sniffing eagerly, their eyes avidly on the peccary steaks that sizzled and gave out a tantalizing aroma as Sasha held them over the fire. They shouldn't have been hungry, however, as Lauro said they'd just been fed.

"Down! Lie down!" Sasha growled at them; then he turned back to the steaks, which were nearly done.

The dogs retreated an inch or two but continued to eye the crackling meat; saliva dripped from their muzzles.

"Have a drink if you wish, boys," Sasha invited as the two men hesitated, obviously waiting for just such an invitation. "Bring some *piquy* for the senhora."

"Sim, patrão, I oblige most gladly. Like a lightning flash!" Lauro rushed off and called over his shoulder, showing his white teeth in a big grin: "Piquy for the senhora, cachaça for the men!"

Rosando, who unlike the cocky little extrovert Lauro, always seemed ill at ease in my presence, was about to follow when Sasha, to give him something to do, asked him to take the baked cassava roots out of the oven. Rosando gratefully complied.

"You and Lauro both ate with your families, I suppose?" Sasha asked perfunctorily. They always ate earlier than we; their wives had supper waiting for them in their huts down-river by the time they quit work, as their children were put to bed early.

"Sim, we have eaten." Rosando halted to look back stolidly; his voice was as expressionless as all Indians' speech is supposed to be.

Sasha shoved the peccary steaks on a covered platter to keep warm at the end of the grill and served the arancuão breasts. In the meantime I had trimmed the palm hearts and poured over them a native wine vinegar. Rosando returned with the baked cassava roots on a shovel. He waited silently to one side until I picked up a fork and, smiling at him, speared the crisp, hot roots and transferred them to an earthen bowl on the table. Then Lauro arrived with a bottle of cachaça and two glasses—one empty, the other partly filled with a yellowish liquid. That was my piquy, a pleasantly sweet native liqueur made of a wild fruit; a light "woman's drink."

Sasha and I sat down; Lauro handed me my piquy, then poured some rum for Sasha. After a whimsical toast to *The River Gypsy,* Sasha returned his empty glass to Lauro, who promptly filled it to the brim for himself. He and Rosando squatted on the ground a few feet away with the bottle—the stolid Rosando patiently waiting his turn, as usual.

The two always seemed to be greatly pleased at a chance to spend the hour during which we ate dinner loafing and talking with us—and not entirely because Sasha usually allowed them to tap the rum barrel. Sasha dignified such occasions by announcing they were to talk over their next day's work, though he would grin sheepishly when I kidded him about calling another bull session. The sessions were morale builders, he would retort; Lauro and Rosando welcomed a chance to spend a few leisure hours away from their heckling wives and squabbling children. It was like a night out with the boys, Sasha would add banteringly; I should feel flattered that they apparently considered me regular and one of the gang.

We finished the arancuão; Lauro, watching, quickly jumped up and brought the peccary steaks. And at his direction Rosando lumbered over and removed the plates of our first course. At least on these nights when we were not alone we were waited on.

"How about some maté now, Lauro?" Sasha suggested as we began on our steaks.

Lauro turned to Rosando and relayed directions—in a quicker, more clipped Portuguese than he used to Sasha or me. And Rosando, with a nod, heavily lifted himself up from the grass and left.

The peccary was succulent; the birds had been delicious, too, for that matter. And with the palm-heart salad, the baked cassava roots, and the piquy, it was an excellent meal, I thought.

Rosando plodded back with the maté gourd, and Lauro took over.

"I presume this will be—vaqueiro-style maté, Lauro?" Sasha smiled. This was a stock proceeding every time Lauro prepared the maté, for Lauro never forgot he was a former vaqueiro.

"Sim, patrão—vaqueiro-style maté." Lauro grinned.

Rosando in the meantime had picked up the little sack of dried maté leaves which he had brought with the gourd; he held it open for Lauro, who placed several of the dried leaves in the gourd and covered them with cold water.

Everyone drinks maté in the Mato Grosso. For that matter, it is a popular drink throughout all of South America. The maté leaves come from the tree of the same name, which grows wild throughout the continent. Maté contains caffeine and is a noticeable stimulant. The natives prepare it, as Lauro was doing, by first steeping the leaves in cold water for a few minutes. They then suck the cold water from the gourd by means of a silver tube and expectorate it. Finally hot water is poured into the gourd, and after a few minutes of additional steeping the maté is ready to drink.

Whenever you visit a native hut in the Mato Grasso, as a gesture of hospitality you immediately are handed the family maté gourd, with the family's prized silver tube for sucking up the liquid. And it is considered bad form to wipe off the saliva of the preceding drinker before you put the tube in your mouth.

By this time Lauro and Rosando had replaced the cold water

in the gourd with boiling-hot water from the kettle steaming on the grill. They had poured out the cold water, however, instead of eliminating it in the native manner—in deference to what they considered my quaint and incomprehensible ideas.

"Vaqueiro-style, eh?" Sasha smiled as he observed the steam tumbling from the gourd Rosando handed him.

"Sim, patrão," Rosando answered with an awkward, bashful smile. Then he squatted on the ground again, looking as if he were embarrassed at having thus impulsively broken his long silence. Lauro dropped down beside him and after Sasha and I had gingerly sipped from the gourd he peremptorily took his turn. He closed his lips over the silver tube sticking from the neck of the gourd, then winced when the scalding maté reached his tongue. He lowered the gourd and, with a mischievous grin on his black face, instantly spat the mouthful of maté at one of the dogs lying half asleep a few feet away. The dog yelped and jumped up, then, with a reproachful look at Lauro, moved farther away and lay down again.

Lauro pretended to look disappointed; he shook his head sadly.

"I apologize to the patrão; this is not vaqueiro-style maté. Vaqueiro maté should be so hot," he went on lugubriously, "that when you spit it on a dog he *runs* away howling!"

While we had been eating it had suddenly become dark, and the darkness brought with it the gratifying coolness of the tropic night. The flickering firelight from our grill made the surrounding jungle seem blacker by contrast. The moon had just begun to rise, and the stars were bright and seemed almost measurably near. The abruptness with which night came in the jungle would always seem strange to me. There was no dusk as we know it in a temperate climate; when the sun dropped beneath the horizon it was night, full-blown in darkness—as if the earth had suddenly plunged into a black, bottomless well.

I looked across the table at Sasha; Lauro and Rosando were sprawled on the grass; the dogs lay sleepily stretched on their bellies, their heads between their front paws; occasionally one snapped irritably at a fly or mosquito, although the smoke from our fire, drifting thinly this way and that, kept most of the bothersome insects away.

"Well . . ." I happened to catch Sasha's eye after a short silence,

24

during which he had seemed deep in a reverie; I smiled teasingly. "Does this seem too domestic to you? Being saddled with a wife and building a permanent home? Are you sorrowing for the freedom of your bachelor days?"

Sasha grinned back half guiltily.

"As a matter of fact, my dear," he admitted, "I *was* thinking of my bachelor days. Though not—ah—grieving too much."

"Really? I knew it!"

Sasha sighed.

"Not even my thoughts can be mine alone any more." He grinned ruefully. "Am I really that transparent, Edith?"

I considered. "Well—at times! However, I wouldn't worry. Not many of your thoughts are what one might term—reprehensible."

Sasha winced.

"Please, Edith, my dear!" He shook his head reprovingly. "That's enough to give any husband a psychosis—to accuse him of being harmless!"

I smiled. We had been speaking English, and so Lauro and Rosando had been unable to follow our conversation.

Rosando raised himself from the grass long enough to put more wood on the fire. The flames leaped high, and for a moment the night about us was thrust back, and the trees in the encircling fringe of the jungle were vividly outlined. Through a break in the high bushes on the bank the moonlit surface of the broad river gleamed. From a group of flowering *piuva* trees came the grating cry of a toucan calling his harem.

I turned back to Sasha.

"I'm sorry I unwittingly bruised your tender ego. I promise I won't do it again—at least not in exactly the same manner." I grinned and took another small sip of maté; then, switching to Portuguese, I added, "But please inform me, esteemed husband, which of your gay and free bachelor days were you remembering when I surprised that brooding look in your handsome eyes?"

A pleased expression immediately crossed the faces of Lauro and Rosando. They looked like a couple of dogs pricking up their ears.

"I was just thinking," Sasha said, also in Portuguese, "of my days in the diamond fields, and how different a life this is." He paused thoughtfully. "I was wondering what would have happened if I'd stayed there longer."

"You'd probably be a millionaire by now," I suggested brightly.

Lauro and Rosando grinned broadly; they thought, I knew, that Sasha already was quite wealthy, what with all the guns he owned, his many carpentering and ironworking tools, his outboard motors, and his cameras. Why would he want more wealth?

"No." Sasha shook his head. "That is highly improbable. I might not even be alive today."

He had told me, though only sketchily before, of various incidents in the diamond fields of the northeastern Mato Grosso, where he had spent some time with his brother Ernst years before I met him. His brother had been killed after a diamond-field brawl.

"Was it always that dangerous, Sasha?" I asked. Then I bit my lip and added hastily, "The region, I mean?"

Sasha shrugged.

"The region where we were, along the Rio das Garças and the Rio das Mortes, was jungle," he said slowly. "And the jungle can be dangerous—anywhere."

"The Rio das Mortes . . . River of Death!" I interrupted. "What an ominous name."

Sasha smiled wryly.

"Many men have found it so," he said, looking past the campfire with thoughtful eyes. "It is just inside the territory of the Chavante Indians—the most savage of all the jungle tribes. So far, they have tortured and killed *every* man who has attempted to go upriver to them—missionaries, explorers, hunters, and prospectors."

I had heard of the Chavantes.

From the river there suddenly came the startling bull-like roar of a night-fishing bull heron. I jumped involuntarily.

"Rio das Garças," Lauro interjected happily. "That is where the *sucurí* swallowed the vaqueiro! *Não,* patrão?"

Sasha grinned.

I remembered that story, which Sasha had told me the first time I came down to the jungle.

A few years ago metropolitan South American newspapers had carried a news story reporting that a huge boa constrictor killed in

26

the jungles of "the wild Mato Grosso," when slit open, was found to contain the body of a cowboy—complete with poncho, sombrero, and spurs!

"In proof of this story," the dispatch had ended naïvely, "the prospector who made the discovery exhibited money he had recovered from the dead man's pockets."

The tale, of course, had been a whopper. Afterward Sasha had heard the prospector in question, one Carlo Alvarez, bragging how he'd stuffed a visiting journalist in a frontier-town bar who'd asked for "exciting stories from the diamond fields."

But, as Sasha pointed out to me, the fact that Rio de Janeiro, Buenos Aires, and Lima newspapers all unquestioningly printed the story as truth illustrates the typical attitude toward the Mato Grosso. South Americans still look on this vast, uncivilized heart of their continent as a dangerous, fantastic region where anything can happen.

"Remember, patrão"—Lauro grinned eagerly at Sasha, pleased that he could contribute to the conversation—"remember the sucurí we killed?"

His eyes alight, he got up quickly to refill the gourd with hot water, then sprawled before the fire again. That was one good thing about maté—the leaves retained their strength through a half-dozen water refills.

Sasha nodded and smiled. He turned to me.

"That's right. Lauro and I ran across a big boa constrictor a couple of years ago."

"Ugh!" I said distastefully. I added as facetiously as I could, "How big? Big enough to swallow a vaqueiro, complete with poncho, sombrero, and spurs?"

"Well"—Sasha grinned—"he almost swallowed Lauro! Isn't that right, Lauro?"

Lauro raised himself up from the ground to squat on his bare black heels; his teeth shone in a broad grin as he nodded vigorously. Then his face became very serious as he addressed me. "That is true, senhora! The patrão saved my life!"

"Oh—really?" I said, a little taken aback.

Sasha shrugged disparagingly, then added flippantly, "He'd probably have found you a pretty tough meal, anyway, Lauro. And disgorged you pronto—complete with poncho, sombrero, and spurs!"

Lauro laughed loudly; and even Rosando grinned at that.

"Sim, patrão!" Lauro agreed.

"We were crossing an arm of the Xarayes Pantanal, some distance west of here," Sasha explained. "Lauro was walking ahead of me in the high marsh grass. Suddenly he shouted, 'Sucurí! Sucurí!' And then he stumbled and fell!"

Lauro, his eyes shining as he relived the moment, excitedly agreed, "That is true, senhora! That is true!"

"And a boa constrictor as thick as a tree trunk reared out of the grass and lunged at Lauro," Sasha continued. "Luckily I had my gun ready, and I quickly blasted a hole in its head with a double charge of bird shot. Otherwise I'm afraid the snake surely would have grabbed Lauro!"

"Sim, senhora! That is true!" Rolling his eyes, Lauro repeated the words in a frenzy of excitement. He'd had a lot of cachaça.

"As it was," Sasha added with a faint smile, "we both had to move quickly then to escape being crushed by the thrashing about of its heavy coils!"

I shivered.

"How big *was* it?"

Sasha took a sip of maté before answering.

"Well, when we finished our duck hunting several hours later we came back the same way," he said. "The snake was completely dead by then, and we measured it. It was twenty-seven feet long. And I pried its jaws apart and found they opened wider than a man's shoulders!"

So a boa constrictor *could* swallow a man. . . .

I was silent for a minute; then I inquired lightly: "Do you think Rupert will ever get that big?"

Rupert, of course, was our small pet boa constrictor. I had first heard of him when Sasha had teasingly told me—on our way back to the jungle after we had been married—that the baby boa constrictor was his wedding gift to me. At the time I had thought he was joking, but I soon learned that he wasn't. Rupert did exist—although Sasha had also given me a fine riding horse as a more serious wedding present. Sasha had tamed Rupert and encouraged him to stay about the place in order to keep the rats and mice away. I had grown so I could tolerate Rupert, but I didn't think I ever could become fond of him.

(However, I knew I didn't dare indicate any distaste for the little snake. After all, I supposedly had "won" Sasha by finally overcoming my fear of snakes and taking a wriggling, headless one in my hands. Sasha would never let me hear the end of it if I backed down now. In fact, at times I suspected that he kept Rupert mainly to bait me—and that he was very much amused by my queasy valor.)

Lauro and Rosando both laughed at my words.

Sasha drawled, "Well, I don't think you need worry for at least twenty years. Rupert doesn't seem to be growing very fast."

"And by the way, where is he now?" I asked, glancing behind me with extreme casualness. I didn't mind Rupert quite so much if I always knew where he was.

Sasha laughed—at me, I suspected. "He's undoubtedly sleeping somewhere. As usual."

"Sim, that one is sleeping," Lauro assured me emphatically.

I made a face at Sasha.

Just then Lauro's name was shouted in a peevish woman's voice. We all turned; the shout was repeated, and Lauro answered reluctantly. A moment later his plump but still attractive wife, Cenaria, approached out of the darkness. She smiled nervously and jerked her head in a quick bow to Sasha and me, then asked our pardon for disturbing us. Barely waiting for it to be granted, she marched up to Lauro and glowered at him.

"When are you coming home?" she demanded brusquely, planting her hands on her mammoth hips.

Lauro rose slowly, looking at us with an embarrassed expression; then he frowned at his wife.

"Why do you ask that, woman?" he growled.

"There is much to be done at home!" she retorted, scowling. "Need wood for the fire. Need water. Need man around. Why do you not come home?"

"I have been talking to the patrão, that's why, woman!" Lauro replied belligerently. He added importantly, "The patrão wanted to talk with me."

"So?" Her eyes narrowed in disbelief; then, half fearing she may have offended her husband's boss, she turned to Sasha with an embarrassed expression and began to apologize. "I—I am sorry. If the patrão——"

Sasha cut short her flustered stammers with a reassuring smile.

"No, no, Cenaria, it's all right," he said smoothly. "You take Lauro home with you now. He should get to sleep. We have to get up early tomorrow; we have a lot of work to do." As Lauro started moving slowly away Sasha waved at them both. "Good night!"

Cenaria turned and bobbed her head, and Lauro uttered a muffled "Good night, patrão y senhora."

Rosando hurriedly stood up. "I—I think I will go home too, patrão," he mumbled.

Sasha grinned. "Do you think your wife is worrying about you too, Rosando?"

Rosando's face cracked in the beginning of a smile, but he did not reply. Instead, with a "Good night, patrão y senhora," he, too, strode out of the firelight and disappeared in the darkness.

We were silent for a moment.

"Cenaria is certainly jealous of Lauro, isn't she?" I mused. "Insisting that he spend every bit of his spare time with her. . . . And they've been married for years!"

"Yes." Sasha grinned again. "Lauro surely inspires love in his ladies." He looked at me for a minute with a calculating expression, then asked teasingly, "Are you going to be that jealous of me after we've been married for years?"

I scoffed: "Huh! I'm not now!"

"Hmmm . . ." Sasha said. "Here I thought you were the jealous type."

"Well, I'm not!" I protested. I thought it over and added, "At least not in the jungle—with no competition." I paused. "However," I added with a smile, "I agree completely with Cenaria on how to handle erring husbands. I don't think her method could be improved on, dear."

Sasha guffawed, and I laughed with him.

Lauro had taken a lot of ribbing from us about that, and he had taken it good-naturedly. But I'm certain that if anyone else had kidded him as much as we he would soon have been carving another notch on his gun. . . .

The affair had happened months earlier, after we returned from Rio. Lauro, who is quite a ladies' man, had been finding fairly frequent excuses to visit a tiny backroads settlement two days' distant. Cenaria finally could stand it no longer. So one morning at dawn, seething with anger, she took her six children to Rosando's hut and dumped them in his wife's care; then she mounted the family mule, armed with an eighteen-inch razor-sharp machete.

She arrived at sunset the following day and of course had no trouble locating "the house" in the tiny settlement. According to Lauro's sheepish recital to Sasha some time later, she burst in upon him just as he was dandling his jungle Jezebel on his knee, while the two of them, each waving a mug of rum, were harmonizing on a ribald vaqueiro ballad.

"So!" shrieked Cenaria. "This is how you are true to me!"

And with that she rushed at him, swinging her wicked machete.

The other woman screamed and fled, but Lauro stood his ground and tried to grapple and argue with his spouse—with the result that she slashed a ten-inch gash across his abdomen and was still shrieking and wildly swinging, eager for more blood, when his inamorata returned with the local facsimile of a constable.

But Lauro refused to allow the man to "arrest" Cenaria.

So Cenaria meekly surrendered her machete to her spouse, and after a little bandaging the two of them lovingly rode home together. . . .

We had been silent for several minutes.

Both of us finally had had enough maté. Sasha arose to put more wood on the fire, then sat down again. He smiled at me, obviously still in a conversational mood. I wasn't sleepy either, though as we got up at dawn we usually went to bed early.

"But maybe if you *had* stayed longer in the diamond fields," I mused, reverting to our original topic, "you *would* be a millionaire now."

Sasha laughed scornfully.

"The famous Vargas diamond is the largest ever found in Brazil. In fact, it's the third largest in the world. I understand the New York diamond company which now owns it values it at one million dollars." He paused to let that sink in—then added dryly, "Yet the three men who found it got only two thousand dollars each! They were broke less than a year later."

"I see what you mean," I said. "But why did they sell for so little?"

Sasha shrugged.

"The prospectors were all at the mercy of the few diamond buyers who periodically trekked in by pack horse to pick up stones. They wouldn't pay more than five dollars a karat for the finest-quality ones—stones worth easily a hundred times that much!" He snorted disgustedly. "A small handful of stones would bring just enough to buy the necessary food and supplies to carry you through a few more months' digging!"

I shook my head slowly. It certainly sounded futile.

"That's why I finally deserted the diamond diggings," Sasha said; then he added bitterly: "I tried to persuade Ernst to leave, too, but he insisted on staying. If he'd left when I did, he'd probably still be alive!"

The conversation always seemed to get back to Ernst, and I hated to have Sasha thus reminded of his unfortunate older brother. I tried to think of something to say.

I wanted to say something comforting or consoling, but I felt that anything I could say would only make him feel worse. So I sat there groping for words that wouldn't come, feeling stupid and tongue-tied and wishing I could just get up and put my arms around him.

In our silence the sounds of the jungle seemed unusually loud. Tree frogs cheeped, and insects rasped. The night was raucous with the cries of swamp birds, all out fishing in the river in the moonlight. The hoarse bellow of an alligator shook the air.

Abruptly Sasha flipped his stick into the fire and turned to smile at me.

"Except for trimmings strictly tropical—such as that alligator —it was almost exactly like the California gold rush in the days of '49," he drawled. "Or don't you want to hear any more of my diamond days?"

"Of course I do—silly!" I said quickly. "Go on, dear."

I was very glad that his mood had changed.

"You see," Sasha continued, "the diamond hunters, like the gold miners, came from all parts of the world—and a fair share were murderers and escaped convicts, men who wanted to hide themselves in the jungle and at the same time have a try at a fortune. It was a man's world, except for a few women camp followers—abandoned hags, the dregs of the red-light districts of Rio, Bahia, and Pernambuco."

"It sounds pretty rough," I said, raising my eyebrows.

"Well—" Sasha grinned—"it wasn't exactly pastoral. Not a peaceful Pennsylvania countryside. Not with hostile Indians and boa constrictors and vampire bats—and, of course, tigers. And we were working right in the river with the alligators, electric eels, and piranhas."

"Electric eels?" I echoed. I hadn't known there were any of those, and I could see Sasha was now enjoying his reminiscences. "Oh, tell me about them!"

Sasha stared at me with mild amusement—he realized that I was purposely drawing him out. He grinned.

"Well, the diamonds were all alluvial stones," he began, "found in the sands of the river beds. The rivers were deep, often as deep as thirty feet, and the current was strong. So as a technique, diving was not practicable. Instead, each prospector drove a long pole upright in the section of the river bottom he'd staked off for himself—and then climbed down the pole with a basket to bring up the sand."

"Mm-m-m-m—clever!" I murmured.

Sasha grinned and made a little bow.

"At the end of the day," he resumed, "each man washed out his little heap of gravel piled up on the bank, with a perforated pan. And with only the larger pebbles left, he looked carefully for the diamonds. These came in all colors—yellow, black, blue, and rose, as well as the finest colorless gems."

"It sounds fascinating," I said.

Sasha snorted. "It wasn't," he said shortly. "It was damned hard work. And usually dull and boring, except when accidents happened. Which they often did. For the men all worked naked in the water, since that was most practical. And the river, as I just mentioned, was full of alligators, piranhas, and electric eels."

'Which you promised to tell me about!" I reminded him.

"Have patience, little girl," Sasha said loftily. "Papa is just coming to that part."

"Yes, sir," I said meekly. I clasped my hands under my chin in a pose of rapt attention.

Sasha stifled a grin and frowned.

"Usually," he continued, "we managed to safeguard ourselves against piranha attacks by arranging a distraction. We'd kill an alligator and slash off the tip of its tail, then anchor it in midstream with ropes, just above where we were working."

I nodded in approval of the device but didn't interrupt.

"And of course the alligator was barely moored when all the piranhas around were drawn by its blood. They'd fight in hundreds to eat their way inside their armor-plated victim!

"At the end of the day, when we'd draw in our ropes"— Sasha leaned forward and crossed his arms on the table— "dozens of gluttonous piranhas would be flopping about inside the alligator's bony shell like rats in a barrel, so stuffed they couldn't make their way out again through the small hole in the end of the tail!"

I shivered a little, for I was thinking of the unfortunate swimmer I had seen eaten by piranhas.

Sasha stopped talking and looked at me narrowly.

"Go on," I said quickly. "Continue, Sindbad, I'm tough!" I grinned. "Don't you know I live in the Mato Grosso?"

Sasha got up and stood by the fire a moment.

"Well, do you still want to hear about the electric eels?" he asked abruptly.

"Naturally," I said, "*if* you've finally come to them."

Sasha smiled and sat down again, sprawling lazily.

"There's really not much to the story," he began slowly, "but here goes. The electric eels run up to six feet long, and five sixths of their length is devoted to their electricity making. They can deliver a terrific electric shock—one sufficient to kill a man or a mule. And not only that—they can send this shock a considerable distance through the water; you don't have to touch them to be electrocuted!"

"What a wonderful pet!" I smiled. "With a couple of tame

ones hanging around in the river, we could have electric lights in our houseboat, to say nothing of a radio—maybe even a refrigerator and an electric iron."

"*Very* clever," Sasha retorted sarcastically.

"I'm sorry," I said meekly. "Please tell me more about the electric eel."

Sasha stared hard at me and then abruptly got up again and started pacing in front of the fire.

"One of the prospectors, a young Norwegian, died because of one, although technically he was killed by piranhas. He'd been fishing and hooked an electric eel. The eel's powerful charge, conducted by his wet fishline, stunned him—and he fell into the river, where the piranhas set upon him." He paused, then explained, "They'd been so numerous for several days in that section of the river that we had been unable to work at all."

He ran his hand through his hair and went on: "The man came to the surface shouting for help. He was close to the bank and managed to reach shore before we could throw him a rope. But when he staggered out we saw that his belly had been eaten away and his entrails were hanging out!"

"Ooooh-h-h! How horrible!" I felt a little nauseated.

Sasha wheeled and looked at me.

"Well, anyway," he said quickly, "the poor devil stumbled to his gravel heap and picked up his revolver and blew out his brains."

I mulled this over for a while. The electric-eel story had turned into another story about piranhas. Finally I asked, "But weren't there any funny happenings in the diamond fields? Was *everything* so dangerous and—and deadly?"

"Funny?" Sasha smiled with amusement. "Of course there was hilarity, my dear. Especially at the end of the day, when each man was panning his pile of gravel. You'd see a prospector bending over his washing pan; suddenly he'd pick out a pebble and gleefully wave it aloft. *'Diamante!'* he'd shout. *'Diamante!'* And then, grabbing his six-shooter, he'd start exultantly shooting at the sky. And every naked prospector for several hundred yards around would drop his pan and rush over to admire the find."

"I should think there'd have been a lot of stealing, with all those diamonds," I put in. "Especially with murderers and ex-convicts all over the place."

Sasha shook his head emphatically, then sat down.

"No, you are wrong. There were two thousand men of a score of different races in that diamond camp, all of them armed. Naturally, they didn't get along perfectly. Yet, in spite of the great incentive to theft in the diamonds, there was—surprisingly—no stealing. However, there were constant killings, of course. For instance"—Sasha slapped at a mosquito—"the day Ernst and I first rode into camp an Italian doctor, an exile, was being buried. He'd been shot. When we asked why, one of the men shrugged and explained: 'The good doctor made an unlovely accusation. He was playing at cards and intimated that there had been cheating.' "

"The poor man," I murmured. "They probably *were* cheating the pants off of him! Doctors are usually so naïve." Then I remembered what Sasha had said about the men all working naked. "That is, if he wore pants."

Sasha looked pained. "Senhora Siemel!" he protested.

"To go on"—Sasha got up and placed a couple of pieces of wood on the fire; the red coals abruptly burst into bright flames again, and the darkness about us retreated—"another man was killed less than a week later. That one was done in by a woman camp follower—one of about twenty who worked the camp. The miners held an impromptu trial for her right on the spot. And, incidentally, the outcome of the trial proved the fact that the chivalry of frontiersmen is pretty much the same the world over, from the Yukon on down. Even though it sometimes takes an odd form."

"Well, hurry up, tell me!" I urged impatiently.

"Yes, dear," Sasha resumed with maddening slowness. "As a matter of fact"—he cleared his throat a bit self-consciously—"as a matter of fact, I was personally involved in that incident."

"Sasha!" It was my turn to pretend shock. "With a woman camp follower? A—a professional woman?"

Sasha regarded me coolly for a deliberate moment, then apparently decided not to tease me.

"I was involved slightly, but not in the way you're thinking.

36

The dead man was found in his tent one morning with his head split open by an ax," he continued. "The woman he'd been living with was immediately seized and taken before an impromptu court composed of three camp leaders. The court convened on a hillside near the river—several hundred bearded prospectors crowded about in a solemn semicircle, their arms crossed, most of them smoking.

"The woman," Sasha rambled on, "was a drab, weary-looking old hag. She made no attempt to deny the charge. 'Of course I killed him,' she said stolidly. 'The dog left me for another woman.' "

Sasha rubbed his knuckles against his chin.

"Without any discussion of the circumstances the three judges quickly voted to send the woman back to a frontier town under guard—to be executed by a firing squad!"

"A firing squad!" I exclaimed. "I thought that only happened to traitors. . . . How brutal!"

Sasha nodded. "That's what I thought. And while the hundreds of other prospectors nodded and shouted *their* approval of the verdict, I impulsively pushed forward and faced the crowd. 'Please, amigos,' I said. 'Listen to me. This unfortunate woman —must she be executed by a firing squad? Surely there could be some less severe punishment. The degradation to which life has brought her is punishment in itself! Won't you'—I looked about into the scowling, disapproving faces and ended lamely—'won't you— reconsider?' "

"Sasha! You did that, really?" I exclaimed. "How gallant! My dear Don Quixote."

Sasha looked embarrassed and a bit crestfallen, as if he suspected I was ribbing him. I hastily reached across the table and groped for his hand. "I mean it, Sasha!"

Sasha sighed. "Well, to continue . . . The judges, of course, refused to change their verdict. But after the guards had left with the woman the court's chairman took me aside. 'We really don't kill women,' he explained. 'But we couldn't acquit her; it would set a bad precedent. Remember, it's a long way to Santa Rita, and she still has her trade. Don't worry, she'll make a bargain!' "

Sasha chuckled.

"Sure enough"—he leaned back and clasped his knee, smiling reminiscently—"the two men delegated to take her through the jungle and turn her over to her executioners returned in less than a week. They blandly reported that their prisoner had escaped."

"How slick," I said after a moment. "And still the form of justice was served." I grimaced. "But it's an ugly story just the same."

We both were silent. The fire had subsided into glowing red embers. The moon was high in the star-splashed sky above. It silvered the mile-wide river before us with a prodigal hand. Distantly we could hear the angry, womanlike scream of a mountain lion, the only thing at variance with the peace of the night.

We both arose and, hand in hand, wordlessly moved toward our grass hut.

The interior was pitch black. I struck a match and lit our lamp—a regulation wick in a small bowl of capibara fat. Sasha had recently shot one of these large marsh guinea pigs (they grow to 120 pounds) and had told me that the natives used its fat instead of candle tallow, so I'd insisted on trying it; besides, we were out of candles.

I partially undressed and washed. I first had to skim off a couple of huge brilliantly colored moths that had fallen into the pail of water and drowned.

Then I took off my riding boots and socks and walked about barefoot on the earthen floor while I found and climbed into my pajamas. Our hut was the only place it was safe to go barefoot because of the hookworm prevalent in the ground. Sasha had taken a tip from the Mato Grosso Indians and made a floor in the hut of powdered clay from an old anthill. The muriatic acid in the glandular secretion with which the ants cement the walls of their earthen homes keeps hookworms away.

Sasha was washing his face. Then abruptly there was a tinny clatter and the slosh of water spilling. Sasha uttered a peevish ejaculation.

"What happened?" I demanded curiously.

Sasha laughed. "Oh, Rupert was sleeping in the corner and I didn't see him. I set the pail squarely on top of him."

38

"Oh."

Sasha blew out the light, and I could hear his hammock creaking as he crawled in and said good night.

After a silence of some minutes I asked hesitantly, "Sasha—seriously, Sasha, do you miss that kind of a life now? I mean, miss being a bachelor—and all those adventures?"

There was no answer. I decided Sasha must be asleep. Undoubtedly he was dreaming of his gay bachelor days, too—darn him.

I went on in a small voice, forlornly talking to no one at all:

"Sasha, I suppose you'd—still *rather* be single—and working around in diamond fields—with women camp followers!"

An alert, amused chuckle came suddenly out of the darkness. Sasha reached across the space between our hammocks and clasped my hand. "No, my dear," his deep voice rumbled, "I infinitely prefer being here with you."

Another month had passed—a month of long, sun-baked, drowsy days, each so like the others that they blurred together in my mind.

I stood for a moment staring thoughtfully through the wide screened window in the living room of our nearly completed houseboat. From beneath the projecting eaves of the sharply sloped roof I could see the deep blue sky, unmarred by the slightest shred of cloud, and the broad, silently flowing river shimmering all around me. Sasha and Lauro were sawing logs into boards on the bank. I could hear the shrill whang-whang-whang of the kerosene-powered circular saw suddenly drop an octave as it snarled doggedly through a long length of log, then rise again with an earsplitting shriek. I had spent months doing my housework to the ungodly sounds of construction.

It was cool indoors, for above the tin roof was a superstructure of palm thatch, and the houseboat was tied close to the high riverbank where the trees and bushes partially shaded it. Whenever an occasional slight breeze came down the river I could feel it pass through the large screen doors at either end of the houseboat, and I could hear it rustling the palm thatch and see it moving the tips of the long fronds hanging over the eaves.

And the illusion of coolness was heightened by the sound, beneath the heavy floor boards, of the river slapping gently against the five long dugouts upon which the houseboat rested.

I idly touched the fragile petals of the magnificent purple orchid growing at the right of the window, then compared it with the one at the left. Both were nearing full bloom. I turned and glanced about at the others—exotic splashes of color every few feet around all four walls of our large living room—nearly a score in all, purple, brown, and golden, and in all stages of bloom. I wondered what the girls with whom I had gone to boarding school in Philadelphia would say if they knew I had orchids as house plants. As a matter of fact, orchids were nearly as commonplace in the jungle as daisies and buttercups at home. And frequently when Sasha and I went for a short ride, as we often did in the coolest parts of the day, just after dawn or before sunset, I would persuade him to stop when I saw a particularly beautiful blossom I wanted.

The orchids were ideal house plants, of course, since they required absolutely no care. In the jungle they grow parasitically on the limbs of certain trees, but they are parasites only to the extent of using their host as anchorage; they draw all their sustenance from the air. Therefore, Sasha would merely chop off the section of tree limb which held the orchid and tack it up on our houseboat wall; the orchid would continue to grow as well indoors as it did in the deeply shaded jungle.

As the screech of the buzz saw continued unrelentingly I picked up my broom and resumed sweeping. My broom was a product of Sasha's handicraft; to a section of straight inch-thick sapling, Sasha had tied a bundle of twigs, binding them with the strong, soft inner bark of the caraguata, or wild-pineapple, thornbush. (Our baskets and hammocks, which we had bought from natives, were woven of the same bark.) And as I swept the fresh-smelling mahogany floor of the living room with my twig broom, which was a bit noisier than a factory-made broom and looked like the kind no witch is complete without, I regarded our brand-new houseboat home and marveled that this was I, in the heart of the Mato Grasso jungle, being more domestic than my own dear mother back in Philadelphia. I smiled to myself a bit ruefully at

40

the thought. But we really did have a nice little home-on-the-water.

And it wasn't so little, either. The living room, which was also our bedroom, was fifteen feet wide and twenty feet long; it occupied the central part of the houseboat, the "house" structure of which was fifteen feet wide and forty feet long, not counting the deck around it. There was another fairly large room at each end of the living room. The one in front, unused as yet, could serve as an extra bedroom whenever Sasha entertained visiting sportsmen clients while completing preparations for a tiger hunt. The room in the rear Sasha already had fitted up as his workshop, and in it he kept his cameras, outboard motors, carpentering and iron-working tools, his vise, axes, and a kerosene blowtorch. Behind the workshop were two small storerooms. Sasha planned that when we traveled on the river the roomy workshop would become quarters for Lauro and Rosando and their families, and the two small storerooms would house his eighteen hunting dogs. (I wasn't particularly looking forward to traveling this way; it sounded a little too much like Noah's ark.)

I swept underneath the mahogany dining table and moved the two matching mahogany chairs which Sasha also had built. Since we had moved the table indoors, Sasha had worked on it evenings until its surface was fine and glossy, rubbing it down with the leaves of the *lixeira* tree, which are so abrasive that the Indians use them to polish the weapons and ornaments they make of wood, horn, and bone. Sasha planned eventually to make several more dining chairs for use when we had sportsmen. But there were so many more necessary things to finish on the houseboat.

I stooped to sweep under my bunk—Sasha had built two roomy ones end to end for us; during the daytime they were lounges, or jungle-style sofas—and as I did so I started, for in the half-darkness there I saw two close-set eyes glittering at me. It was Rupert, of course. Sasha had insisted on bringing him with us to the houseboat.

"Rupert!" I muttered resentfully. "Why don't you become a snake in the grass? Go away and find a mate."

I poked my stiff broom about under the bunk, and Rupert sleepily uncoiled his eight-foot length and slithered closer to the wall, all the while eying me unblinkingly, even when the broom twigs scuffed him. For some reason his stare made me slightly uneasy. Which was foolish, of course, for a boa constrictor no larger than Rupert was harmless so far as human beings were concerned. In fact, one as lazy as Rupert was largely harmless even so far as rats and mice were concerned, which fact I had several times pointed out to Sasha.

Though, to be completely fair, I must admit Rupert had had absolutely no opportunity to exercise his mouser talents since we had moved aboard. One of the many advantages of living in a houseboat instead of a house was that this way, anchored a few feet from shore, we were invulnerable to invasion by rats, mice, ants, termites, and other crawling land pests. The houseboat's only connection with the bank was a narrow plank walk which we let down during the daytime, when it was improbable that these unwelcome visitors would attempt to use it. And at night we pulled our plank drawbridge aboard and were as secure from invasion as any medieval knight in his moated castle.

Not that termites would have been much of a problem, anyhow, for Sasha had assured me that mahogany was one of the few woods which was termiteproof and wormproof. This was one of the reasons he had built the entire houseboat, including the thirty-six-foot dugouts on which it floated, of mahogany. He had chosen every material which had gone into it for strength and ability to resist the factor of decay, which goes on at a much more rapid pace in the tropics than elsewhere. He had even decided against using steel nails, knowing how fast they would rust in the heavy dampness and unending rains of the wet seasons. Instead, he had purchased a large quantity of brass screws and had used them throughout.

As I swept under the other bunk I glanced back at Rupert; I was disconcerted to realize that he was following my movements with his head; his beady eyes had never left me. A bit uneasy, I bumped my elbow against the bunk.

"Damn," I muttered; I reminded myself that if I hadn't allowed Rupert to get on my nerves this way I wouldn't be so clumsy. I wondered resentfully why I let him bother me. I had been used to him a long time now.

When I finished sweeping I wiped off the mirror and dusted the books in our built-in bookcase—another product of Sasha's fine hand for cabinetmaking.

At that moment a woman's voice called from the riverbank:

"Senhora! Senhora, may we have permission to come aboard?" the voice said.

I moved to the screen door. On the bank were Cenaria and Antonia, Lauro's and Rosando's plump wives. With them was Maria, one of Cenaria's small daughters by her first husband. Cenaria held a basket on her head piled high with fruit, and Antonia was returning our laundry. Little Maria was hanging onto her mother's shapeless but clean cotton dress.

"Come in, Cenaria! Enter, Antonia!" I greeted them politely.

"Thank you, senhora." Cenaria's round, light-skinned face beamed with her smile; Antonia, much darker and, like her husband Rosando, undemonstrative, merely bobbed her head stiffly; little Maria was scowling. In single file they mounted the narrow plank walk and crossed over the intervening eight feet of water. Their bare feet padded noiselessly across the deck and through the doorway as I held the door open. (All Mato Grosso natives go barefoot; as a result virtually all have hookworm.) I waved to the table, and the women trudged over and deposited their armloads.

"You finished early, Antonia!" I exclaimed as she put down the laundry—khaki shirts and trousers for Sasha and me, cotton underwear, handkerchiefs, socks, towels, tablecloths, bed linen, all of which she had soaped and rubbed by hand at the river's edge early that morning, while kneeling on the bank and watching warily for piranhas; she had then spread the clothes over the grass, where they dried quickly in the broiling sun. The clothes were neatly ironed; both Cenaria and Antonia were trained to use a charcoal iron.

"Sim, senhora," Antonia replied with a bashful, pleased smile. She busied herself rearranging the clothes, to cover her embarrassment at my compliment.

"Cenaria, what fine fruit!" I stood watching her empty her basket. There were *ginipapos,* which look like large greenish-gray peaches and have a sweetly acid taste; *goiabas* (from which the widely sold guava jelly is made), which look like gigantic plums and are yellow outside and pink inside; papayas and *jaboticabas*, a unique, large, cherrylike fruit which grows, without stems, directly on the limbs of the tree and thus gives the bark the odd effect of being studded with giant rubies. Cenaria added a couple of palm hearts from the bottom of the basket, then smiled happily.

"Much fruit today, senhora! Rosando"—she turned to beam on the silent Antonia, to indicate that the credit was Antonia's, since she was Rosando's wife—"Rosando went out early and picked it, four, five leagues away."

And immediately I thought: Why don't I can some of these luscious wild fruits which grew so abundantly throughout the jungle? I could easily make preserves and jams and jellies, as housewives did at home. That is, if I had some Mason jars. It was impossible without Mason jars. Maybe next year Sasha could get me some.

Cenaria touched one of the palm hearts and looked up at me slyly.

"Senhora, there is plenty of palm beer now!" She smiled invitingly. "Does the senhora desire some? Lauro can get it."

"Well, that's nice," I said. "Maybe a little palm beer would be good for a change."

"My man will bring the senhora some," Cenaria said decisively, as though Lauro would have no say in the matter.

Palm beer is a mildly intoxicating beverage which nearly all Mato Grosso natives drink, as it is manufactured at the cost of no labor whatsoever. The beer is a by-product of the popular appetite for palm hearts, for after the tender heart has been carved from the center of an acuri palm's luxuriant crown of fronds, the sweet sap automatically collects in the hollow thus made and ferments. The result is palm beer, available by merely climbing the tree and scooping it out of nature's fermentation vat with a gourd. The Bororo Indians have cut the labor involved in getting it to the irreducible minimum. A Bororo merely shinnies up the tree with a hollow reed in his mouth and sips palm beer on the spot until he can drink no more.

"Thank you, Cenaria," I said. "Sasha will enjoy some palm beer."

All this while nine-year-old Maria, Cenaria's eldest, had been clutching her mother's dress, twisting bashfully about on one bare foot and staring at me.

"Mama," she said abruptly, still keeping her eyes on me, "Mama, I'm hungry!"

"Maria!" Cenaria spoke brusquely and tried to disengage the child's hand from its grip on her garment. When Maria refused to let go, she slapped her.

"*Mama!*" Maria began to cry, and—still hanging tightly to her mother's dress—began rubbing her eyes with both fists. "You *hit* me!"

"I can get something for her——" I began hastily.

"Não, não, senhora," Cenaria protested hurriedly; she had a firm grip now on Maria's shoulder, and she started to shove the child toward the door. Antonia, who had not said a word, smiled at me again, bobbed her head, and began moving after Cenaria.

"We will go home now to eat," Cenaria explained. "Lauro will come soon. Maybe it is time, so he will come with me now."

She was right, for it was almost noon, high time for the men to quit work for lunch and a siesta through the hottest part of the day. And, to prove the correct timing of her visit, at that moment the piercing scream of the buzz saw dropped pitch in a descending whine, faltered, and died. The ensuing silence was broken by a loud, jovial outburst from Lauro—as always when quitting time arrived.

Cenaria and Antonia already had the door open and were backing out, but I could see little Maria's face still showed her disappointment at not receiving anything from me, and I remembered there was a piece left of a cake I'd made a couple of days before. I quickly got it and offered it to the child, who smiled and snatched it in her grubby little hand. She said nothing but beamed her pleasure.

"Thank you, senhora," Cenaria supplied quickly, looking embarrassed; she scowled at her daughter and aimed a slap which the child expertly dodged. "Maria is a bad girl!"

Sasha and Lauro arrived at the foot of the gangplank. Seeing his wife on the deck, Lauro stood on the bank and shouted at her to hurry because he was hungry. And Cenaria, with an annoyed frown, shooed her daughter before her across the gangplank; Antonia followed. Sasha, after a moment of amusedly watching them all climb the bank, came aboard and strode into the living room; the screen door slammed behind him. He pulled me toward him briefly, crushing me to his damp shirt front; then he stepped back and held me at arm's length, took out his handkerchief, and pretended to mop his brow.

"Well, my dear!" He grinned in high good humor. "Isn't the day laborer worthy of his hire? Aren't you going to feed him?"

I was conscience-stricken.

"I'm sorry," I said. "I've been so busy—so busy that I guess I just didn't realize it was nearly noon."

Sasha placed his hands on his hips and frowned at me.

"You have been waiting for me to do the cooking again!" he said with mock ferociousness. "It that it, *mulher?*"

"Don't call me 'woman'!" I snapped. "Who do you think I am? Some Indian squaw you bought for a bottle of rum?" I added ungraciously after a moment, "Well—what do you want? There's nothing but that eternal beefsteak."

Sasha rubbed his hand thoughtfully over his beard. "We've had nothing but steak lately. I've no appetite for any more."

"Nor I."

Sasha's face brightened.

"This is the time to tap our fish reserve." He grinned and snapped his fingers. "A small hunk of bread, mulher, while I prepare my fishline."

I made a face at him but got the bread.

Sasha had discovered that he could train our neighbors in the river to become regular and useful visitors by feeding them frequently from the deck. He had thus "tamed" a sizable school of fish known as *piraputanga,* which were delectable. When fed, they would surface in large numbers and could be hooked one after another. But finesse was necessary, for they were shy and easily frightened.

I stood beside Sasha on the deck facing the open river and peered into the water, which was fairly clear, although the bottom was invisible.

"I don't see any," I murmured unhelpfully.

46

"Don't be so impatient. After all, I haven't started yet." Sasha gave me an amused look.

He began tearing the bread and kneading it into tiny pellets which he tossed into the water. They started to float slowly away with the current. Then suddenly a fish broke the surface and gulped one; another appeared, and the next instant the water directly below us became a merry-go-round of flashing silver bodies as dozens of the fish, each a foot to two feet long, swirled about fighting for the bits of food.

"See!" Sasha flashed me a glance of triumph. "And now for the strategy."

He gave me the remaining bread and I continued breaking it up and dropping it on the water as he had done, to keep the school there. In the meantime he covered the point of a fishhook with bread and lowered it, by a short hand line, to the water. It hadn't touched the surface yet when it was gulped—and Sasha immediately jerked the eager fish out of the river and swung it onto the deck. He repeated this until he'd caught six piraputangas within not much more than the same number of seconds. That was all we needed; I dropped the remaining bread crumbs on the water, there was a short flurry of fins, and then the school disappeared and the water was quiet.

The technique, as we had learned by experience, was never to allow a hooked piraputanga to struggle in the water, for then the rest instantly became frightened and dashed away—and they would stay away for days. But if the fish was jerked out the moment he was hooked, before he had had a chance to struggle and thus telegraph his predicament to his fellows, we could catch as many as we wanted.

Sasha quickly filleted the fish on the large kitchen table which we kept on the rear deck. When he had finished he gathered up the remains, which were already attracting flies.

"We shall now summon our sanitation department," he announced in a businesslike voice.

He referred to our garbage collectors, who usually showed up and waited within a few feet of the houseboat—not only ready, but eager and panting—to collect our food scraps after each meal.

I turned to watch.

Sasha picked up a fish carcass and flung it into the river about ten feet from the boat. Then he picked up another and tossed it after the first, and a third, and a fourth.

But the second carcass had barely struck the surface when out near a large mud flat there was a sudden splashing, and from what had been a quiet, innocuous-looking stretch of water there emerged nearly a dozen large alligators, lunging through the water with clumsy haste. Three arrived simultaneously, and two of them quickly gulped a carcass apiece. The third was swallowing his when another greedily grabbed at the tail still hanging from his jaws and got the larger part of his fish. He uttered a bellow of rage and lunged furiously with wide-open jaws at the encroacher, who backed water, his jaws wide open, too, and hissing like a snake.

At that moment the water boiled suddenly, and there was the metallic glitter of a swarm of small fish churning and leaping about in a maelstrom before us. The other half of our garbage-disposal service—the piranhas—had arrived. Though few in number, they dashed heedlessly among the alligators.

Sasha tossed the remaining fish carcasses in their midst.

The nearest of the big saurians lurched awkwardly forward. But the vastly faster, vicious little piranhas beat them to it, and in an instant were furiously crowding about the tidbits, tearing them to pieces.

The disgruntled alligators clumsily withdrew and subsided, sinking a few feet away so that only their large bulging eyes showed above the water's surface; and for several minutes they watched us silently, waiting to see if there would be more. The piranhas vanished as mysteriously as they had come.

Sasha addressed the alligators solemnly:

"That's all, commissioners!" He peremptorily waved them away. "Come back again this evening."

I laughed. "Do you think they understand English?"

"Naturally," he retorted. "Portuguese, too. They're apt students. Watch them leave now."

And of course the alligators, realizing by now that there would be no more handouts, leisurely began returning to their favorite mud flat, pairs of eyes trailing wakes behind them.

48

I grinned. "Well, smarty, how about helping me carry this stuff ashore?"

We still did our cooking on the riverbank, using the open grill and the anthill oven. As soon as Sasha would have time to make the one-thousand-mile round trip to Corumbá, he planned on bringing me a real stove—a wood-burning iron range complete with oven —which we would install on the houseboat.

"Immediately, my dear," Sasha agreed. He quickly filled a washbowl from a pitcher of river water—we used river water for all purposes, including drinking, as Sasha considered it perfectly pure; he scoffed at the occasional visiting sportsman who wanted to boil it to kill the germs.

He scrubbed his hands, using soap we had made ourselves. (We made soap by dissolving caustic soda in water, adding beef fat, and boiling the yellowish-white mixture; after it thickened somewhat we cut it into cakes. If we desired a harder soap we merely added resin before boiling it.) Then we went ashore, where it took only a few minutes to fry the fish fillets and some cassava cakes and heat a kettle of water for maté.

We returned to the houseboat with the food, and I set the table while Sasha obligingly washed some fruit and palm hearts —whistling boyishly as he did so.

After the glare of the noon sun the inside of the houseboat was pleasantly dim and cool. We sat down; Sasha placed maté leaves in glasses and poured the preliminary cold water over them. I tasted my fish and it was delicious. By this time we both were half starved, and we ate silently. I finished before Sasha and leaned back with a contented sigh, then selected one of the peachlike ginipapos and bit into it. Its acid-sweet taste made it an ideal dessert fruit. Sasha suddenly took a bit of fish up in his fingers and held it over the side of the table.

"Sit up! Beg for it!" he said, grinning. Then he dropped the morsel.

There was the flash of a long, serpentine neck as a flat head shot upward; its jaws opened wide and gulped the falling morsel; then it drew back again. How long had Rupert been there without my seeing him? I shuddered mentally as I pictured the snake gliding up noiselessly behind my back, and immediately I was resentful because Sasha had enticed him to the table without warning, causing me to be thus disagreeably startled. And at the same time I felt provoked with myself for feeling the way I did. I had forced myself to tolerate Rupert's comings and goings for months; I'd even pretended to be, like Sasha, half fond of him. But now . . .

"Why must you always feed him?" I demanded. I'm afraid I spoke somewhat querulously. "He'll never catch any rats or mice if he isn't hungry!"

Sasha looked up, surprised, from his glass of steaming maté.

"There aren't any rats or mice on the houseboat," he replied simply. "You don't want Rupert to starve, do you?"

I almost retorted with a defiant "Why not?" but thought better of it. Instead, I made an oblique attack.

"When you drop food on the floor," I said petulantly, "I'm the one who has to sweep it up."

Sasha glanced down at the coiled, motionless snake watching us with its beady eyes, as though hanging on every word.

"I don't drop food on the floor, dear." He smiled in amusement. "Rupert never misses!"

"Oh, Rupert—Rupert—*Rupert!*" I said in exasperation, mimicking him. "You talk about that—that serpent as if he were a person! I'm sure you prefer him to me!" Angrily I threw the ginipapo I had been eating onto my plate, pushed my chair away from the table, and stalked across the room. I found myself at the window which overlooked the open river, and I leaned my chin on my hands with my elbows on the window sill. I stared moodily across the water, brassy and blinding in the broiling midday sun.

There was a heavy silence for several moments.

Then Sasha's chair scraped back from the table. I didn't move, even when I felt Sasha's arm across my shoulders and his beard tickling my cheek. He turned me around, gently but firmly.

"Good lord, let's not quarrel about a snake," he said in a worried tone. "You've been working hard, and it's hot." He led me across the room toward our bunks. "Come, lie down and take your siesta like a good girl, and then you'll feel better."

I made no attempt to resist; I felt, at the moment, completely enervated and sapped of initiative. But when he half lifted me

50

into my bunk and began gently pushing my shoulders back
against the pillow, that was too much.

"I'm not sick," I protested, resenting his silly concern.

Sasha shrugged. "It's siesta time, anyway. Sleep for a couple
of hours. We'll find out then."

I scowled as he put his hand on my forehead to feel if I had a
fever and then—apparently satisfied I hadn't—studied me for a
final quizzical moment before going to his own bunk.

I lay not moving for several minutes, annoyed with myself and
annoyed with Sasha—annoyed especially with him for that masterful way of his with which he immediately assumed I was "sick"
or "overtired" because I had been slightly critical, putting me in
the wrong, of course. Naturally, I told myself with heavy sarcasm,
he couldn't be wrong. Never! He and his damned Rupert! "Love
me, love my snake": that was practically grounds for divorce.

And where was Rupert now? From Sasha's slow, regular
breathing I could tell he had fallen asleep already. Glad that he
couldn't laugh at me, I sat up quietly and looked across the room.
Rupert was nowhere in sight, and I felt a momentary alarm.
Maybe he was under my bunk again! I wanted terribly to lean
over the edge and look, but I dreaded having my suspicions confirmed and meeting those glittering eyes. I morbidly imagined the
snake lying motionlessly beneath me, quietly waiting, biding his
time. Then I gripped the side of the bunk hard and gritted my
teeth. What *was* the matter with me? Rupert was perfectly
harmless. I'd never been really afraid of him before, or even
uneasy.

I must force myself to think of other things. Of home, and my
mother, for instance. I hadn't had a letter from Philadelphia for
over a month. It had been that long since we'd seen the mail boat
—the small, overloaded launch which valiantly made the five-hundred-mile trip upriver through the jungles from Corumbá. It came
approximately once a month, except during the height of the
rainy season, when we received no mail at all. Accordingly, it was
a big occasion whenever we did get mail. I wondered how Mother
was, and I thought, too, about my riding horse, Sparks, and my
old Scotch terrier, Peter. I wondered if anyone was exercising
Sparks, and I thought a bit sorrowfully that nobody else ever

would do it exactly the way he liked. I felt a sudden pang. Would I ever again see Mother, and Sparks, and good old Peter?

Then with a start I realized what I was doing. Surely I couldn't be homesick? I'd felt rather proud of my adaptability in *not* being homesick. All right, maybe I was a little homesick. But this hadn't happened before in all the time I had been with Sasha, for wherever Sasha was, of course, was home now.

A large yellow-and-black butterfly lit on the window screen above my bunk, and I watched absently as it opened and closed its wings, slowly, rhythmically, as if breathing with them. There was a sudden roar from one of Sasha's caged ocelots, of which he now had three in our little zoo a short distance down-river. Sasha turned over in his sleep, and his breathing became more audible, though, thank God, he never snored.

I wasn't sleepy. I dwelt on this somewhat bitterly and self-pityingly, resenting it that Sasha should be sleeping when I wasn't. He could have stayed awake and talked to me, I thought. It was little enough time he spent talking to me! When he wasn't sleeping he was working—or going someplace—or wanting to go someplace.

And why didn't that stupid, slow mail boat arrive? It was always late. It must be at least six weeks now since it had come. I squinted at the calendar hanging on the wall beside the mirror, across the room. Yes, it was six weeks yesterday. We had received five letters from Mother then, besides a letter from a prospective hunter and some advertising circulars. So that sluggish, impossible old mailman was already two weeks late, and heaven only knew how much longer we'd have to wait. I remembered the last delivery. Sasha had been on a short expedition upriver with Lauro and Rosando to get more mahogany logs, and I had had the fun of reading all our mail first. Then a sudden thought struck me. SIX WEEKS ago!

The thought hit me with the impact of a small lightning bolt. I sat erect in my bunk and leaned forward to look at the calendar again. Then I hastily scrambled up and strode across the room to turn back to the preceding month. I counted the days off.

"Heavens to Betsy!" I muttered, half aloud. "It *is* six weeks!"

I was so dazed at the thought that I found myself sitting on my bunk without knowing how I'd gotten there.

Maybe that was why I was so—so jittery—so unreasonable! Maybe that was why Rupert bothered me so much more than he used to! Maybe that was why . . .

I suddenly *had* to tell Sasha. I stood up. My legs felt shaky, but I felt an enormous exhilaration. I flew over to Sasha and plumped myself down on his bunk, then unceremoniously began shaking him.

"Sasha! *Sasha!*" I shouted. "Wake up! Wake up quickly, I've got something to tell you!"

"Huh?" Sasha stirred sleepily without opening his eyes.

"Wake up! Darling!" I yanked his beard. *"Sasha!"*

"O-o-o-w! Stop it!" Sasha opened his eyes wide and looked at me accusingly. "Just because you're still peeved about Rupert, you don't have to get violent." He rubbed his chin.

"Sasha—Sasha," I stammered, almost breathless in my excitement. I leaned over him.

He sat up abruptly.

"What is wrong, Edith?" he demanded, alarmed. "Tell me at once!"

"Nothing is wrong, silly!" I gulped, to catch my breath, and beamed on him. "Oh, Sasha, what—what would you like to have most—in all the world?"

Sasha blinked, then cocked his head and looked at me through narrowed eyes.

"What is this? A guessing game?" he said irritably. "Is that all you woke me up for? To ask foolish questions?" He lay back on his pillow and closed his eyes again.

"Oh, *Sasha!*" In a burst of annoyance at his sleepiness I beat my fists against his chest. "Sasha—*don't* you understand?" I smiled at him.

He slowly shook his head.

"Oh, you're so thickheaded! So stupid!" I retorted, exasperated. Unable to sit still with the excitement of my secret, I flounced about on the bunk, then drew my feet up and sat on them, cross-legged, in a very unmaternal pose. I regarded him then with what must have been a smugly beatific smirk. "Sasha," I said sweetly, "don't I look different?"

He stared at me hard, then—still baffled—shook his head once more.

"Sasha," I said, "we're going to have—a visitor—in—well, in a few months!"

"We are?" Sasha echoed; he stared back at me dully. "Who? Your mother? Did the mail come?"

"Oh, nuts!" I retorted, all my exuberance abruptly deflated. I reached out and roughly pushed his head sideways into the pillow. "You lunkhead! What do I have to do—start knitting little garments?"

Sasha's jaw gaped, and he stared at me unbelievingly.

I nodded and began feeling suddenly flustered—like a blushing Victorian bride.

We sat for a long time, talking and planning, and progressed to a point where we agreed that he would be a boy, that we would teach him to ride and swim by the time he was two years old, and that we would take him along on tiger-hunting trips from the age of six months. We would name him Alexander, which was Sasha's real name, and we would call him Sashinho, which means "Little Sasha."

CHAPTER 2

ONE AFTERNOON A FEW DAYS LATER THE MAIL BOAT FINALLY arrived. I happened to be on the houseboat deck, filling a pitcher with water from the river and talking to Sasha, who with Lauro and Rosando was working directly opposite on the bank. They were laying a plank deck on a barge which they had built by joining, side by side, two of our thirty-six-foot dugouts. The barge, twelve feet wide, would be towed behind the houseboat to carry our animal cages and heavy impedimenta whenever we moved our water caravan.

But when the small mail launch, its low gunwales almost awash, appeared around the river bend a half mile downstream and slowly chugged toward us, the men all dropped their tools with a clatter and hurried up the gangplank to join me on the houseboat. The four of us waved and shouted at the launch like a bunch of excited children. And Ricardo, for that was the name of the mailman on our lonely jungle route, raised his right arm in solemn acknowledgment of our enthusiastic welcome. And then we waited impatiently for minutes more while Ricardo's laboring old engine slowly cut down the distance between us.

When its final chug-chug had died with an exhausted wheeze and the dilapidated launch had slid silently the remaining few feet across the smooth water to the side of the houseboat, Lauro and Rosando quickly stooped to make it fast to the houseboat rail. Although neither of them ever expected or received any mail (as a matter of fact, neither could read or write), they always were as anxious as we to see the mailman—for both, Lauro especially, were eager to get the latest frontier-town news.

"Welcome, Senhor Ricardo!" Sasha smiled broadly as he greeted the slight, frail-looking little man. "You bring us much mail, I hope!"

Stiffly conscious of his dignity as the representative of the Postal Department of Brazil, Ricardo removed his sombrero (which he always wore, despite the launch's faded striped awning that amply protected him from the blazing sun) and bowed formally, first to Sasha and then to me.

"I thank you, senhor," he replied imperturbably.

He hitched higher the heavy cartridge belt from which his six-shooter hung and swept his deep-set, fierce black eyes guardedly over all of us, as if to make certain we weren't bandits in disguise who might rob him of the Republic's mails. Then, though his narrow, dark face remained as implacably stolid as before, the heavy, drooping mustache beneath his large hawklike nose twitched slightly.

"Sim, senhor." There was a suspicion of unfreezing geniality in his hollow, almost cadaverous voice, a voice which sounded as though it had grown rusty with long disuse over many years of lonely journeys up and down the jungle river. "Sim, senhor, I have much mail for you. For both you and the senhora!"

"Oh, wonderful!" I exclaimed, beaming on him; it required will power to restrain myself and allow the poor man to give us the mail in his customary deliberate, ceremonious fashion—the only break in his monotonous, lonely existence.

"Sim, senhor. There are many letters," Ricardo assured us again weightily. He stooped and opened a worn leather mailbag wedged amid the kerosene tins which occupied most of the space in the launch—fuel for his long trip. He extracted a thick bundle tied with a dirty piece of cord, then placed it on one of the kerosene tins while he retied the mailbag carefully and with madden-

56

ing slowness. At last he picked up our packet of letters (I was practically ready to snatch them at this point), straightened up, and with another faint twitch of his enormous mustache—which was the closest he ever came to a smile—he once more bowed with ceremony and presented the little bundle to Sasha, saying pompously:

"The mail, Senhor Siemel!"

"Thank you, Senhor Ricardo." Sasha smiled and returned the bow as he accepted the packet; quickly he broke the string that bound the letters and began flipping through them, handing mine to me as I hung over his elbow. But absorbed as he was, Sasha did not forget the amenities. He smiled hospitably and urged, "You will stay the night, of course, Ricardo?"

"I thank the senhor." Ricardo again bowed; then he shook his head slowly and reluctantly. "But não. I can still get back to the Descalvados Estancia landing before darkness comes. It is better that I begin my return trip and spend the night there."

The Descalvados landing was nearly thirty miles down-river.

"You must go on?" Sasha said politely, tearing his eyes from the letter he was already reading. I had completely forgotten poor Ricardo, being in the midst of the first of seven letters from Mother; she was telling me what success she'd had in shopping for the chintz and patterns I'd asked her to buy for me in Philadelphia so I could make curtains for our houseboat and slip covers for the bunks. I forced myself to look up politely too.

"Sim, senhor. I must go on. It is my duty," Ricardo answered gloomily.

"But you will have a drink of cachaça before you depart, não?" Sasha continued to keep his eyes off his half-read letter with what I considered amazing will power.

Ricardo sadly shook his head and sat down again in his launch.

"Thank you, senhor, but não. The darkness comes sooner than one expects, always."

"No cachaça?" Lauro echoed incredulously. His face fell; not only was he to be cheated of hearing the latest gossip from Corumbá's frontier bars, but Ricardo's determination was even bilking him of a legitimate excuse to tap Sasha's rum barrel.

"I am sorry, Ricardo," Sasha said. "But you, of course, know what is best." He turned to me. "Are our letters to the States stamped and ready? We don't want to—hold up the mail."

"I'll get them; I have them all ready," I said quickly, trying not to smile at the humor in Sasha's choice of words.

Sasha and I wrote our letters erratically, whenever we found the time, though I usually managed to write Mother once a week. But of course none of these letters could be mailed until the mail boat arrived, and so they accumulated for weeks.

I tied our seven weeks' production of letters tightly with twine, hurried out on the deck, and handed them to Ricardo.

"You will guard them with your life, of course?" I asked teasingly.

"But naturally, senhora." Ricardo gave me a hurt, reproachful look before he turned to open his second mail pouch and insert our letters with meticulous care. As he tied the flap he repeated, with emphasis, "But *naturally*, senhora!"

I felt guilty and explained hastily that I had no doubt of his devotion to his duty.

Rosando untied the launch's mooring rope from the houseboat rail and tossed it among Ricardo's crowded kerosene tins. After an exchange of farewells Ricardo stepped importantly behind the grease-encrusted one-cylinder engine, gave the flywheel a practiced jerk, and was rewarded with a cough, a choking sound, and then a strengthening, steady chug-chug-chug-chug. The heavily loaded launch moved slowly out toward the middle of the river, directly into the glittering path cast on the water by the sinking sun.

Sasha smiled and waved his hand.

"Good-by, Ricardo," he shouted. "Good luck!"

The launch was already about one hundred yards away, looking little and lost on the huge expanse of water. Ricardo, seated in the low-lying stern with his hand on the steering rod, twisted his slight, thin body so that he faced us. Under his wide sombrero all that was visible of his face was his ponderous nose and enormous mustache. But when I shaded my eyes to look against the sun I thought I saw the mustache twitch slightly as he swept his arm up in a solemn farewell.

58

Sasha buried his face in another letter; a moment later he turned to me.

"That countess is definitely coming to hunt with us. Jerry Dill writes she plans to leave Rio on the tenth. Let's see"—he began muttering to himself—"three days by rail from Rio to Porto Esperança—two days by river steamer to Corumbá; she should just be able to catch the steamer. Then he's arranging for her to come up to the Descalvados landing in a chartered launch. And traveling day and night, they could make the five hundred miles in about five days. Ten days in all. That means she'll be due at Descalvados on the twentieth." He paused and looked up. "Why, today's the nineteenth! We're certainly lucky the mail came. She's due to arrive tomorrow!"

I heard what he said without paying much attention, for I was busy ripping open my third letter from Mother. A piece of paper fluttered out and fell to the deck, and I hastily stooped to retrieve it. It was a check for five hundred dollars!

"Sasha! Look!" I exclaimed, exultantly waving it in front of him. "Look! Money from Mother!"

He turned, took the check, read the amount, and then handed it back. He leveled an accusing glance at me.

"Did—you—hint—for—that?"

I shook my head vigorously.

"Why, of course not!" I was emphatic. "All I did was mention in a letter that on account of the war you didn't expect many sportsmen would be coming down to hunt with you this season, except maybe a few Brazilians and Americans, and so we would be forced to live on whatever we could find in the jungle." I stared back at him with wide-eyed innocence.

Sasha shook his head deploringly.

"You don't consider that a hint?" he asked a bit grimly.

"Of course not! I was merely telling Mother how we were getting along. She likes to know everything that happens to us. You wouldn't want me to lie to her, would you? And we can certainly use the money!" Having delivered this double riposte, I quickly changed the subject. "What was that you just mentioned about the countess?"

Sasha showed me the letter from Jerry Dill, the friend who

managed the Eastman Kodak branch in Rio and who had been one of the witnesses at our wedding.

"According to Jerry," Sasha said, "the countess is practically here!"

"No, Sasha! Really?" I pretended I hadn't heard before.

"She should arrive tomorrow!"

Jerry's letter had been written weeks earlier, and it was possible, of course, that the countess had changed her plans since then. Jerry had first written Sasha about her months ago. She had told him she was a writer and wanted to do a book about Sasha, if he would take her on a tiger hunt without charge. (Sasha ordinarily charged fifteen hundred dollars for a month's hunt and then supplied all guns, ammunition, camping equipment, and food —"guaranteeing" at least one tiger.) Jerry had suggested that possibly the publicity from such a book might bring Sasha more sportsmen. Sasha had agreed, after talking it over with me, and had written Jerry to send on the countess. Because of what subsequently happened, I won't identify her except to say that she was an authentic countess from one of the smaller eastern European countries, a refugee living in Rio.

I hastily scanned the letter, then handed it back to Sasha.

"What're you going to do?" I asked.

"We'd better drop everything and get ready to go on a hunt, naturally."

"Am I going along?" It was a question, but the tone in which I said it dared him to refuse.

Sasha raised his eyebrows. "Do you think you should?"

"If you're referring to my condition," I said heatedly, "that's absurd. I feel fine. There's no reason why I can't go."

Sasha grinned. "All right, all right! I didn't say you couldn't."

He handed me the rest of the mail and then went ashore with Lauro and Rosando to begin preparations for the hunt. I went indoors to curl up on my bunk and read the rest of my letters—three more from Mother, one from each of my married older sisters, and a statement from the Philadelphia bank in which I still had a very small checking account.

The next morning Sasha and Lauro started out at dawn to meet the countess, taking an extra riding horse for her and two pack horses for her luggage. But whether she would be waiting when they arrived at the Descalvados landing was anybody's guess, for Sasha could only estimate the time required for her five-hundred-mile launch trip upriver.

In the afternoon I and Rosando and Antonia set out in the opposite direction with Sasha's eighteen hunting dogs, an extra riding horse, and an oxcart loaded with supplies. We even took along two milch cows, with their calves, to supply us with fresh milk. We were bound for Sasha's base hunting camp on the south fringe of the great Xarayes Pantanal, or marsh, in the heart of the best tiger-hunting territory. Lauro's wife, Cenaria, was left at home to feed the animals in our little zoo, as well as take care of Rosando's children and her own—a job I certainly didn't envy her. We were taking Antonia along to do the cooking—and to "put on a little dog" for the countess. Rosando, with his wife beside him, drove our lumbering team of oxen and the heavily loaded supplies cart. I rode with the extra horse and Rosando's horse on lead ropes.

Our trip was uneventful. Because of the slow oxen, we moved at a snail's pace. We camped that night near a little stream at the edge of the jungle. And the next day we started out in the cool dawn and kept moving over the sun-baked, dried-up marshlands until the broiling midday sun forced us to give our animals and ourselves a two-hour rest in the shade of a copse of piuva trees. It was nearly dark when we finally reached the base camp, where Sasha and his men three years earlier had built two fairly large grass huts and a small corral. The camp was ideally located in a small clearing on a rise of ground surrounded by a heavy growth of piuva, *paratudo,* and mahogany trees—some of the last rose to a height of nearly two hundred feet. A stream ran nearby, affording us a convenient water supply.

A bevy of macaws and parakeets, which apparently had been making the clearing their headquarters, fluttered through the trees above and scolded us raucously during our camp-making activities, until—discouraged by the drifting smoke from the fire, and our obstinacy in the matter of moving on—they eventually departed with a few final squawks.

It was too late to do much that night. We hobbled the horses

and oxen and turned them out to graze, put the calves in the
corral to keep the cows from straying, then fed the dogs, had a
hasty meal of charqui ourselves, and retired early.

Sasha, in the meantime, was having some highly disconcerting
experiences, although I wasn't to learn of them until twenty-four
hours later, when his party rode into camp with the countess and
her luggage.

He later related the events to me in a somewhat stunned manner when we were alone.

The countess had not yet arrived when he and Lauro reached
the Descalvados landing. But, very luckily, she appeared later that
same day. She proved to be a lean, nervous woman in her forties,
with an odd shade of auburn hair and an affected manner,

Sasha said that, although he didn't think much of it at first,
the decided coolness he observed between the countess and the
three boatmen who had brought her upriver should have warned
him. He got more of an inkling from the language she used in a
squabble which arose as she was paying them off.

She refused to pay the amount originally agreed on, accusing
the shocked elderly pilot of trying to drown her by what she
termed his reckless handling of the boat; she slandered the boat
itself by calling it a dirty, leaking old tub; and she finally intimated, not very subtly, that if she hadn't kept her eyes constantly
on her luggage he and his men would have stolen most of it. She
concluded her tirade against the abashed and humiliated old man
by extracting from her money belt an amount considerably short
of that which he had claimed as his due and threw it at him,
telling him that was all he deserved and all he was going to get.

After thus rudely dismissing her launch pilot she turned to
Sasha and in a patronizing manner explained in Russian that
"these natives are all thieves!" (Jerry Dill may have told her that
Sasha was a fluent linguist and spoke six languages, including
Russian—or she may have chosen Russian merely to impress him.
She herself had a quite adequate command of several languages.)

Before the countess had arrived Sasha had stopped at the Descalvados ranch house to try to borrow two vaqueiros who knew
something about hunting. (Since the countess was planning to

write a book about her adventure, Sasha wanted to make this a full-scale tiger-hunting expedition, omitting none of the details. Besides, he needed extra helpers because he was going to try at the same time to capture alive a pair of tiger cubs for a Canadian zoo.) John Ramsay, Jr., the ranch owner, had not only obligingly agreed to lend Sasha two of his men but had insisted that Sasha and the countess spend the night at the ranch house before starting out.

And, as the sun was already setting when the countess arrived, they accepted the invitation.

At dinner she immediately endeared herself to her host and his charming wife by refusing meat, declaring that since she had come to Brazil she had stopped eating it.

"Brazilian meat," she stated with finality, "is poisonous!"

As two generations of Ramsays had devoted their lives and the five-thousand-square-mile Descalvados Estancia entirely to the raising of beef cattle, this was the ultimate insult. And "poisonous" or not, in the cattle-raising Mato Grosso, the largest part of everyone's diet is meat.

When Mr. Ramsay, who was an ardent admirer of Sasha's fearlessness in fighting tigers with a spear, asked him to describe one of his most dangerous fights, the countess interrupted to lecture Sasha on the "barbarousness" of using a spear.

"Shooting a tiger," she pointed out condescendingly, "is the *only* merciful way."

When Sasha ventured to reply that there were times he'd been face to face with a wounded and infuriated tiger when a gun would have been useless and his spear had saved his life, she blandly changed the subject. She gave glowing accounts of her own finesse in hunting hares with greyhounds on her estate in Europe.

A ranch hand had just killed a tiger which had been preying on the herds. He was stretching the skin the next morning and, thinking the countess would be interested, Sasha took her to see it. She glanced at the skin and raised her eyebrows contemptuously —because there were "*two* bullet holes" and they weren't "right between the eyes."

Early in the morning Sasha had sent Lauro and the two extra

men, Manoel and José, ahead with the countess's considerable luggage so as not to be delayed by the slow pace of the pack animals. For the countess had impressed Sasha with the facts that she was an expert horsewoman, loved riding, and desired, above all—as she airily declared—to "canter, canter, canter, over the countryside!"

But Sasha was amazed to find out, within a short time, that she was no rider at all; she was obviously uncomfortable after they'd gone only a short distance. As tactfully as he could Sasha suggested that they rest by dismounting and walking for ten minutes, and she agreed. When it came time to remount, he offered to help her into her saddle.

"No, no!" she tittered, shrinking back. "I never let men touch me!"

So they had to walk their horses for another fifteen minutes until she could find a tree stump from which she could mount alone!

As she refused to use a spur on her horse because it was "shockingly cruel" (and few Mato Grosso horses will mind an unspurred rider), what should have been a single day's ride to the base camp where we awaited them required two full days—even though they took a short cut. It was fortunate, Sasha said, that they caught up with Lauro and the two vaqueiros that first afternoon, so the five were together when it became dark and they had to make camp. If the men hadn't been there to serve as chaperons, Sasha explained with a wry grin, he was convinced the countess would have spent the night astride her horse. As it was, she insisted on borrowing Lauro's six-shooter and sleeping on her side of the fire with the gun strapped to her waist. Her transparent excuse was that a tiger might approach during the night to investigate the fire, and she wouldn't want to miss the chance of shooting it. She was a "very light sleeper," she added pointedly.

All of this, of course—plus Sasha's budding conviction that he had, to say the least, a very odd character on his hands—I didn't learn until hours after the five of them arrived. When they rode into camp late in the afternoon I expectantly ran out to meet them; I had looked forward with considerable pleasure to meeting the countess. After all, I hadn't seen a human being from "outside" since we had left Rio, right after our marriage. I had hoped that this visiting woman writer, even if she was a countess—for after all, she was going to be our guest; Sasha wasn't charging her a cent for a month's hunt—would be as amiable and as entertaining as Katherine Elling, a brusque divorcee with a Rabelasian sense of humor whom we had taken hunting just before we had been married and who had been the last white woman I had seen. But in this I was speedily disillusioned.

Sasha greeted me with a broad smile and an enthusiastically shouted "Hello, darling! We've arrived, finally!" He dismounted and tossed his reins to the ground. Lauro and the vaqueiros, grinning cheerfully, jumped down, too, and began unloading the pack horses. The countess remained stiffly in her saddle, coolly regarding me as if I were some zoo captive, until I felt my warm smile beginning to fade. Sasha strode over to take the reins of her horse so that she could dismount.

"Countess," he said in a voice smooth with amiability, "this is Edith, my wife."

I smiled again.

But the countess merely raised her eyebrows as she continued to stare at me.

"Ah—Madame Tiger Hunter!" she murmured with a slight smile and an air of supercilious amusement. Then she dismounted slowly, paying no more attention to me than she would have to a stableboy or some equally lowly servant on her east European estate. I was embarrassed by her rebuff, although I was willing to forgive it as being due to her different background, telling myself that she probably didn't really intend to be rude. However, to cover up my moment of disconcertedness, I spoke to Sasha hurriedly, asking if they had had any trouble and telling him we had half expected them the previous day. Sasha started to reply.

"Senhor Siemel," the countess rudely broke in, addressing him rather arrogantly in Portuguese, "what have you prepared for my quarters?"

Sasha pressed my hand in a quick gesture of understanding,

then turned to the countess. With a casual apology for keeping her waiting he led her toward the huts in the clearing. As I walked beside him he asked whether Rosando had had time to rethatch the roofs, and I explained that he'd been busy all day and that the huts were now in fine shape.

Antonia was on her knees, building a fire, and she looked up as we approached.

"This is Antonia, Countess," Sasha said casually. "Antonia will cook for us. She is an excellent cook."

Antonia stumbled to her feet and, clasping her hands before her, smiled with shy friendliness.

"Hm-m-m-mm," the countess murmured as she literally looked down her nose in cold appraisal of the flustered woman.

"Where is Rosando, Antonia?" Sasha asked hastily.

Antonia pointed across the clearing.

"Ah, patrão—an hour ago he went by foot that way." She smiled anxiously. "Rosando thought he would find a deer."

"That is good," Sasha replied. "Splendid."

We moved on to the doorway of the first grass hut; it was the one where I had slept the night before, and I mentioned this to Sasha. Sasha looked up to appraise Rosando's work in covering the two sides of the steeply sloping roof with new palm fronds, then nodded absently, evidently satisfied with the rethatching job. He turned to the countess.

"This is the women's quarters, then," he said, waving toward the square roomy hut—really no more than a heavily thatched rainproof roof on poles, as the four sides were but sketchily walled with marsh grass to admit the cooling breezes. "Lauro will hang a hammock for you when he brings your luggage."

The countess looked aghast.

"You have no separate quarters for me?" she said in a horrified voice; her eyes flashed. "I must have separate quarters, Senhor Siemel! I demand it! This is an impossible situation!"

There was a moment of tense silence; I looked at Sasha and he evaded my glance; he stroked his beard noncommittally and pursed his lips. Then he turned to the countess with disarming equanimity. "I had thought that since we are roughing it, our two huts would be sufficient. Forgive me, Countess." He spoke

66

politely, but I knew him well enough to see the veiled mockery in his eyes.

He turned to move away. "Some of the men will start work on a third hut at once."

"I should hope so!" The countess imperiously tossed her auburn hair, then smiled primly. "I have never lived in a hovel before. It will be an *adventure!*"

Carefully avoiding my eyes, Sasha murmured something about going to find Lauro and turned and strode away; I, too, withdrew quickly—ostensibly to help Antonia.

And so, with no time to rest after their long ride, Lauro, Manoel, and José were put to work building a third grass hut. They took time out only for a hasty supper when Rosando returned with a deer, and finished the hut late that night. It was smaller than the other two but more heavily thatched about the sides, insuring greater privacy. And the countess, when her luggage had been moved in, withdrew to it without so much as a "Thank you!" or a tardy apology for the extraordinary exertions caused by her demands. The exhausted men went to their hammocks, too, but Sasha and I sat talking nearly an hour by the fire—mostly about the countess.

"At least now," I commented sarcastically as I bade Sasha good night, "there's no danger of her being contaminated by being forced to sleep under the same roof with the cook and me!"

Sasha smiled thinly, then kissed me lightly and strode to the hut he would share with the men.

When Sasha and I went on a hunt alone we occupied one of the huts and the native men the other. But when a sportswoman was included in the party all the men took one hut and the women took the other. The latter arrangement was necessary this time, even though the countess now had a separate hut, because Antonia was along.

The next day, out of consideration for the countess and her undoubtedly tender bottom after her two-day ride, Sasha decreed that we would not go hunting immediately but would rest instead. However, to keep the countess from becoming bored, Sasha gave her a .22 rifle and a box of super-speed cartridges and sent her out with Lauro to shoot alligators in the stream. She had said she wanted to take home a couple as trophies—though God knows why.

Hours later they returned, with the countess petulantly declaring that the gun Sasha had given her was no good. She had shot an entire box of cartridges and hadn't hit an alligator! Sasha and I were astounded, for alligators are such slow and stupid creatures that you can kill them with a club. When Sasha later questioned the usually voluble Lauro about it, he merely shrugged, looking somewhat dazed.

So the next morning Sasha decided to test her marksmanship. On the edge of the clearing he set up a foot-square target and asked her to shoot at it from a distance of fifteen yards. I wanted to see this and managed to cross and recross the clearing on various duties. Believe it or not, she didn't hit that absurdly easy target once in ten tries!

And she wanted to hunt *tigers!*

It was Sasha's rifle that was at fault again, of course.

"I am not accustomed to your guns, Senhor Siemel," the countess declared haughtily as she returned the rifle after her ten misses. "If I had my own handmade guns with me, *mon Dieu,* it would be different! Mine have beautiful balance."

"But these are quite good guns, Countess," Sasha replied mildly.

"They are factory-made!" the countess sniffed. With an indifferent shrug she moved across the clearing to her hut.

I approached Sasha with a malicious grin. He looked at me and shook his head slowly. Perversely enjoying the situation, I complimented him on his self-restraint, for I knew what pride he took in his guns; they included the very best American, German, and English firearms and represented a considerable investment; and since he was an expert gunsmith, they were always in the finest condition.

However, Sasha was determined to see the deal through. So, starting that same afternoon, we rode out each day with the dogs over good tiger territory. But after a week we still hadn't found a fresh trail.

And the countess, as we had anticipated, became more and more disagreeable. From the very first day she complained continually—about her hammock, the mosquitoes, our native helpers, our horses and guns and the food.

She still refused to eat "poisonous" Brazilian meat, and though we tried to provide enough other food for her, there wasn't too much available in the jungle except wild game. However, she had brought along a trunkful of chocolate and concentrated foods, canned and dehydrated, and she ate these in the seclusion of her hut. She had brought her own tea leaves, too, and she brewed the tea herself, refusing to let Antonia touch it.

At variance with this fussiness and contrary to my previous ideas about European nobility, the countess was not physically clean. During all the time she was with us she never once bathed —and the weather was extremely hot. Nor did she have any of her clothing, either shirts or underwear, laundered—although Sasha had told her Antonia would do her washing in the nearby stream whenever she wished.

And then there was the incident of the milk.

Taking milch cows along on a tiger hunt so the countess could have fresh milk daily sounds, I know, as though Sasha slightly overdid his cushioning of visiting sportsmen against the rigors of camp life. However, Sasha himself would have been the first to admit, a bit smugly, that he missed no opportunity to provide everything possible to set up his hunting expeditions on the grand scale upon occasion. Besides, it afforded him a chance to demonstrate how completely he had mastered the problems of living in the jungle.

Sasha and his men originally had captured our milch cows by lassoing the half-grown calves of wild cattle—cattle which long ago had escaped from the ranchers' herds and taken their chances in the marshes with the tigers, pumas, ocelots, and wolves, and as a result had become as wild and tough as buffalo.

Milking such redoubtable animals required a masterful technique—you virtually had to be a trained bullfighter and a practicing psychologist.

Our technique was rather sensationally demonstrated the first and only time the countess watched us. Manoel and Antonia were busy elsewhere, and the countess and Sasha merely watched. But each cow engaged the united efforts of all the rest of us, including

Lauro, Rosando, José, and myself. Months earlier, in my mania to prove myself equal to the jungle's hardships, I had insisted on doing the actual milking once the cow was readied for me, and I had been doing it most of the time since—that is, on the somewhat infrequent occasions when our desire for milk, cream, and butter impelled us to make the strenuous exertion.

I insisted on doing the milking this time, too, in spite of my condition and Sasha's objections; he remained near me with a worried expression.

When we began operations the two longhorns were standing beside the calves' corral, just barely tolerating their offspring's suckling through the fence.

Warily coming up behind one of the cows, Lauro and Rosando simultaneously tossed their lassos over her dangerous three-foot spread of horns and dragged her—decidedly reluctant and bellowing loudly—to a sizable tree and tied her head tightly to it. This, of course, nullified her ability to turn on the men and gore them. But it left her kicking and thrashing about with her equally deadly hind legs. The next step was to lasso them and keep the rope taut, thus immobilizing her at both ends. This was imperative, for if the cow could break loose, she would turn on the hapless milker and gore him and stamp on him, cutting him to ribbons.

However, even after being rendered helpless at the front and rear, the cow would fight back by refusing to let down her milk for a human milker.

"Now, José," the sweating Lauro directed as he hung onto the tightly snubbed lasso securing the cow's hind legs, "now rope the young one!"

José quickly lassoed the cow's frightened calf and dragged it to its mother's teats, where, after a moment, it started suckling. This calmed the fighting, bawling cow somewhat. After a few minutes the roped calf was dragged away from the teats, and its head was tied against the cow's hindquarters, so she could feel it rubbing against her flank. And then I hastily stepped up with my pail and started milking. As the cow's head was tied so tightly to the tree that she couldn't turn to look backward, she thought her calf was still suckling and so let down her milk.

70

(*Above*) General Theodore Roosevelt, Jr., with jaguar he shot and (*below*) jaguar wearied by the chase.

When after all of this the first squirts of milk dinned tinnily against the bottom of the pail, the countess turned to Sasha and languidly observed:

"But it seems so inefficient and unnecessary, Senhor Siemel. The peasants on my estate did it much more quickly. Why, the stupidest little milkmaid"—from the cool amusement in her voice I knew she was directing this at me—"managed perfectly well alone!"

I felt a sudden wash of anger welling up within me; I turned to scowl at her. Just at that moment the calf let out a loud and doleful bawl. And the cow, realizing that it was not her calf who was taking her milk, suddenly gave a mighty bellow and heaved and bucked and then kicked so hard that even though three men were holding the ropes she knocked both the calf and José to one side. I half dodged, half tumbled to safety, out of the way of the sharp hoofs. The pail spilled, of course. And I heard the countess's tinkling laughter behind me.

"Senhor Siemel"—she spoke airily as she started moving away—"you really should see one of my clever little milkmaids!"

Sasha had his arm around me and was anxiously asking if I was all right.

Lauro stood looking at me, then glared at the disappearing countess and said defiantly:

"I don't like that one, patrão!"

Naturally there was no use trying again to milk that cow, so the men let her loose and roped and tied the second one, and we were able finally, without too much difficulty, to fill the pail a third full.

The pay-off came, however, when Sasha poured a large glassful and presented it to the countess. She was quite effusive in her thanks, and I thought she was trying to make amends for her callousness. She explained to Sasha that she had hardly expected to have the good luck to get milk regularly in the jungle but that she would have missed it greatly if she hadn't. And then she dipped her hands in the milk and washed and massaged first them, and then her face, with it!

"My skin is *so* delicate," she informed her gaping, almost horrified audience, "that I simply *must* bathe it in milk!"

Needless to say, so far as the countess was concerned, our two cows gave no more milk for the remainder of the hunting trip. We were always either too busy to milk them, or when we did try, we found that their calves already had exhausted the supply.

However, we were all much more preoccupied with tigers, or rather the lack of tigers, than we were with cows and milk.

After ten days of luckless rides out from camp with the pack, threading the fringes of the jungle and beating through the high brown grass of the dried-up marshlands, the countess began making more and more sarcastic gibes about Sasha's hunting ability. He tried to explain to her that tiger hunting *is* like that—uselessly, because she had the annoying habit of paying absolutely no attention whenever anyone attempted to explain or in any way reply to a criticism she had made. In fact, she gave the impression of not even *hearing* the reply, and she was completely heedless of any advice, even after she had solicited it.

We were sitting around the campfire after another day of riding behind the pack. Sasha, somewhat discouraged himself by this time—because the countess was heckling him almost constantly about his failure to find a tiger for her to shoot, and doing it in Portuguese, so that our natives could not fail to understand her remarks—tried again to explain to her that tigers couldn't always be found on order.

"There's no reason to give up hope yet," he said encouragingly. "Luck is such a·huge factor in hunting. And your luck can change overnight." He smiled. "I remember a few years ago—within a period of only eight days—I killed eight tigers, one puma, and two ocelots!"

The countess raised her hairline eyebrows and smiled cynically.

"Really, Senhor Siemel?" She extended her long carved-ivory cigarette holder and daintily flicked the ashes from her cigarette. "You amuse me. You of course have witnesses—and signed affidavits?"

I was sitting, hugging my knees, on the other side of the fire, staring morosely into the flames and watching the sparks ascend like fireflies toward the black patch of sky above us that seemed so small and crowded by the huge trees of the encircling jungle. And when she said that, for a moment I felt an impulse to pounce on the witch and claw at her. Maybe I could claw out some of that infuriating, patronizing, insulting offensiveness. And then I bit my lip hard and told myself to calm down or my emotions might have a harmful effect on my baby.

Sasha, however, drawing on his store of stoic calm—it amazed me that this was lasting so long, for he was very sensitive and on occasion I had seen him display a hot temper—ignored, or pretended he hadn't heard, her intimation that he was lying.

A sudden strong breeze stirred the tops of the towering trees barely distinguishable in the thick darkness overhead, and the updraft caused the dying flames to leap with new life. Lauro, stretched out with his chin on his hands, sleepily gazing into the fire, abruptly nudged Manoel. And Manoel, for once not bragging to the men about his hunting exploits, lazily moved a few feet to reach for a fresh log. A dozing hound yelped as he stepped on its tail. From the stream came a distant splashing and the sharp squawk of a water bird.

I began thinking of my baby. In about seven months . . . I began to picture what he would look like—for of course he would be a boy—and my eyes, glazed in thought, dwelt on Sasha's face. Sashinho, I decided, would, of course, have Sasha's fine forehead, his high, intelligent, thoughtful forehead, his frank, honest blue eyes, his wavy brown hair. I wondered whether babies were born with curly hair or all had straight hair at first. . . .

Sasha's deep, well-modulated voice was pleasant.

" . . . So hunting is as much a matter of luck as a matter of skill," he resumed. "Take, for instance, Theodore Roosevelt, Jr. Colonel Roosevelt was one of the best hunters I've ever known, and certainly the best sportsman."

The countess flicked the ashes from her cigarette.

"Really?" she murmured in a very bored manner.

Sasha pretended her ejaculation was one of encouragement.

"And yet he had the worst luck of any sportsman I've hunted with in twenty years. He came down here early in 1935. He wanted to kill a tiger and a tapir, to set up a habitat group for the American Museum of Natural History in New York. And we hunted every day for nearly a month—for twenty-eight days, to be exact—before we even *saw* a tiger!"

I looked over at the countess. She was patting the head of one of the dogs, obviously paying little or no attention.

"The main reason, of course, was that we were hunting during the wrong season," Sasha continued, determined to be completely honest, even though his admission neutralized to some extent the effect of his argument. He cleared his throat. "Colonel Roosevelt came here in what normally would have been the beginning of the dry season. But unfortunately the rainy season lasted longer than usual, and the entire region was still badly flooded. Which made hunting extremely difficult."

He gave the countess a bland look and added, "But Colonel Roosevelt never once complained about the hardships or our hard luck. And when he finally got his tiger he said it 'had been well worth the waiting!' "

Sasha concluded abruptly: "So you see, Countess, there's no reason to worry. Our luck may change tomorrow!"

The countess yawned, ground out her cigarette against her boot heel with deliberation, and stood up before replying.

"I fail to see any connection between your Colonel Roosevelt and myself." She gave an affected laugh. "*My* time is valuable! *Good* night." And with that she sailed off disdainfully to her hut.

I picked up a stick of wood and hurled it into the fire so violently that a shower of sparks flew up. "And to think that Jerry Dill did this to us!" I groaned.

Then there was the incident of the *novatos,* the fire ants, whose bites sting like a burn for hours afterward. These ants live in the hollow trunks of novato trees, which consequently are known as fire-ant trees. If you carelessly brush against a fire-ant tree, the ants swarm out immediately and drop on you by the hundreds, with extremely painful results.

When we rode single file through the jungle, the countess loved to play gracefully with the leaves of trees. Several times she had thus jarred the branches of a fire-ant tree. She, herself, was already past and out of the ants' way by the time they swarmed out. But since at Sasha's suggestion I always rode behind her, to keep her from straggling even more than she did and becoming lost, I invariably got the indignant ants all over my head and shoulders and was badly bitten.

74

Twice I pointed out this fact to the countess and politely asked her to stop. But she merely laughed merrily and continued to grab for every branch within reach. I complained to Sasha at that point, and he spoke to her too. She became incensed.

"But it happens I *enjoy* doing it!" she stated arrogantly, as though that settled the matter. And she continued.

By this time I found myself developing a great dislike for her. In fact, her only likable quality, so far as I was concerned, was her genuine fondness for dogs and horses. Yet her kindness to animals did not extend to the wild life. Sasha several times reprimanded her for holding impromptu target practice on birds and small animals as we rode along—for unnecessary and indiscriminate killing was something Sasha abhorred and always discouraged. But she was such a poor shot, the wild life really was in no great danger.

After more days of unsuccessful hunting, finally one morning the dogs broke away excitedly on a trail. We rode furiously after, and I soon found myself up with Sasha in the lead; then we happened to look back and saw that the countess was half a mile behind. Sasha waved at her and shouted, urging her to hurry. But she had obstinately refused to wear spurs, so her horse continued to plod along at a slow pace. Exasperated, Sasha told Lauro and me to follow the dogs and try to hold the tiger until he got the countess in place for a shot; then he rode back. But she refused to let him jog her horse. As Sasha later wryly told me, she informed him she was "in no hurry; the tiger must wait."

However, by this time Lauro and I had found out that it wasn't a tiger after all; contrary to all their training, the dogs had been chasing a peccary. We called off the pack and galloped back to tell Sasha.

The countess smiled at him and ·carefully inserted a cigarette into her ivory holder, waiting for him to light it.

"I *knew* it wasn't a tiger," she said sweetly.

Two weeks now had passed without any luck. Then early one afternoon we chased up a tiger while we were riding through the dried-up marshland, and he made immediately for the thickest part, disappearing completely into brown grass eight feet high. The dogs plunged forward.

We started to ride after them through the high grass, which came up to our chins when we sat our horses, and we tried to see where the tiger and the dogs were but could locate them only by the movement of the grass, for they were completely invisible. Then Sasha said something to me about the countess's marksman-ship—under such conditions.

"Good lord," he muttered, "I'd give her a shot at a treed cat; but on the ground, with all of us in this grass . . ."

He wheeled his horse and rode back. I saw him take away the rifle she carried and instead give her a six-shooter revolver; I heard him telling her to use it only for her own defense.

"Stay back," he cautioned her. "Stay back as far as possible!"

Then he rejoined me and we spurred our horses to catch up with the dogs. Lauro and Sasha took the lead, I was behind, and the countess was much farther back.

The dogs were excitedly baying; apparently the tiger had turned and was making a stand—although neither the tiger nor the dogs were visible in the high grass. Sasha and Lauro and I dismounted; Sasha had his spear unsheathed.

All at once I saw the tiger rushing at him from a distance of less than eight feet. Sasha barely had time to swing his spear to-ward the big cat when it dived for his legs—and the blade caught it in the mouth. I shivered with excitement, my hands tense on my rifle, as I watched from not more than forty feet away. The tiger withdrew, snarling, and dodged back into the brown sea of grass, out of sight again. I could see Sasha waiting, his spear poised tensely, expecting another attack.

Suddenly there was a deep guttural roar, and a tawny spotted streak charged into our midst. It seemed to come directly for me. Almost blindly I raised my gun.

I shot.

Lauro shot.

I shot again.

The tiger staggered, coughed, and abruptly slumped over, dead.

Sasha and Lauro hurried up. I was still trembling. And the dogs rushed in, growling, to tear at the dead tiger's carcass.

"Nice shooting, Edith," Sasha said, coming over to clasp my hand.

"Well"—I smiled up at him rather shakily—"I don't know who killed it. Lauro shot too!"

"Não, senhor," Lauro interjected with uncustomary modesty. "The senhora killed him!"

We beat the yelping, growling dogs off and examined the dead tiger, which was an average-sized male. Lauro stooped and pointed out a wound near the tip of the long tail.

"See, senhor, this is where my bullet hit him!" He grinned and shook his head lugubriously. "That didn't kill. If the senhora wasn't a good shot, she would be inside the tiger by now!"

I smiled; Lauro was trying to make me feel good. I had a pretty good suspicion that that tail wound was my first shot, when I had been too excited to aim properly. Though certainly one of the two other telling wounds in the tiger's body had come from my gun.

Abruptly there was a shout from some distance away. It was the countess.

With an impatient exclamation Sasha quickly remounted his horse and rode back. I mounted also and followed him at a slight distance, while Lauro started skinning the tiger.

The countess obviously was angry. When I rode up Sasha was apologetically explaining that he had only asked her to stay behind for her own safety and that of the others; that a tiger in such high grass was no job for any amateur.

She was looking at him icily.

"That was extremely stupid of you!" she suddenly flung at him. "I could have finished that tiger off with a single shot. But undoubtedly you wouldn't have held me back," she added maliciously, "if your wife weren't so jealous of my hunting!"

"Well, really!" I started to sputter; then I quickly bit my lip and, as if by accident, I raked my horse's flank with my spur and he lunged off—back toward where Lauro was skinning the big cat. I didn't want to get involved in an open quarrel with her; Sasha was having too much of a headache with her as it was. But to accuse me of being jealous of her hunting ability was the most ridiculous thing I had ever heard. Hunting ability! Why, she couldn't even shoot straight! And so far as my being jealous of her in any way—that was fantastic! She must have been having hallucinations. I reined up beside Lauro and sat my horse, pretending to watch him as he squatted in the bloodied grass, expertly wielding his machete as a skinning knife, and I fumed inwardly.

Then I heard the countess's and Sasha's voices behind me, becoming louder and sounding angrier. They rode up and drew rein beside us, still talking; the countess was shaking her riding crop emphatically at Sasha.

"I must say, this tiger hunt has hardly progressed as I anticipated!" she railed, her voice tense with barely restrained hysteria. She leaned forward in her saddle with her chin lifted haughtily. "Indeed, my good man, this hunt has hardly progressed in any manner! As a—as a *guide,* you have been a great disappointment to me!" She flicked Sasha's hand with her crop, as if she were rapping the knuckles of a recalcitrant peasant. "I should have had a shot at seven or eight tigers by this time! Instead of which"— her voice rose to a shrewish pitch—"I have lived two weeks in your primitive camp under the most harrowing and degrading conditions—conditions to which *I* am unaccustomed, let me assure you—and been bored to tears and insulted, a victim of your wife's jealousy—and although I have endured all this patiently, I haven't even had one shot at a tiger!"

"But—but, Countess——" Sasha tried to interrupt unsuccessfully.

"Instead"—she looked at what Lauro was doing and swept on wrathfully, gasping with the force of her outburst—"instead, you call me over to see the revolting, bloody carcass of an animal that someone else has shot already! That *several* other people have shot already! If you had had the decency to wait for me—— I understood that this hunt was being held for *me*"—her voice dripped sarcasm—"not for the members of your household! If you'd had the decency to wait for me, there would be only one bullet hole in that miserable hide!" She contemptuously waved her crop at the half-skinned tiger at her horse's hoofs and went on: "You have behaved outrageously. I have never seen such poor sportsmanship in my life! This is enough. I am returning to Rio at once!"

"Just as you wish, Countess," Sasha interjected coldly, his lips set in a tight line. My spirits immediately rose. Were we finally to be rid of the witch? I carefully avoided her eyes and concentrated on watching Lauro.

"And I certainly have no intention"—the countess half snorted, half laughed, in what was meant to be an expression of bitter contempt—"I certainly have no intention of putting you in my book!"

Sasha inclined his head with stiff dignity.

"That, my dear Countess"—there was a fiery glint in his narrowed blue eyes, and I could tell by the way he sat his horse, ramrod-straight, that he was fairly seething with anger, though his voice was calm—"that, my dear Countess, at this point is a matter of the utmost indifference to me!"

I felt like cheering him.

"Senhor Siemel," she retorted with frigid hauteur, "I shall expect you to arrange for my transportation to Corumbá—immediately!"

And with that she wheeled her mount and, quivering with outraged dignity, abruptly started off through the high brown grass in the direction of our base camp. Her withdrawal, however, was made slightly ludicrous by the fact that instead of dramatically galloping off she moved away at a slow jog—frothing rage racing off astride a tortoise.

When she was well started I met Sasha's eyes.

"Don't tell me we're actually getting rid of her!" I was delighted.

Sasha smiled grimly.

Lauro had hacked off two sizable sections of the tiger's ribs; these he wrapped in the heavy tawny hide—we would barbecue the ribs for dinner—and tossed the bundle across his horse's withers. He aimed a kick at a couple of the dogs that were sniffing hungrily at the remains of the carcass—Sasha never allowed the dogs to eat the meat of any carnivorous animal unless it had been cooked, because most carnivores were infected with filaria, a tiny wormlike parasite—and wiped his bloody machete with a handful of grass. He looked up at Sasha with a sly glint in his black eyes.

"Patrão," he said eagerly, "tomorrow when the she-devil rides, I think her horse will throw her!" He grinned mischievously as he pictured in his mind what he was planning, then hinted at what he meant: "Perhaps a little thornball underneath her saddle?"

Sasha shook his head sternly.

"No, Lauro. No," he said. "Remember, she's still our guest!"

" 'Guest' is right," I observed ruefully. "She's not paying a damn cent! And now we're not even going to get any publicity out of it, either!"

On the way back we soon overtook the countess, who was still plodding along. As she completely ignored our presence, the situation was somewhat awkward. Sasha and I fell back and walked our horses some distance behind her, discussing whom we best could spare to take her down to Corumbá. Lauro, however, had spurred his horse and was riding ahead of her as we entered the jungle, nearing the camp.

Suddenly there was an outraged shriek from the countess, and she began wildly slapping her head and shoulders and tearing at her shirt.

"*Nom de Dieu!*" she spluttered.

We cantered up hastily, just as Lauro was explaining with effusive apologies: "It was my stupid horse, *Condessa*. He stumbled with his foot in a hole and knocked me against this fire-ant tree!" He lifted his hands in a gesture of helplessness, then shot a quick look of childlike innocence at Sasha and me.

"Lauro, I want to speak to you when we get back to camp," Sasha said ominously, but his eyes sparkled.

Early the next morning Rosando and his wife left with the countess and all of her baggage. The night had failed to thaw the lady's frozen aloofness, and our farewells were strained. After reaching our houseboat the three of them would transfer to one of Sasha's larger dugouts, equipped with an outboard motor, for the long trip down-river to Corumbá. Having to send Antonia along was a final annoyance, for it cheated us of our cook and laundry woman. Despite the fact that time and again Rosando had proved himself perfectly trustworthy in every way, we knew that unless his wife went along as chaperone the countess would be fearing rape beneath every tree.

Sasha had no intention of terminating the hunt just because the countess had left. For one thing, he hadn't been on a tiger hunt for a long time. He had been working steadily for months, building the houseboat; he felt, and I agreed, that he owed himself the relaxation and fun of a good month's hunt. Besides, we still hadn't captured the cubs to fill the order from the Canadian zoo.

My duties had increased, since with Antonia gone someone else had to do the cooking, and I seemed elected for a large share of it, although José had some skill in that line and usually helped me. Manoel was proving quite a disappointment. Not only was he lazy and inclined to dodge irksome jobs by wandering out of call on some vague errand, but he had long ago become a tedious bore with his bragging stories of his skill as a hunter. And according to Lauro, he griped constantly because Sasha had failed to take him along on our hunts with the countess, assigning him instead, with Rosando and Antonia, to the "woman's job" of un-exciting camp duties and drudgery. He was "a hunter—not a handyman."

So Sasha, who was now in a particularly good mood since he had finally got rid of the countess and could hunt just as he wished and without the constant need of anxiously worrying over a tenderfoot, decided to humor Manoel and said he could go along with us on the hunts henceforth. José alone would stay at the camp during the day to guard our livestock—which otherwise would be defenseless prey for any prowling big cats or wolves— and our cooking utensils, spare guns, and other equipment— which, being largely metallic and bright and shiny, would attract the bands of little monkeys which occasionally swept through the treetops, chattering and squeaking and extraordinarily curious and kleptomaniac.

It wasn't until after several days of leisurely, unsuccessful hunting that the dogs again ran across a fresh tiger trail. It was in the damp rusty-red mud on the sloping bank of a small stream, where the tiger had come to drink. Lauro dismounted to examine the footprints.

"It is a tiger, all right, patrão," he announced with a broad grin. "But a small one."

"Only a small one?" Manoel echoed. He snorted disgustedly;

then, with a fine show of contempt, added, "That fails to interest me!"

"But a cub is exactly what we want," Sasha reminded him smilingly. "Two cubs, that is. Remember?"

Lauro quickly unleashed the dogs and remounted.

The dogs barely nosed the trail and then raced off, yelping excitedly. We cantered after, pounding through tangled caraguata thorn thickets, splashing across a shallow lagoon, riding recklessly through a sizable patch of thickly foliaged acuri palms, and then headlong over a meadow lush with waist-high swamp grass for three or four miles.

"Aiyya-a-a-y!!" Lauro bellowed, standing up in his stirrups and leaning forward on his horse.

The rest of us, equally uninhibited, whooped like Indians.

Valente, Sasha's master dog, was far ahead and running like a streak. The other dogs were tiring already and some distance behind. Sasha dug his rowels into his horse's flanks, and I spurred mine too.

Then abruptly Valente, about a mile in the lead, turned into the jungle and disappeared among the trees. The other dogs raced after and also plunged in. Skirting several more thorn thickets and a group of obelisk-like anthills, we pushed our sweating, lathered horses through the high grass toward the ragged fringe of the jungle.

At that moment we heard the deep baying of Valente. And then the other dogs joined in, hysterically barking and howling.

"They've treed him!" Sasha cried exultantly.

I leaned across my pounding horse's withers and grinned at him. He could always interpret from his dogs' voices alone, when they brought a tiger to bay, whether it was on the ground or up a tree. With the tiger at bay on the ground, the dogs knew it might at any moment make a rush and pounce on them, and their baying, therefore, had a distinct note of fear, combined, however, with a grim gameness to fight. But with the tiger treed, the dogs knew from experience that it would remain contemptuously looking down on them and, less afraid, they gave voice in a recklessly brave and challenging tone.

We reached the edge of the jungle and rode in. It was fairly open, unlike the deep jungle which would have been impenetrable except on foot. But we had to proceed slowly, picking our way over creepers and vines. We were guided by the frenzied voices of the dogs. The going became more and more difficult, and I thought we would have to leave our horses behind.

Then abruptly we saw the tiger.

It was just a half-grown cub stretched lazily on a limb of a quebracho tree, about forty feet above the ground, gazing calmly down at the pack of dogs, who were howling and leaping at the base of the tree in a paroxysm of excitement. As we came up the cub looked at us curiously a moment, then yawned in our faces. Obviously he had never seen a human before and had no fear of us. Like most Mato Grosso tigers, the only thing he ever had had cause to fear, perhaps, was the combined wrath of a large drove of vicious, scissors-tusked peccaries—and they were easily evaded by a single bound into a tree.

Gazing at us in a bored but curiously kittenlike manner, the cub occasionally turned to glance down reproachfully at the dogs making such a bedlam at the foot of his tree.

Abruptly Lauro gave an ejaculation of surprise.

"Patrão, patrão, look higher!" he shouted excitedly, pointing up into the branches. "There is another one up there!"

I peered into the dense foliage overhead.

About twenty feet above the first cub was a second, sitting on a limb and watching us alertly.

"What luck!" Sasha exclaimed. "This makes up for the last few weeks!"

Manoel, the eager tiger hunter, stared up at the higher cub, then turned to Sasha and with a cocksure grin promised:

"I'll go up and knock that one over the head and bring him down in my pocket!"

Sasha, I noticed, looked at Manoel a bit oddly but refrained from comment. Instead, he shouted at the dogs, trying to make them reduce their earsplitting clamor. We dismounted, and Sasha instructed Manoel to tie our horses' reins securely to trees a short distance away; he told Lauro to stay where he was and keep an eye on the cubs; then, motioning me to follow, he started off deeper into the jungle.

"You feel all right, Edith?" Sasha asked as I swung into stride beside him; he looked at me anxiously, as if fearing I might momentarily turn green or faint. Probably he was a little conscience-stricken about the manner in which he had given himself over to the excitement of the chase, letting me fend for myself until that moment.

"Of course, silly!" I retorted. I felt wonderful. But it *was* nice to have him worrying over me.

I hastily grabbed his arm to save myself from tripping over the thick trunk of a parasitic vine. Sasha drew his machete from its scabbard at his waist and hacked at the chokingly heavy undergrowth. A few more steps, and then we halted and looked around us.

It was deeply shaded and cool where we were. Many of the trees rose to a height of one hundred and fifty to two hundred feet, and their foliage met and meshed so thickly above us that the ground was kept in a perpetual dusk. Far overhead, only tiny serrated bits of blue sky were visible.

"That looks as though it'll do," Sasha said abruptly, pointing to one of the lower limbs of a paratudo tree, dwarfed beside several giant mahogany trees. He thrust his machete in its scabbard and started climbing the tree he had chosen.

I knew what he sought—a straight, light pole, twelve to fifteen feet long, with a crotch at the end. In a moment he had hacked off the limb and it fell; he climbed down and trimmed it quickly. Then we started back, our guide the voices of the still vociferous dogs.

The two cubs were stretched out in the tree almost exactly as we had left them. The one on the lower bough was leisurely washing his front paws with his tongue, occasionally pausing to peer down at the yapping dogs below, as if he wished to goodness they would stop their uncouth noisemaking and be off about their business so he and his brother could resume the game of tag they had been playing out in the sun among the anthills and the thorn thickets and the high brown marsh grass.

Sasha took a lasso which Lauro had brought from his saddle and hung the open noose over the forked end of his pole; then he coiled the rest of the lasso loosely about the pole. He had

Manoel get another lasso and explained what he was to do; then he warned me to stand back. With the lasso stick in his hand, he started climbing a medium-sized piuva tree which grew conveniently close to the tigers' tree. He halted when he was approximately as high above the ground, in his tree, as the lowest-perched cub. Watching the young tiger closely, he addressed it in a combination spider-to-a-fly and bedside-manner tone.

"Now, my pretty one, don't be frightened," he began soothingly as he cautiously moved his long pole so that the forked end, from which dangled the open noose, approached the cub's head. "I won't hurt you, youngster. Don't be afraid."

Lauro, Manoel, and I stood below in a semicircle about the base of the tigers' tree, staring upward. I held my rifle, a Savage .22 High Power. Lauro and Manoel had left theirs under another tree, but both wore their six-shooters.

"Why don't you sing him a lullaby too?" I suggested in a nervous attempt at a joke.

Manoel tipped his sombrero farther back on his head, thrust out his chest, and hooked his thumbs in his cartridge belt. He rocked swaggeringly on his widespread bare feet so that his huge spurs jingled.

"Wait until that one comes down," he promised with a confident grin. "I will show him who is his master!"

Lauro gave Manoel an annoyed look; apparently he had heard too much of this sort of thing.

The noose dangling from the forked end of the stick in Sasha's hand was slowly approaching the young tiger, who—completely oblivious of the threatening danger—continued absorbedly to wash first his front paws and then his forelegs with his tongue.

On the tree limb twenty feet above him, his brother was arching his neck and peering down, naïvely curious about what was going on.

With the unusual clarity with which you often see such things during a tense moment, I was noting with admiration the handsome pattern of the cub's skin (the black rosettes that so dramatically enhance a jaguar's tawny hide are irregular and frequently resemble the inky imprint of a half-opened hand) and thinking what a fine winter coat it would make. That is, if we *had* winters requiring coats in the jungle.

At that moment Sasha's dangling noose, swaying slightly as he shoved it forward, brushed against the cub. The young tiger raised his head and innocently swiped at the lasso with his paw, as if it were a bothersome fly, then returned to his ablutions.

Sasha had withdrawn the noose a foot or so when the cub had struck at it; he held it motionless. Then, slowly, deliberately, he moved it again toward the cub's head.

"Easy—e-e-easy," he intoned as he did so. He sought, of course, to attract the cub's attention sufficiently so it would raise its head again.

And the cub looked up at the words, turning to regard Sasha, ten feet away in the neighboring tree, for an unfrightened moment, then stared with a puzzled expression at the dangling noose approaching again. His long tail began to twitch to and fro, rhythmically. He was beginning to become a bit nervous.

At that instant Sasha dropped the noose over the cub's head. In a fraction of a second he had pulled it tight, dropped the pole, passed his end of the lasso over a nearby limb, and jerked hard.

The cub was ripped from his perch. And a moment later a half-choked, spitting, clawing ball of tawny spotted fur was swinging like a pendulum from the limb of Sasha's tree, trying with frantic contortions to free itself.

As we shouted enthusiastically from the ground Sasha began playing out the free end of the lasso and lowering the young tiger.

"He's all yours, Manoel!" Sasha called down, panting a little from the weight of the cub, which must have been at least one hundred and fifty pounds.

Manoel swaggered confidently forward, carrying his lasso. He paused to be sure that we were watching him, then grinned. "I shall tie a knot in the young one's tail!"

By now Sasha had lowered the wildly twisting and struggling young tiger almost to the ground, and Manoel started carrying out Sasha's earlier instructions. While the three of us watched with somewhat cynical amusement—for Manoel had bragged too much during the past weeks—he fumbled awkwardly about, trying to tie the cub's thrashing hind legs, while still avoiding being ripped by the sharp claws. The cub was frantically clawing with its front feet at the tight noose, trying to get it into its mouth. I observed that Sasha was beginning to look annoyed at Manoel's clumsiness and obvious timidity. If Manoel didn't hurry——

Suddenly Manoel let out a shriek of fear, dropped his lasso, and ran.

The cub, which had chewed through the noose, ran too—but in the opposite direction.

However, in a frenzy of terror Manoel raced to his horse, leaped on its back, and spurred it wildly—completely oblivious of the fact that the horse was still tied to a tree!

And before Lauro—who was laughing so hard he was choking and unable to talk—could convince Manoel that the young tiger had fled and he actually was in no danger, the poor horse, from rearing and bucking against its close-hitched halter rope, was as lathered and sweating as if it had been galloping for miles.

Sasha had been thrown off balance when the cub dropped to the ground but fortunately had managed to grab a limb and save himself from falling; he now quickly climbed down.

We didn't lose the escaped cub. The dogs had eagerly taken after it the moment it chewed itself free; they brought it to bay again in another tree only a short distance away. Although Sasha had some difficulty slipping the noose over its head a second time, for it had become wary, he finally succeeded. This time Lauro tied the cub—tying the hind legs and then the forelegs, and finally lashing the rope tightly around both knots to draw all four legs together. We thrust the well-secured animal into a makeshift sack contrived from a saddle blanket and heaved it across Sasha's saddle. The second cub was still high up in the original tree, and we lassoed, tied, and bagged it similarly, with no more difficulty.

All this was done, however, to the accompaniment of loud and pitiless ridiculing of the luckless Manoel by Lauro. And Manoel, who felt his disgrace deeply, slunk about—for once without a reply —allowing Lauro to bully him mercilessly.

After the second cub had been trussed up and bagged, Lauro first tossed it across Manoel's saddle. Then he quickly switched it to his own horse, apologizing effusively.

"I am exceedingly regretful, my brave vaqueiro!" Lauro pretended extravagant concern for his co-worker. "For the moment I forgot young tigers give you the running sickness!"

When we were mounting to ride out of the jungle Lauro stared at Manoel long and hard.

"Do my eyes deceive me?" he exclaimed, turning to us with feigned consternation. "Our Senhor Manoel is untying his horse!" He shook his head with a baffled expression. "And here I thought he always rode with his *cavalo* roped fast to a tree!"

The final insult to Manoel came after we reached our base camp with our two handsome but dangerous young captives. While Sasha and I retired to our hammocks for a short rest before dinner, Lauro drafted José to help him build two small wooden cages for the cubs. And while they worked he must have briefed José on all the details of the day's hunt.

For that evening at dinner, as soon as we had seated ourselves around the campfire—the *pièce de résistance* was five muscovy ducks we'd shot on the marsh coming back—José approached the glum Manoel, holding his hands behind his back.

"It is an old saying, Manoel," José began, "that the wise man eats the stork to lengthen his neck. And he drinks the blood of the bull to grow strong. So I have saved this for you."

He drew his hands from behind his back and with a solemn, completely dead-pan expression ceremoniously presented Manoel with a tin plate piled high with fried ducks' wings.

"A master tiger hunter must be swift. If he cannot run fast enough, he should grow wings!"

I began to feel sorry for the poor man. I knew he must be feeling intensely ashamed of his cowardice, especially since he could be certain every cowboy on the enormous Descalvados Ranch eventually would hear of it.

Early the next morning we were awakened by the mournful howling of the tiger cubs in their cages. So while the men were collecting firewood and building a fire, Sasha and I fed the cubs ourselves.

They were restively pacing up and down in their small cages when we came up, and the saplings which formed the bars had been well chewed during the night.

"They're such graceful animals," I remarked to Sasha as we

88

stood watching them. "I wish I'd had a camera along yesterday. I could have gotten some beautiful pictures when they were up in the tree. Darn it!"

Sasha pursed his lips and nodded. Then he added dryly, "It's certainly too bad we didn't get some movie film of Manoel and the cub!"

I stooped before the nearest cage and, bringing my face close to the hardwood bars, puckered my lips and emitted what was meant to be a friendly feline purr. The cub inside raised his head and gave a throaty growl. His eyes looked angry and menacing.

I stood up and shook my head in disappointment. "No friendship there."

Sasha had told me he had never been able to induce a tiger cub to be friendly, although he had captured more than twenty over a period of years and had raised many to maturity; sooner or later, all had become dangerous.

I thought back over what I had learned about tigers from Sasha, who knew a great deal about the subject, since he had killed more than two hundred full-grown tigers, as well as over one hundred pumas, in his role as a professional tiger hunter for the cattlemen.

Sasha had told me that tigers are ruthless individualists, seldom ever hunting in pairs, except when mating. And after the female has her litter of one to five cubs, she is forced to protect them from their father, who would eat them if allowed near. A full-grown Mato Grosso tiger frequently weighs up to 350 pounds and is ten feet from nose to tip of tail; and although somewhat smaller than an African lion, it is faster, Sasha maintains, and equally as ferocious. By actual "clocking" he has proved that a tiger can charge thirty feet in one fifth of a second! Paradoxically, tigers have increased rather than decreased as a result of the beginnings of "civilization" in the Mato Grosso's vast swamplands and jungles. For the tigers find the ranchers' herds much easier prey than the wild deer, peccaries, and tapirs. At the time Sasha established his headquarters within the boundaries of the Descalvados Estancia, tigers were killing six thousand head of cattle yearly from the ranch's herd of one hundred thousand. Sometimes a single tiger killed up to twelve head of cattle in a night, just for sport. A tiger once chased by a hunter invariably becomes wily. And tigers can become man-killers. A tiger who in self-defense has killed a human frequently develops a taste for Homo sapiens.

Dwelling on these things, I stared back into the unwinking, cold yellow eyes of the young tiger in the cage.

"If we had our stockade built now," Sasha said thoughtfully, "we could get some really good movies of these cubs. We'll have to start on it as soon as we go home."

I agreed. Sasha had long wanted to build a high, escapeproof enclosure around a half acre or so of the wooded riverbank near our houseboat, where he could loose wild-animal captives to photograph them uncaged and roaming free amid natural surroundings. He planned to build this as North American pioneers had built Indian-proof stockades around their frontier forts—by setting thick strong poles upright in a trench, so close together that they formed a solid log wall nearly twenty feet high. The area he planned to enclose included a piece of thick woods and even a section of a small stream, so it would make a pretty little park. Sasha planned to build a catwalk high up around the stockade so we could take movies of the animals easily and without their knowledge.

"We have so many things to do," I half protested. "And you don't have the houseboat finished yet."

Sasha grinned and was about to reply when we heard a sharp cry in a tree behind us. We turned just in time to glimpse a furry mask and the glint of two eyes. There was a movement among the leaves, and it disappeared. The cry was repeated, and then I saw the head and furry, hunched-up body of a brownish-red, raccoonlike animal gazing alertly down at us from another, lower limb.

"A *cuati!*" Sasha exclaimed. He smiled. "You don't often see them this close to a camp."

"Why, he looks just like a teddy bear!" I said, delighted. I'd seen one before, but only from a distance.

I had an idea, and I started off on the run toward our hut, calling over my shoulder, "I'm going to get a camera. Don't let him get away!"

Sasha grinned. "I'll tell him you want him to wait!"

Lauro and José, who were starting to prepare breakfast, looked mildly astonished when I dashed up breathlessly and ran into our hut (Sasha had moved in with me, since Antonia was gone), but I didn't bother with explanations. I quickly loaded our movie camera with film.

Sasha was lounging comfortably under the tree when I returned.

"What did you do, take time out for breakfast?" he demanded a bit peevishly. He rose to his feet.

"I had to put film in the camera," I protested. I searched the tree with my eyes, but the cuati had disappeared. I turned on Sasha disappointedly. "Oh, you let him get away!"

Sasha grasped my shoulder with one hand and pointed into the thick foliage overhead. "See—on that crooked limb, close to the trunk."

After puzzling for several moments I could just barely discern a darker shadow among the leaves.

"I can take movies of the tree itself, no doubt!" I said sarcastically.

"Now, *wait* a minute," Sasha said in the tone one might use toward an impatient child. He stepped back from the tree several paces and drew his heavy revolver.

"But you're not going to shoot the harmless little creature?" I protested, horrified; I was amazed that Sasha would do such a thing, for he always was so passionately contemptuous of anyone who needlessly killed the small animals or birds of the jungle.

"Naturally not," Sasha replied. "But I'll bring him out of the tree for you. Get set with your camera."

There was a loud report, and a chip flew from a branch just beneath the cuati.

What happened in the next few seconds is almost indescribable. The cuati tumbled out of the tree and landed at my feet, his furry body rolled into a tight ball. And the next moment the air was full of falling cuatis—all rolled into tight, furry balls— twenty or thirty of them, hurtling down from a dozen heavily leaved branches above. I shrieked and dodged and covered my head with my hands, lest they fall on me. And the young tigers in the cages just a few feet away, frightened by the gunshot and excited by the resulting shrieks and confusion, began to snarl and growl and leap in rage at the wooden bars of their cages. And above all the noise and pandemonium I heard Sasha's hearty laughter.

"Get your pictures! Get your pictures! Quick!" he choked, still laughing at my violent reaction.

Almost too late, I drew myself together and remembered I had a camera in my hands. Almost too late—for barely had I started the film whirring on its spool when the cuatis lying motionless all about me almost simultaneously unrolled and streaked away in all directions.

When Sasha finally stopped laughing he told me I'd just witnessed the cuatis' famous stratagem—they travel in bands, and when one of them is threatened they all tumble simultaneously to the ground and play dead to divert attention and give their threatened fellow a chance to escape. "A noble gesture," he concluded, still smiling.

I set my movie camera on the ground and straightened up.

"Well, it seems rather stupid to me!" I snorted. "You attack one, and so the rest obligingly drop down and lie prone, waiting their turn. I should think——"

I was interrupted by a shout from Lauro.

"Patrão, patrão!" He came running up excitedly. "Manoel is gone!"

"He's always gone," I said cynically.

"But his horse and his garupa are gone too," Lauro insisted with heat. "He must have left during the night!"

"What?" Sasha looked startled.

"All of his things are gone," Lauro repeated.

"They are?" I said blankly. "Do you suppose he's gone for good, then?"

"Well," Sasha mused, "it's strange he didn't wait to collect his pay." He laughed suddenly and said a bit reproachfully, "Lauro, you must have made his life unbearable. It's all your doing!"

Lauro looked momentarily chastened, then grinned.

"But, patrão, I have saved you some money!"

At that moment one of the tiger cubs emitted a dry cough, and the sound seemed appropriately sardonic.

We never saw Manoel again.

CHAPTER 3

THE FOLLOWING DAY LAURO AND JOSÉ STARTED BACK WITH the oxcart, which was loaded with the caged tiger cubs and all the bulky equipment we had brought for the countess's hunt. They took along the eighteen hunting dogs and the milch cows and their calves. As soon as they arrived at the houseboat they were to build larger, more comfortable cages to hold the cubs until such time as we could ship them to the Canadian zoo.

And Sasha and I, left alone in the jungle, started out with just two pack horses—on our long-delayed honeymoon.

We were now not too far from the territory of the Bororo Indians, whom Sasha had first promised to take me to visit when we were returning from Rio after our marriage. It had been impractical to make the trip at the time, since it was the middle of the rainy season and the flooded jungle was almost impassable, and afterward we had started building our houseboat and had been much too busy to leave. But I was determined not to miss this opportunity—even though it broke my heart to think that we had already used all our film taking pictures for the countess and her damned book. And Sasha, after some halfhearted arguing against making the trip while I was pregnant, finally consented. The truth was, I think, that he was just as eager as I.

It was five days' ride to the São Lourenço River, along which the Bororos live in widely scattered villages. The route was entirely through deep jungle. We often rode for hours in its semi-dusk without actually seeing the sun, for the centuries-old trees—many ten feet in diameter at the base, soaring upward to heights of two hundred feet—grew crowded so close that they choked off most of the light.

Riding in the hushed gloom of these ancient forest giants beneath a ceiling of motionless, interwoven foliage was like crossing an enormous empty cathedral whose cavernous heights and vaulted arches were lost in deepening shadows. Dust motes eddied lazily in occasional shafts of slanting light. And the silence was awesome, brooding, haunting.

This was because there is little life in the deep jungle. As the forest floor is too heavily shadowed for grass to grow, herbivorous animals stick to the more open jungle fringes, the grassy largos, and the edges of marshes and rivers. And carnivorous animals frequent the territory of their prey—the herbivores and the fish-eating swamp birds. Seldom do any animals seek the gloomy deep jungle, save as a refuge in which to lose themselves when pursued.

Sasha assured me that there was no danger in our visiting the Bororos unescorted. For although these Indians are shy of meeting white men, they are friendly to the rare visitor, in contrast to the hostile Chavantes and Yanayguas, who waylay and murder strangers, and whose horrible tortures of their doomed captives have been the subject of many chilling jungle campfire tales.

As we rode I thought over what Sasha had told me about the Bororos with a great deal of anticipation. He had said their fantastic customs would convince any visitor that he had stepped into a land of nightmares.

When on the fifth day we reached the São Lourenço, we rode upstream beside it for some hours. We were walking our horses single file—Sasha led, I followed closely, and the two pack horses trailed us on lead ropes—picking our way carefully through the heavy rank undergrowth at the river's edge. Abruptly Sasha turned in his saddle.

"Edith," he said in a low, rapid voice, "look ahead! About three hundred yards ahead!"

I tore aside a thickly leaved creeper vine blocking my view and stared eagerly up the river. At first my eyes were unable to single out anything in the billowing, tangling vegetation that stretched interminably before us. Then I saw a slight movement in the vast tapestry of greenery, and suddenly the startling figure of a naked man whose entire body gleamed a violent, fiery orange-red! He was staring full at us, standing erect and motionless, with one arm thrust forward, balancing a tall bow and unsheathed arrows upright on the ground.

An instant later he was gone. And from the thick green wall into which he had vanished there came a shrill, piercing whistle, as if in warning. I turned excitedly to Sasha.

"Was that—— Is that a Bororo?" I gasped.

Sasha nodded and smiled, amused, apparently, at my reaction.

"He was a Bororo—undoubtedly posted outside a village," he said matter-of-factly; he reined his horse to a more plodding walk. "We'd better go slowly now. He's racing to warn the tribe of our approach!"

"Oh!" I looked at Sasha somewhat anxiously. "You—you don't think——"

"Calm yourself, my dear," he said reassuringly. "I told you the Bororos are a friendly people. The chief himself will be out to welcome us soon."

I said no more, but I was unable to quell a tense feeling of nervous expectancy.

Our horses stretched their necks to crop at the low-hanging tree foliage as we sat them with loose reins.

Several minutes later Sasha gave a grunt of warning.

"Here they come," he said lightly. He straightened up in his saddle and adjusted the cartridge belt about his waist, from which hung his heavy Magnum revolver.

I must have been even more nervous than I realized, for I found myself wishing desperately, and rather ridiculously, for a compact mirror.

Striding toward us through the dense, luxuriant greenness came six giant Indians, their faces and naked bodies all the same shining, lurid orange-red. (I knew this was because they smeared themselves with a paint made from mashed urucú fruit seeds nd fish oil, but the knowledge made the effect no less startling.)

The Indian in the lead, who had a magnificent, broad-shouldered physique, was at least six and a half feet tall. He looked much taller even than this, owing to his towering feather headdress, an enormous fan-shaped affair of blue, yellow, and red feathers, rising perpendicularly from the crown of his head to bring his total height to nearly ten feet! All of the other Indians were over six feet tall, but none wore a headdress. And all save the leader, who obviously was the chief, carried six-foot bows and arrows equally as long. Their greased and glittering straight black hair was cut in low bangs across their foreheads in a sort of Dutch-boy bob. But, counteracting this demure effect, each wore, through a hole pierced in the septum of his nose, a white monkey bone, and a bone button was thrust through his underlip. (I knew these were monkey bones, as Sasha had described them to me long before. And he'd explained that the hole in a Bororo's underlip enabled him to give a unique whistle—undoubtedly the whistle I'd just heard—which was a tribal identification.)

The chief stiffly extended his right arm in a silent greeting and halted a few feet away. The other, armed Indians grouped themselves about him protectively, then stared at us.

"*Bom dia*, Archie!" Sasha said heartily from his saddle as he raised his arm to return the chief's salute. (He had told me the Bororos refuse to disclose their names to an outsider, believing that to do so would give the stranger some evil power over them, so his practice on former visits had been merely to assign the chief a name of his own choosing, for convenience. And his reason for speaking Portuguese, of which the chief undoubtedly understood nothing, was to maintain "face"; although Sasha knew something of the Bororo language, he preferred not to speak it; he would lose prestige if he ineptly attempted anything at which the Bororo excelled him.)

"How are you, Archie?" Sasha added in an exuberant half shout; he grinned amiably at the chief and started to dismount. "You're looking even better than the last time I saw you!"

The chief's impassive face cracked in the semblance of a smile; it was obvious he was responding to Sasha's tone, not his words.

As Sasha strode past me, back toward our pack horses, he replied to my questioning look with the explanation:

"We're in luck! This is the same Bororo tribe I visited four years ago."

"But—does he remember you?" I half whispered back. For I had been unable to intercept any sign of recognition in the stolid Indian's manner.

"Oh, certainly!" Sasha said confidently. "The chief is just not very demonstrative."

He stopped beside the nearest pack horse and began opening a saddle bag.

I rather timidly returned my gaze to the oiled and painted savages standing like statues—only their glittering black eyes seemed alive—a few feet away. I noticed now that what the chief wore suspended from his neck was a handsome amulet made of four tiger teeth. He also wore a necklace of enormous armadillo claws.

Sasha brushed past me again, carrying a quart of cachaça. He walked toward the chief, who broke into a pleased grin at the appearance of this prospective gift. The other Indians silently moved closer, eying the bottle avidly.

And I could no longer avoid noticing something about which Sasha had kidded me every time we discussed visiting the Bororos: The men's only concession to modesty was a tiny, and quite inadequate, section of hollow reed, worn where it would do the most good. Furthermore—in accordance with the tribal taboo on hirsuteness which compelled them to keep themselves plucked bare of even their eyebrows and eyelashes—they were completely denuded of all body hair.

Sasha and the chief were busied with the now-opened cachaça bottle.

I noted, with an inner amusement, that our welcoming delegation was not wearing "formal dress." The one-and-a-half-inch-long bit of hollow reed each man wore—I recalled the dimensions from Sasha's description—was called a *ba*. But these men were wearing only their ordinary, everyday *bas*. There was another kind, I knew, with a two-inch decorative flag attached to it, which was worn for all ceremonial occasions.

Horrors! I told myself, feeling slightly hysterical and silly. Didn't the chief know his protocol? Or didn't he consider us important enough for formal attire? Of course we had come unannounced. Possibly if we had sent an emissary ahead . . .

I was trying hard to maintain a blasé but dignified pose as I idly sat my horse, with nothing else to look at while all these very masculine men milled about in the raw just a few feet away, around Sasha and the chief and, most particularly, the bottle of rum. And then abruptly Sasha turned and spoke to me.

"We shall go now to the village," he announced. "The chief will escort us."

I nodded with dignity, assuming that was all that was expected of me.

Sasha and the chief came toward me, leaving the other Indians standing where they were. With a wave Sasha indicated me and made his introduction in Portuguese: "Tiger man's wife!" From my saddle I achieved an uneasy smile at the expressionless chief. I knew, from Sasha, how completely unimportant in the Indian world women are. The Bororos consider a female merely an adjunct of a man, even denying her a personal name. But the chief, with a barely perceptible flicker of his black eyes, seemed to indicate that he understood Sasha's meaning and was prepared to tolerate my presence.

He turned again to Sasha and spoke briefly in a deep, dignified voice, in what must be described—as I'm certain Indian speech always has been described—as guttural monosyllables. Then he raised his hand toward his waiting warriors and spoke commandingly. In silence they set off through the heavy jungle growth in the direction from which they'd come.

Sasha remounted, gave his horse a light touch of the spur, and started after them; the huge chief strode beside him, his three-foot brilliant feather headdress reaching higher than Sasha's head as he sat his horse. I followed with the trailing pack animals.

The chief remained magnificently silent as he strode imperiously at the head of Sasha's horse. The gleaming and naked warriors trotted noiselessly ahead—most of them hidden from sight. The only sounds were the soft swish and silky slap of the lush, heavily leaved undergrowth and parasitic vines through which we were

98

threading—and almost literally tearing—our way, for our horses' hoofs made no noise on the thick carpet of rotting vegetation beneath the crowded jungle growth. Occasionally I would see a delicate purple or golden orchid clinging half hidden to a lower limb of one of the enormous trees, its vivid color momentarily startling in the thick gloom of monotonous mossy greens. The heavy canopy of the jungle so completely enclosed us and shut off our view that we suddenly burst into the little clearing on the riverbank which was the site of the Bororo village before I had any idea that we were near it.

When we did precipitously enter the clearing, which occupied a slight rise of ground, the warriors in the lead announced our approach with shouts. And then I had an exciting glimpse, over Sasha's shoulder, of a score or more of naked and painted Indians —men, women, and children—turning to stare at us from the doorway of a small, conical-roofed grass hut to one side—one of several dozen such huts grouped around an open space in the center of the clearing, upon which fronted a much larger two-story log structure with a thatched roof.

The chief said something to Sasha in his deep, unhurried voice; Sasha turned to make a reply.

But I failed to hear what he said, for at that moment I was startled by the sight of a dozen or more large birds, completely stripped of their feathers and as ugly as only naked birds can be, racing between the huts and squawking angrily, chasing an incredibly famished-looking dog, who ran before them with his tail between his legs, howling miserably, as if in dire fear of his life. The obscenely naked birds, I suddenly realized—more from the noise they made than from their appearance—were macaws, the birds whose magnificent brilliant plumage makes them such exotic inhabitants of the jungle; macaws like our own pets, Rainy and J. Pluvius! The birds whose vivid three-foot tail feathers composed the chief's headdress . . . Heavens! Was that why——
Just then the harassed dog, yiping dolefully, streaked past us and made for the other side of the village again, with the denuded birds noisily in close pursuit.

Later Sasha told me that the Bororos keep flocks of macaws solely for their highly prized plumage and that, as a consequence,

the poor birds are always as naked as the Indians themselves—
and grow new crops of feathers only to be plucked again.

But there was no time for this explanation now.

At that very moment there arose from inside the grass hut
where the Indians were clustered a most agonized human shriek
—long drawn out and ending in such a pitiable, tremulous moan
that I was certain someone was being terribly tortured. The shriek
was repeated, even more heart-rendingly, and I leaned forward
over my horse's withers to demand of Sasha in a shocked voice
that he ask the chief what in heaven's name was happening.

The chief boomed out some terse comment of his own accord,
but Sasha apparently did not understand.

And then Sasha, with his characteristic immediate regard for
any creature in trouble, was spurring his horse forward toward the
hut. I rode after him, quaking inwardly. The chief quickened his
stride to keep up with Sasha's horse. Sasha dismounted. Nervously
I followed suit, keeping close. As we approached, the outer fringe
of Indians broke and made way for the chief, staring curiously
at Sasha and me. Those crowded within the wide doorway were
too absorbed to notice us.

I stared.

Just inside lay a naked male Indian in a hammock, writhing
and jerking convulsively and screaming at intervals, obviously in
almost unbearable pain. He became suddenly rigid and loosed
a spine-chilling, quavering wail that seemed to start in his very
bowels and lasted for a full minute. The Indians standing close
about him stared dolefully, murmuring and shaking their heads
in what obviously were expressions of sympathy. But I could see
no wound on the man's body. Then I became conscious of Sasha
at my side muttering, "It must be snakebite. I'd better get my
serum." He made a move to withdraw, then turned to the chief
standing silently behind us.

"Sucurí, Archie?" Sasha used the Portuguese word for "boa constrictor" as he gestured toward the writhing, moaning man. "Sucurí?"

I was becoming acutely conscious of the overpowering, rancid
smell of the close-packed Indians about me—a pungent, heavy
odor compounded of stale sweat and the fish oil which they used

as a base for their orange-red body paint—and I moved back a bit from the crowd.

The chief, whether he happened to understand that single word of Portuguese, or whether he merely guessed Sasha's meaning, shook his head. Not a muscle in his impassive face moved. But with a tolerant dignity that seemed by its very casualness to hint at an inward amusement at our ignorance, he pointed first at a little potbellied Indian child standing among the onlookers, and then at the agonized man in the hammock. He repeated the performance and intoned a single word twice.

A sheepish grin spread over Sasha's face; he turned to me.

"Stupid of me!" He chuckled. "I should have guessed it. But I've never witnessed the performance before. I didn't recognize the symptoms. The man is having a baby!"

"He's what!" I gasped. Then I remembered what Sasha had told me once and grinned sheepishly too. "Oh, so that's it!" I looked up at him and added meaningfully, "I'd better watch. Maybe I can get some pointers." Still smiling, I craned my neck to peer through the crowd at the writhing and shrieking man in the hammock.

Just then there was a slight commotion among the onlookers behind us, and we turned. Three naked Indian women had just come out of the thick jungle in back of the village. One was carrying a tiny baby, which began immediately to wail. And the group of Indians instantly broke into smiles and a hubbub of congratulatory expressions—all directed at the man in the hammock, the baby's father. In the meantime the mother timidly approached her husband, silently exhibited the naked infant—a boy—then hastily disappeared with it into the dark interior of the hut. I had moved near her as she made her way through the crowd, eager for a look at a newborn baby. I turned to Sasha when she had disappeared and was disconcerted to find him watching me in a highly amused way.

I grimaced. "How ugly! A little monkey!"

Sasha shrugged. "All newborn babies are ugly, I'm told." He smiled teasingly. "Even white babies."

I tossed my head.

Then he took my arm and drew me back a step or two. For

the mother's disclosure that the newborn infant was a male had been the signal for noisier and more enthusiastic demonstrations toward the father. And more Indians, drawn by the excited babble of shouts and laughter, hurried from among the huts at the far end of the village. Many pressed gifts on the new father, gifts which Sasha identified as they were presented—such as a decorated mussel-shell scraper, a polished bone knife, a small fire bow for kindling fires. And he, accepting these as his due, lay back in his hammock, now quiet but exhausted and pale from his ordeal, wanly but proudly smiling. Finally, with some last fond glances at the father, the crowd of well-wishers began to disperse.

No one had paid the slightest attention to the baby's mother!

As a matter of fact, a half-hour later I saw her, with her newborn infant tied to her back, silently serving supper to her husband, who lay in his hammock, luxuriously convalescing.

As we turned to move away with the chief I looked up at Sasha.

"If that isn't the finest demonstration of typical male callousness and complete lack of consideration!" I blurted indignantly. "A typical selfish, egocentric male!"

Sasha grinned. "Tut-tut, my dear. You misjudge the poor Indian. He is sincerely convinced he is helping his wife."

"I don't believe it!" I scoffed.

Sasha insisted, however, that the Bororo males have a plausible reason for this bizarre act. They believe they are making childbirth easier for their wives by thus bearing the pains for them. Therefore, when a Bororo woman feels childbirth near, she informs her husband, and he drops into his hammock and begins his graphic imitation of a woman's labor pains—while she slinks quietly out of the village to have her baby, unattended, in the underbrush. Later a couple of village women find her and bring her and the baby back.

In the meantime the chief had been speaking gruffly to the men who had accompanied us into the village, speaking in short, deep-voiced bursts of sound and from time to time emphatically nodding his head, as if giving orders—and I was fascinated by the way in which his three-foot feather headdress (which Sasha had

Jaguar cub before capture.

Young wood ibises on nest.

told me the Bororos call a *paracu*) impressively accentuated each commanding nod.

Among the score or more of naked men and women still standing a short distance away, staring impassively at us, were several children. And as I glanced over at them a little girl standing beside her mother—the child must have been at least eight years old, for her head reached to her mother's shoulders—turned and nonchalantly took her mother's nipple in her mouth and began suckling! I was amazed, especially so because the mother had an infant slung over her back (in a heavy basket-weave net which she had tied over one shoulder and under the other arm), and I should have thought the baby's prior rights would have been respected.

"Is that—customary at that age?" I asked, a bit awed.

Sasha grinned and nodded. "Yes, I've seen it before."

The Bororo women and children, I noted, wore no nose bones, but they had their hair cut in the same Dutch-boy bobs as the men, slicked down with fish oil; and they, too, were daubed from head to toe with the same orange-red greasy paint—as much for protection from mosquitoes and other insects, Sasha had concluded, as for decorative purposes. And although the children were quite naked, the women, like the men, wore a slight concession to modesty—in their case, a two-inch square of hand-woven cloth suspended from a string about the waist. Like the men, of course, they were plucked of all hair save that on their heads. The young girls had nice figures and regular features and, like all the tribe, were tall and slender. One or two could even have been called beautiful. But the older women!

After noticing several "matronly" types in the staring crowd I made the inevitable comment about what a virgin territory this would be for a brassière salesman, for the breasts of some of the older, shapeless hags—and I'm not exaggerating a bit—actually hung to their waists.

Sasha laughed.

"They planned it that way!" he retorted. And then he proceeded to tell me that the overworked women (like all Indians, the Bororo males merely make war or hunt; the women do every-

thing else), as an efficiency measure, purposely stretch their breasts
so they can sling them over their shoulders and thus nurse the
baby tied to their backs, without interfering with the pursuit of
their multiple domestic duties—grubbing for roots, weaving, cooking
the family dinner, or serving it to their lords and masters.

"Well," I finally observed, "it's an idea—if rather unique."

Sasha nodded without replying. His face had what I termed his
"experienced explorer" look—a somewhat superior amusement at
my naïve reactions, coupled with an I've-seen-it-all-before, indifferent cynicism.

There was a short silence.

"Do you think it's possible"—I spoke seriously, pretending to
be genuinely perplexed—"that *I* might be that busy—after Sashinho
comes?"

Sasha, to my satisfaction, looked a little taken aback.

But at that moment the chief, having finished his colloquy with
his warriors, turned to us. He said a couple of words to Sasha
and repeated them, then waved his hand toward the far end of
the village.

"All right, Archie," Sasha replied, nodding as if he understood
perfectly—as perhaps he did, for he wasn't entirely ignorant of
the language. In an aside to me he said: "I think the chief is
taking us to his home. For dinner."

"Really?" I murmured politely. "How nice."

The chief stood with his arms folded while we gathered up our
horses' reins; then we led our mounts and our two pack animals
single-file behind him through the village. The men to whom the
chief had been talking hurried off, and the crowd of men, women,
and children who had been watching us silently made way for
our little cavalcade. Sasha strode ahead beside the chief, and I
(like a true squaw) followed just behind him—a little disconcerted by all the staring eyes now that I didn't have him right
beside me.

We crossed the broad open space of hard-packed level ground
in the center of the village, back of which was the large, two-
story rectangular building, walled with palm trunks thrust upright in the ground, that I had noticed when we had first arrived.
Its steeply sloping palm-thatched roof must have been thirty-five

104

feet above the ground. Sasha turned to me and, in the manner of a proper Cook's tour director, obligingly explained the open field:

"The village playground. This is where they hold their feasts and dances. Except during the rainy season, when they stage them on the ground floor of the community hall." He nodded toward the large building.

I looked, then asked: "And the second floor?"

"That's the young men's dormitory," Sasha said over his shoulder without pausing in his stride. "All the boys must live there until they pass their tribal initiation rites at puberty. Then they are allowed to marry if they wish and build huts of their own."

We passed the community hall and began weaving our way between more of the small single-family huts. At length the chief stopped before the largest one, indicating it was his home. It was built like the others: a circular wall of vertical palm trunks and interwoven grass, a steeply rising conical roof thickly thatched with palm fronds, a doorless entryway. But the chief's house was perhaps twenty feet high and at least thirty feet in diameter. It also had more open ground around it than did the others. One of the reasons for the chief's need for more room, as I learned immediately, was that he (like the tribe's medicine man) had two wives. Ordinary members of the tribe had only one.

The chief's wives were outside the hut, busily working. One, a pretty young girl with a sleeping infant tied to her back, was on her knees, grating cassava root with a mussel-shell scraper into a painted clay bowl. The other, an older woman who had long lost her beauty, was squatting beside a rock-lined fire pit, skinning a dead monkey. Both, of course, were painted the inevitable orange-red. As we approached they looked up and stared, but the chief didn't deign to notice them.

Instead, he spoke to Sasha, pointed to our horses, and indicated with a wave of his hand a grassy spot behind the hut, just on the edge of the encircling jungle, where, I gathered, we could tether the animals. Sasha thanked him, then he opened one of our pack sacks and rummaged around in it. He closed it and turned to the chief.

"Archie, old boy," he began in a full-blown, oratorical manner (since the chief didn't understand Portuguese, it was only the tone and gestures used which were important), "Archie, because of the unique friendship we have had for each other since I first met you four years ago"—Sasha thumped his chest magnificently, and his phrases took on a mellow sonorousness—"and in anticipation of the hospitality you undoubtedly will extend to me and my estimable, if female, frau, I want to present you with this little token of my esteem!"

With a flourish he handed the chief a brand-new steel machete.

The chief's black eyes gleamed with pleasure as he turned the bright tool over and over in his hands. Then his feathered paracu swept up dramatically as he abruptly raised his head and, with solemn mien, made a lengthy speech of thanks—lengthy, that is, for him.

When he had finished Sasha bowed and smiled to wind up the ritual properly. But he turned to me and said flippantly:

"I dare say that put me in solid! And it ought to prove slightly more effectual on a tough steak than a tiger-thighbone knife."

I had had a difficult time keeping a straight face during Sasha's pompous presentation, for I was thinking he might just as well have been reciting the alphabet, but I said sternly:

"You ought to be ashamed of yourself, Sasha, corrupting the chief with a white man's knife!" I smiled. "That'll probably start the whole tribe downhill. Next time we come they'll be driving Model-Ts and eating hot dogs!"

For Sasha had told me that the Bororos, unlike the other Mato Grosso jungle tribes, have kept both their ancient culture and their blood stream untainted by the white man.

They are nomadic hunters, living on wild animals and fish killed with their bows and arrows, plus wild fruits and roots; they make no attempt, even, to plant and cultivate food. They construct their villages without thought of permanence, for when they have exhausted the game in the vicinity, they leave it and seek an untouched part of the jungle. They have no horses and no interest in acquiring any (they travel entirely on foot), but they do keep dogs for hunting. And, in that they use no metal tools or implements, they are a Stone Age people.

But the Bororos were inspiring in me a far greater respect for the culture of the Stone Age than I'd obtained from my schoolbooks, which depicted the Stone Age man as a skin-clad brute who lived in a cave and divided his time between slugging dinosaurs with his stone ax and dragging his women about by the hair. Sasha had told me that the Bororos clear the trees for their village sites and cut the poles for their huts, using as their only tool the stone ax—a hunk of granite tied in a cleft stick—with which they "gnaw down," rather than cut down, trees, since such an ax head, of course, is hopelessly dull. And to accomplish the amount of building they do for a temporary village, with no better tool than this, certainly is a feat. (They use fires, of course, to supplement their "chopping" at the bigger trees.) In addition, Sasha had earlier shown me the examples he had collected of their fine work in weaving and in making their bows, arrows, and various ornaments. The Bororo bow he had was stained and highly polished, decorated elaborately with narrow bands of feathers and ocelot fur.

The chief had turned to his two wives and was speaking to them—probably, I decided, telling them we were going to stay for dinner. The women said nothing, merely nodding their heads and stealing looks at us as they continued to squat on the ground, busy with their preparations. Then the chief addressed Sasha again. He gestured. Sasha listened intently, then nodded. They started moving away together, and I followed somewhat uncertainly. No doubt the chief, since dinner wasn't yet ready, was going to show us around some more.

Minutes later we halted at a hut before which two men sat cross-legged. One was rubbing down the six-foot length of an unfinished arrow with sandpaper-like lixeira leaves; the other was working on a new bow—scraping fine shavings from it with a mussel shell that had a sharp-edged hole in its center and worked like a crude plane. Nearby several other men were similarly engaged.

Sasha and I watched them interestedly; and the men, apparently flattered at our attention, worked even more industriously. Abruptly Sasha turned to the chief and pointed at the handsome tiger-tooth amulet that dangled against his painted chest—four large teeth in a fine mounting composed of polished mother-of-pearl and a broad band in which many tiny, vividly colored feathers were woven. Sasha drew from his pocket four loose tiger teeth.

"Archie," he said, pointing with the handful of teeth to the chief's amulet and then to the seated Indians, "I'd like to have these made into an amulet like yours. Do you think I can arrange it?"

The chief understood and, with an immediate interest, he took the loose teeth to examine them more closely. Then he nodded, pointed to his own amulet, and returned the teeth; and I could see there was added respect for Sasha in his eyes. He gestured toward the several other Indians, who had quickly dropped their work and jumped to their feet when Sasha had displayed his tiger teeth—and withdrew. And at the chief's departure the other Indians, almost overwhelming us with their eagerness, crowded about and reached for the teeth, and when Sasha somewhat reluctantly let them handle them, they passed them from one to the other with admiring clucks and ejaculations. (Sasha had told me on the way that he intended bargaining with the Bororos to make him a tiger-tooth amulet—their most prized decoration, not only because of the hunting prowess which it indicated but also because it was believed highly efficacious as a charm against all manner of sickness and evil.)

Sasha, thinking they had examined the teeth long enough, finally put out his hand so that the Indians might return them. One after another did so with obvious reluctance. And then there was an abrupt exclamation of surprise from them all.

In Sasha's outstretched palm there were only three teeth! One was missing.

The Indians held out their open hands for Sasha to see that they clearly did not have the missing tooth and with eloquent shrugs and exaggeratedly innocent and baffled expressions conveyed the idea that they were just as amazed as he at its strange disappearance. They even made a great pretense of peering about on the hard-packed ground—but the tiger tooth was not found.

Sasha disgustedly turned to me.

"Well, it looks as though I've been taken for a country boy by these sleight-of-hand artists!" he mourned gloomily. He disconsolately looked the Indians up and down as they stood before him, still indicating with elaborate gestures that they couldn't possibly imagine what happened to the fourth tooth.

"But what could they have done with it?" I wondered aloud, completely baffled. For the Indians, of course, wore no clothing in which the prized trophy could possibly have been hidden. (I never would have supposed that I could become accustomed to seeing naked men everywhere around me, but by now it seemed quite natural and in no way shocking.)

Sasha shrugged and turned to move on.

The Indians had been momentarily immobile, watching him intently. At his move to leave—indicating he had accepted the loss—one stepped forward and eagerly pointed to the hand in which Sasha held the remaining three teeth, then scurried over to pick up a bow lying on the ground before his hut. By unmistakable gestures he indicated he was offering to trade.

Sasha turned to me with a wry grin.

"He knows three tiger teeth are worthless," he observed dryly. He sighed. "Well, I might as well make the best of a bad bargain."

So the trade was made, and the Indian, grinning like a pleased small boy, quickly left, fondling the teeth and followed by his admiring and envious fellows.

Sasha and I strolled away, Sasha muttering disgustedly to himself.

Suddenly the chief appeared at Sasha's side again and spoke somewhat lengthily, then pointed to his stomach. Sasha nodded and glanced a little queerly at me. I decided dinner must be ready, for the sun was beginning to set and in a few minutes it would be dark. My spirits rose, for I was hungry.

But instead of leading us to his hut the chief took us back to the playground. When we reached its edge he halted and gestured toward a small group some distance away—Indians of all ages assembled about a little mound of fresh earth which I'd noticed earlier. Sasha took my arm and drew me to his side. I looked up questioningly, first at him and then at the chief, who stood, impassive and dignified, gazing silently at his tribesmen, who were perhaps one hundred yards away. And they, on their part, ignored us and seemed strangely quiet and chastened, as if waiting for something to happen. Each, I noticed, held a large gourd.

"What—what is it?" I whispered.

Sasha shook his head. "Wait!" he said cryptically.

For a few minutes we stood there silently, and then the sun had sunk completely behind the horizon and it was dark, with only the light from a large lurid moon hanging but a foot above the forbidding black jungle—jungle that stretched away from the clearing in rolling, mountainous masses. Little campfires sprouted up here and there among the dozens of scattered huts around the broad playground. Suddenly, as if the fall of night had been the signal they were awaiting, the small group of Indians dropped to their haunches in a tight cluster about the tiny mound and began a weird, doleful chanting. They swayed from side to side as they squatted, and their chanting, which started on a barely audible low note, raised in pitch and volume, then dropped again and climbed monotonously. It was a weird, animal-like mourning, almost unearthly and incredibly sad; and under that huge bright jungle moon, despite the scattered camp-fires casting their friendly, flickering reflections among the cone-shaped grass huts, it gave me a queer, almost frightened feeling.

"A—a funeral?" I whispered in a half-choked voice, looking anxiously at Sasha beside me.

He inclined his head slowly.

"A small boy. The chief said he died of a pain in his stomach. This is the sixth day of mourning. Tomorrow"—I could not see Sasha's face, but I could detect the cynical yet pitying amusement again in his voice—"tomorrow the *bope* come!"

"The bope!" I echoed with a faint shudder. "The evil spirits!"

I cast a quick glance at the chief, towering in his sweeping feather headdress like a cold ten-foot statue in the darkness on the other side of Sasha, and I was about to ask more questions. But at that moment the Indians abruptly ceased their chanting and swaying. The silence somehow seemed eerier than the wailing had. I squinted to see better. The Indians still sat on their haunches about the fresh mound, but there was a confused movement among them now. They were handling their gourds, and I heard the gurgle of water.

"They're watering the grave!" I whispered excitedly.

Sasha nodded.

Though the night was warm, I shivered, for I was picturing in my mind what would follow. I had been eager to see everything, but now I found myself dreading this. Sasha already had told me a great deal about the tribe's elaborate burial ceremonials, as he had seen a warrior's funeral on one of his previous visits.

He had told me how, after the warrior died, his relatives had wailed and mourned in his hut for a full day and then had buried his body in the village playground—under a scant ten inches of loose earth. For six nights thereafter they had visited the grave at sundown, wailing and chanting over it and pouring on it copious quantities of water—just as the relatives of this child were doing now. The watering, Sasha had explained, was done for the grisly purpose of hastening the decay of the corpse and loosening the flesh. The playground burial and the days of watering were merely a preliminary to the disinterment of the rotting corpse and the principal funeral ceremonies—which, in this case, would begin tomorrow.

Immersed in these thoughts, I flinched as Sasha abruptly put his arm about my shoulder. I looked up at him with an anxious smile. He smiled back reassuringly and said that we would return to the chief's hut now for dinner. We fell into step with the chief. I had lost a little of my hearty appetite, though. . . .

A small fire burned in the center of the chief's hut, and its low flames only vaguely outlined various bows and arrows, bone knives, a heavy war club, and a stiff-looking tiger skin, all supported by pegs on the shadowy circular wall. To my surprise, the hut's bare interior boasted two elaborately carved wooden chairs. These were beautifully made in the semblance of a large bird: its curved back made a saddlelike seat, and its head and tail rose like high pommels.

The chief indicated that one of the chairs was for Sasha, but Sasha smilingly seated me instead. After a moment of disapproval the chief acceded to this arrangement and proffered the other chair to my spouse. As the chief and his young son were now deprived of their customary seats, the boy squatted on a mat on the ground, and the chief sat down on the skull of a longhorn cow. (The presence of this skull mutely spoke of one reason many ranchers feel that "the only good Indian is a dead Indian," but the innocent Indian, coming upon a wild longhorn in the jungle, has no idea that it is anything but another game animal.)

After we were seated the chief's wives brought the pièce de résistance into the hut on the stick by which it must have been suspended over the outdoor cooking fire. They set the stick upright in a hole in the hard-packed earthen floor, then withdrew to a dark corner and squatted there, waiting patiently for us to finish, when I presumed they would make a meal on the leavings.

The bare fact that the entree was roast monkey did not surprise me greatly. I had noticed one of the wives skinning the animal in the afternoon, and I had once eaten monkey meat curried with rice and found it quite palatable. But the treat before us now was a monkey roasted whole, head and all! And standing upright before us impaled on its spit, with its furry skin removed, its flesh fire-blackened, and its teeth showing gruesomely in a wide, impudent grin, it looked exactly like a skinny little black boy! I gulped.

Sasha looked at me, drew out his bottle of cachaça, and shoved it into my hand. Then, with dead-pan courtesy, he carved me a large chunk of the meat.

I went through the motions of eating it to keep from offending the chief, but I filled up on palm heart and cassava cakes.

Afterward Sasha and I were standing outside the chief's hut, admiring the moon and discreetly observing cross sections of Bororo family life disclosed by several nearby campfires, when the chief, in a suspiciously sly manner, approached and called Sasha aside. I anticipated what he wanted, for I knew Indians are seldom satisfied with one drink.

As Sasha turned to join the chief I noticed that the seat of his trousers was stained. A horrid thought struck me, and I twisted around to examine my own derrière by the light of the outdoor fire. Sure enough, my pants also were smeared with orange-red! I thought of the number of times the chief and his son must have sat in those chairs, and I wondered whether urucú stains were removable; I had little hope for the fish oil and resigned myself to smelling like a stale herring for the duration of our visit.

The chief drew Sasha out of sight behind the hut. Sasha afterward told me what happened.

Standing there was the chief's small, grave-eyed daughter, whom we had seen waiting with the women in the hut at dinner—a child no more than nine or ten years old, not yet old enough to wear the two-inch-square "apron" which Bororo women don at puberty. The chief came quickly to the point: Would Sasha like to have his daughter for the night?

Sasha was somewhat taken aback. However, not wishing to affront our host with an outright refusal, he quick-wittedly took advantage of a technicality.

"What do you want, Archie?" he asked seriously.

The chief's answer, of course, was a bottle of rum. And Sasha sighed and said he was sorry but he had no more. The chief's face immediately fell and he ordered his daughter back into the hut. And Sasha, having gracefully extricated himself from the situation, returned to me.

That was Sasha's final version of the incident and the one he swore was the truth. But when he first rejoined me he wore a very smug grin, and as we sauntered away from the hut all he would say in reply to my persistent questioning was that the chief "had just—er—offered his daughter for the night."

"Why, the very nerve of him!" I spluttered. "That—that old——"

Sasha merely continued to grin—which, of course, made me angrier.

"You made it quite plain, I hope, that you weren't in the slightest bit interested?" I demanded.

"Well . . ." Sasha pursed his lips and paused, as if undecided how much he should disclose. Finally, with apparent reluctance, he said: "Well, I sort of mentioned that I already had you along!" Then he regarded me with blandly innocent eyes. "But I thought you weren't the jealous type?"

"You—you mean," I caught him up belligerently, "that if I *weren't* along——"

"Now, Edith," Sasha drawled reproachfully, "I didn't say that."

"No?" I retorted wrathfully. "You certainly implied it!" I looked back in the direction of the chief's hut. "And as for that painted ape who calls himself a chief—— The idea of offering you his own daughter! He ought to be horse whipped! Why, she's just a little child!"

Sasha's mocking smile baited me.

"You mean—if she weren't just a child——"

I should have known better, but I was furious, and I guess I slapped him then. The smack sounded startlingly loud in the darkness. If there were any Bororo women watching, they surely must have been horrified.

Without speaking Sasha felt his cheek and then cast a quick look about us. But only a few slinking dogs skulked the village; all of the Indians appeared to be in their huts. He turned back to me and stared at me hard.

"You are fortunate, my dear," Sasha fairly purred. "That might have been serious. If the chief or any of the Bororo males had witnessed it, I would have been forced to beat you publicly—to keep face!"

There was a silence.

I thrust my tongue out rudely. "You just *try* that, Senhor Siemel!" I challenged. But I felt a little uneasy, for somehow I didn't think Sasha was joking.

He stood there, looking at me rather stiffly, and suddenly I felt ashamed of myself and conscious of the fact that he could have said a lot more than he had, and I felt close to tears at having hurt him. Then, as though nothing had happened, Sasha playfully tweaked my ear and suggested that it was high time we retired to our hammocks.

We turned and started back toward the chief's hut through a particularly dark portion of the village. There was an indignant squawking and the sound of scurrying in the intense darkness underfoot, and I jumped back with a startled exclamation; then three or four of the ugly, plucked macaws were outlined in the ruddy light of a small fire, irritably settling themselves in a new sleeping place. As we walked on I mulled over the subject of our recent quarrel, but it no longer seemed so upsetting.

After all, as I should have remembered, Sasha had told me long ago how different the Bororos' ideas on chastity are from our own. No Bororo father has compunctions about selling an unmarried daughter's virtue to a visiting prospector or hunter. However, if, as a consequence, the girl presents the tribe with a blue-eyed or kinky-haired baby, the medicine man quickly kills it.

According to Sasha, though a Bororo husband and wife remain at least as true to each other as do their counterparts in civilized European and American communities, promiscuity before marriage is common and not frowned on.

Their marriages, in contrast to other elaborate tribal ceremonies, are quite casual and seemingly unimportant—probably a reflection of the unimportant status of women in the tribe. Bororo girls are betrothed early, often when only eight years old, although they do not marry until several years later. When a youth decides upon his bride-to-be, he calls on her parents with a gift, perhaps a large fish, and discusses the matter. If her father consents, the couple becomes engaged. And whenever the young man wants to set up housekeeping, he simply calls again with another gift, and the girl's parents deliver her to his hut.

By this time we had reached our tethered horses on the edge of the clearing. The chief's dwelling, like all the others, was silent, and the fire beside it had burned to glowing coals. The entire village was already asleep. Speaking in low tones, we got our hammocks, ponchos, and mosquito netting from the saddlebags and then moved in under the nearby trees to "make our beds."

The next morning, shortly after our sunrise breakfast of maté and charqui, which we ate alone under the trees, the chief came for us. In his always dignified, reserved manner he informed Sasha that the summoning of the bope, or evil spirits, for the dead boy would take place shortly. The chief apparently harbored no resentment at Sasha's refusal of his daughter.

"Fine, Archie!" Sasha replied heartily. "We'll be right with you."

And in a moment we were striding beside him toward the village playground.

In the bright morning sunlight I no longer felt my reluctance of the night before, and I was now very eager to see this part of the weird burial rites. Today's ceremony would be a colorful pageant that illustrated the dominant influence wielded over the Bororos' lives by the feared bope.

The Bororos do not believe in any Happy Hunting Ground.

Life after death for them is an unhappy, forced wandering about with the bope, a wandering in which their spirits successively inhabit the bodies of such miserable living things as frogs, snakes, and alligators, from which they may eventually progress to become deer, which are the legendary ancestors of the tribe.

The two-hundred-odd members of the tribe already were crowded about the edge of the large playground, waiting in a hushed, excited manner. The chief silently made a way for us through the throng—all naked, of course, and oiled and painted a glistening orange-red.

We had been standing among them perhaps five minutes when abruptly we heard several shrill blasts on a whistle from the far end of the playground, and the elaborate pantomime began.

Eleven male Indians, their bodies painted black and their faces hideous and masklike in black with white arabesques, pranced into the large open space. The leader, whose face was the most grotesquely painted and who in addition wore a cloak and a full swirling skirt of palm fronds, raised his bamboo whistle to his lips and repeated his shrill blasts. This, Sasha explained hurriedly, was the tribe's medicine man, summoning the bope.

Immediately the eleven swept into the paces of a vigorous stamping dance—another symbolic invitation to the bope to show themselves.

As the dance progressed, five of the medicine man's assistants withdrew from the stamping circle, dropped on all fours, and began imitating the heavy lunging and the grunts of a tapir, thus (as Sasha relayed to me in his running explanation) automatically becoming representatives of the bope.

The grotesquely painted medicine man and the remaining five dancers now began, with much waving of arms and shouting, to drive the five bope across the wide playground toward that little mound of fresh earth, to force them to resurrect the dead boy's corpse. This went on for some minutes, and I could hear the sweating and redolent Indians crowded about us muttering tensely among themselves as they excitedly watched the progress of the maneuver. The bope, snorting and lunging about on all fours, reluctantly backed up toward the village. Then, at a signal, they capitulated. Simultaneously the medicine man's other assistants transformed themselves into horses by also dropping on all fours, and the now eager bope jumped on their backs and galloped back to the grave. There they quickly dismounted, squatted about the mound, and clawed at it with their hands—for only a moment, however, as Sasha explained it was merely a symbolic gesture.

While the tribe watched with silent, morbid fascination the medicine man built a large fire and flung into it, one by one, all of the deceased child's belongings as his relatives silently handed them to him: his tiny hammock, his ocelot-skin blanket, a miniature bow and arrows, and several small gourd toys. And while the medicine man burned these, with many muttered incantations, Sasha explained he did this so that the child's unhappy spirit, in company with the bope, could not return through his possessions to haunt his family. Finally the medicine man, with still more muttered mumbo-jumbo, ceremoniously placed his own palm-frond skirt and cloak on the small forlorn grave, then abruptly stalked across the playground and through the crowd and disappeared; his assistants already had vanished. This ended the ceremony.

I turned to Sasha and sighed deeply; I had been particularly affected at the pathetic sight of the little boy's playthings. The Indians crowded on either side of us had begun to talk loudly among themselves and move away. With their attention no longer riveted on the pageant, they again stared curiously at Sasha and me.

"Well"—Sasha smiled—"what did you think of it?"

"It's—impressive," I said. I drew a shaky breath. I'd been so absorbed that I hadn't noticed until now how uncomfortable the hot sun was. My khaki shirt felt glued to me; I pulled a handkerchief from my pocket and wiped my face. The chief began striding away, Sasha turned to follow, and I fell into step beside him, only dimly conscious of the stolid, staring Indians through whom we moved.

We passed dozens of painted, dust-smeared Indian children already racing about in the sunlight and shouting as they played between the little grass huts, chasing the yelping, emaciated dogs with which the village seemed overrun, and the squawking, naked macaws which looked so like absurd caricatures of the naked

Indians. Millions of flies hovered lazily in dense clouds over the sun-baked earth between the huts.

Then I gave a shriek of surprise and grabbed Sasha's arm to keep from falling; a fat little Indian boy about four or five years old had bumped squarely into me. He fell flat on his face between my legs, and the other children, who had been chasing him, abruptly halted in their tracks and stared openmouthed at us, as if fearful of punishment. Sasha stooped to pick up the child.

"Did you hurt yourself, sonny?" he asked kindly as he set the youngster on his feet again.

I smiled down at the boy and pointed to his skinned knee, which was beginning to bleed slightly. I took out my handkerchief to brush the dust from the scraped skin, but the child let out a scared squeal and squirmed from Sasha's grasp. He looked back with a frightened expression just before he disappeared, with the other children, behind one of the huts.

The chief said something to Sasha and shrugged.

Sasha chuckled. "He was afraid you might use your white man's magic on him!"

"Magic? You mean I look like a witch?" I felt slightly disconcerted. "That's not very flattering!"

The chief spoke again to Sasha, then turned and walked back toward the playground. Sasha explained as we strolled on: "He has some business to attend to. But we can do a little more sightseeing on our own."

We rounded a hut before which an Indian sat, so absorbed in what he was doing that he didn't look up, although we were almost on top of him.

Sasha halted with an exclamation, then stooped to look closer at what the man was doing.

"Why," he said slowly, "you red-skinned thief!" He straightened up and glanced at me. "He certainly didn't take long to find that lost tiger tooth!" He looked down accusingly at the Indian and added sarcastically, "So you couldn't even wait until I'd left, huh?"

For it was the Indian to whom he had traded the three tiger teeth the day before—after the one tooth had so mysteriously disappeared. Three of the teeth lay on the ground between the

Indian's legs; the fourth he held in his hands—apparently he was trying to drill a hole through it with a pointed bone tool. Though he couldn't understand Sasha's words, it was obvious from his sheepish expression that he realized his trickery was exposed. He peered up at Sasha out of the corners of his eyes, then quickly returned his gaze to the ground.

Sasha looked exasperated.

"Oh, don't make trouble about it," I urged. "It isn't worth it!"

Sasha started to say something, and for a moment I was afraid he was really going to lose his temper; then he shrugged and took my arm and we moved on.

"Well, anyway, he's got a month's job ahead of him, boring holes in those teeth so he can string them together," Sasha said finally with satisfaction. "I could have done it for him in ten minutes with my little steel drill."

"Which you just happen to have along, of course?" I drawled teasingly.

"Well—no," Sasha admitted with a rueful grin. "But the thought is some slight consolation." He added more cheerfully, "And I did get a new bow out of the deal."

Eventually we wandered back toward our own camp site. As we passed the chief's hut we saw his older wife kneeling beside her young daughter, deftly trimming her hair, and we paused to watch. The child sat submissively, not moving even to brush away the bits of black hair that clung to her bare shoulders and small, unformed breasts. She glanced up briefly to give us a shy, sweet smile.

"There's my rival again," I said a little reproachfully.

The corner of Sasha's mouth twitched.

"She's a pretty little thing," I added with ungrudging honesty.

"Yes," Sasha said dryly. "The next man probably won't have any scruples."

I didn't want to think about that.

"What's her mother cutting her hair with?" I asked hastily.

"The jaws of a piranha." Sasha smiled. "Those razor-sharp teeth make an excellent scissors!"

We watched while the chief's wife finished trimming her child's bangs, and then we walked on to the edge of the forest, where our tethered horses were quietly cropping grass. After a light lunch on food from our saddlebags we crawled into hammocks and pulled our mosquito netting over us to keep off the flies and were soon enjoying our midday siesta.

Late in the afternoon we strolled into the village again by ourselves. As we sauntered between the huts our attention was drawn by a small crowd about one of them; from inside issued weird howls and yells in a gruff male voice. I wondered whether another man was "having a baby." We joined the fringe of the onlookers. Sasha craned his neck to look over their shoulders, then he turned to me and winked broadly.

"There's a doctor in the house," he said. "The medicine man is making a professional call."

"Oh—I must see that!" I eagerly raised myself on tiptoe.

After a little deft crowding between the audience—so entranced by what they saw that they ignored us—we soon had standing room in the front row.

A sad-looking Indian sat on the ground just inside the hut, hugging his knees, and howling and jumping about with fantastically acrobatic contortions was the medicine man. He was made up grotesquely, much the same as he'd been in the morning—his face and body were painted black (the fish oil was mixed with charcoal for this effect), setting off the chalk-white arabesques he had drawn on his cheekbones and breast, and the gleaming white bones in his nose and lower lip. He wore a feather headdress and another cloak and skirt of loose palm fronds. As he jumped about, shouting and yelling and waving gourd rattles—to drive out the evil spirits which had invaded the man's body—his headdress bobbed and his palm-frond skirt swirled ludicrously, and I could see the beads of sweat rolling down his paint-smeared body. And then, to my horror, he started spitting in the sick man's face, as well as alternately blowing and shouting in his ears—still trying, I imagined, to force out the evil spirits entrenched within.

After about ten minutes of this nauseating treatment the horrible creature abruptly dropped on his knees before his patient. Applying his mouth to the man's right leg, he began vigorously and noisily sucking on it for several minutes. Finally he raised his head and spat something into his hand. Then, leaping to his feet, he turned his back on his patient and dramatically exhibited to the circle of hushed onlookers what he held in his outstretched palm. I shuddered when I met his glittering eyes, deep-set in his black-and-white "mask," but I leaned forward to see what he held. It was a handful of insects!

"Ants," Sasha drawled. "He's explaining they're what made his patient's leg ache—and how his magic got them out!"

I shook my head slowly. The medicine man—his cure effected and his patient now actually smiling with relief—arrogantly pushed through the throng of awed Indians and strode rapidly away. The audience began to melt. Sasha took my arm, and we moved away too.

"The medicine man, of course, had those ants in his mouth all the while," I said after a short pause. "Right?"

Sasha nodded. "Of course."

I considered this. I still could see those glittering eyes, as cold and ruthless as a snake's, in the painted mask, and I shuddered.

"What a repelling creature he is!" I said tensely, for there was something sinister and evil about him—above and beyond his getup.

Sasha nodded again without comment.

The sun beat down hotly on us. We were strolling slowly, skirting the edge of the playground. Indian men were sitting in the shade before the grass huts on our left. Some were leisurely working on bows and arrows or bone knives; others were just sitting, staring into the distance.

Indian women, several with babies tied to their backs, were on their knees or moving about, industriously engaged in household tasks. One was mashing urucú seeds with a mortar and pestle. Another was vigorously chopping firewood with a stone ax. A young girl was nursing a baby (on her lap; was she a rebel?) and stringing seed pods together. And two older women stood over a fire roasting several turtles. However, as the poor turtles were still alive and were trying frantically to wriggle out of the flames, the women were very busy poking at them with sticks to keep them on the fire.

Indian children were boisterously playing about. Two boys were wrestling; it was a strenuous form of the sport, for they lunged at each other from a distance of ten feet or more, then clinched and rolled over and over on the hard-packed, dusty red earth. Some smaller boys were practicing archery with tiny bows and arrows, shooting at beetles and the occasional four-inch centipedes, and also at any of the mangy dogs in range. And three little girls were playing with feather-trimmed gourd dolls.

In the bright sunlight it all seemed so carefree and pastoral that it was difficult to believe there were depths of horror and violence underneath the surface peacefulness. Difficult, that is, if I hadn't just witnessed the sinister-looking medicine man's trickery with the ants. That particular cure was harmless enough, but it reminded me of other things Sasha had told me about the Bororo medicine men.

The medicine man, he had emphasized, really rules the tribe. For while the chief (who is usually the largest and strongest male and the bravest hunter) is the tribe's leader in war and on the hunt, the medicine man is more powerful. The medicine man (who is invariably the shrewdest person in the tribe) actually controls life and death. He does this by exploiting the Indians' fear of the evil spirits which dominates their lives.

And naturally, Sasha told me, the medicine man makes a very good thing out of his position. For instance, no big game brought in from the hunt can be eaten until he exorcises it of its evil spirit—and in return for this service he always selects the choicest cut for himself.

Executions are in the province of the medicine man. The Bororos practice infanticide, and it is the medicine man alone who decides whether a baby gives evidence of possessing non-Bororo blood, or whether it appears too weak to be likely to grow up into a strong Bororo; and he carries out his own death sentences. Cripples are killed immediately too. And no one becomes old and feeble among the Bororos, for the medicine man finishes off a member of the tribe as soon as he shows signs of threatening to become a burden to the rest.

In addition, Sasha told me—and I felt sick every time I thought of this—any Bororo mother who gives birth to a baby before her preceding child can walk must hand over the newborn to the medicine man to kill. For when the tribe is on the move through the jungle the women act as pack horses (the lordly males stride ahead with no more than their bows and arrows and clubs), and one baby, plus all the family's household possessions, is adjudged all a Bororo wife can carry.

Our stroll had brought us to the river. The bank, rather high at that point, was nearly deserted. About a hundred yards upriver an Indian was standing in the shade of a huge vine-clad tree, holding an arrow loosely in his bow and gazing intently into the water, waiting for a fish to swim within range; during all the time we stayed there he never moved a muscle. Some distance down-river several small boys were throwing stones at alligators dozing in the shallow water. Huge clumsy-looking storks and several scarlet ibis were wading about on the opposite side.

We sat down on the grassy bank and gazed over the slow-moving river shimmering in the sunlight.

I was still thinking of the medicine man's cure we had witnessed.

"What do you suppose was wrong with that Indian?" I asked Sasha abruptly. "With his leg, I mean."

Sasha looked at me and then shrugged. "Oh, possibly a touch of rheumatism."

I smiled slowly.

Then Sasha told me how he had once watched a medicine man in another village treat a Bororo for snakebite. He'd pranced around, yelling and making faces, just as this one had done.

"And the poor Indian died, of course," I put in dryly.

Sasha smiled cynically.

"No. As a matter of fact," he drawled, "he recovered almost at once."

He went on to explain that in the case of snakebite cures the medicine man can rely on the law of averages. Most Indians don't know which snakes are poisonous and which aren't. In reality, only about one out of every four snakes in the jungle is poisonous (the deadly ones are the bushmaster, fer-de-lance, coral, and rattlesnake). Furthermore, only about once out of every four times does a bite from even a poisonous snake result in death for a human, for whether a snake's venom sacs contain sufficient poison to cause death depends on how recently it has used them. Thus, not more than one snakebite out of sixteen is fatal.

"And for the few cases which he does lose"—Sasha smiled—
"the medicine man always has an alibi. He accuses the victim's
relatives of having mentioned the forbidden word 'snake' in his
patient's presence, thus reawakening and enraging the snake's evil
spirit just after he had succeeded in putting it to sleep!"

Sasha picked up a flat stone and idly skipped it across the water
at the solemn storks on the other side of the river.

I was silent, remembering a really horrible story which Sasha
had told me long ago. It illustrated how completely ruthless a
medicine man can be when he attends seriously ill patients—
those whom he decides probably will, or should, die. In these
cases, Sasha said, in order to enhance his reputation for super-
natural knowledge and power and thus increase his hold on the
tribe, the medicine man first predicts the exact time when his
"incurable" patient will die—and then murders him, to make
his prediction come true! Such murders by the medicine men,
solely to maintain their professional reputation, are far from uncommon, Sasha said. In fact, he actually witnessed the one he'd
told me about.

The patient had been a husky male Bororo, about twenty-five,
who had contracted pneumonia as the result of exposure on a
hunting trip and insufficient food and sleep. With the warrior's
family and friends Sasha watched the medicine man's first treatment. Painted hideously, the medicine man shook his gourd rattles
and went through the customary contortions around the sick man,
who squatted glumly in his hut, his chin on his knees. But after
howling and railing at the evil spirits in possession of the patient's
body and blowing in his ears and spitting in his face for over a
half-hour, the evilly painted faker abruptly halted his performance
and came out of the hut. He swept his eyes over the circle of
waiting Indians. Then he raised his left hand toward the sky.

"*Meri, meri, meri,*" he counted on his fingers. "Three suns
he will see. Then he will die!"

Sasha said that the sick man's wife gasped, then uttered a low,
howling moan, like a dog. The others looked frightened.

The medicine man stood for a long moment savoring the obvious fear of the unknown which he had inspired. Then, looking

124

neither right nor left, he pushed brusquely through the group and disappeared into his own hut.

At sunset on the third day, the warrior, though flat on his back, was still alive. Sasha waited about unobtrusively. Only a few moments after the medicine man arrived the sick man's wife and children filed out of the hut at his orders. In the fast-fading twilight Sasha made his way behind the hut and worked a small opening in the thatched grass, enough to see into the dim interior.

The medicine man stood over his patient and stared down at him silently a moment. Then he muttered something and quickly squatted astride the man's chest. Sasha said that from what he had been previously told, he guessed what was coming next—but he knew that if he tried to interfere he would have the whole tribe on his neck.

Continuing his imprecations against the evil spirit that refused to leave, the medicine man slipped a rope under the man's back, tied it across his chest, and inserted a short stick under the knot. Then, raising his voice to shout at the top of his lungs at the stubborn evil spirit—and, incidentally, to drown out sounds of the sick man's cries—he quickly tightened the rope, tourniquet-fashion, by turning the stick. Sasha said he thought he heard the victim moan piteously as his chest became constricted, but he couldn't be sure, what with the medicine man's shouting and wailing and blowing and spitting. In a few minutes the medicine man came out of the hut and in a loud voice summoned the warrior's relatives, who had been squatting on the ground silently waiting some distance away. They approached him hesitantly, fearfully. Sasha moved nearer.

In an oratorical manner the medicine man informed the gaping relatives that the evil spirit had gotten a very deep hold in the body of the sick man; that he, their medicine man, had struggled mightily to oust it, summoning all his enormous powers; that he finally had succeeded in driving out the evil spirit. However, just as he had predicted when he'd first attended his patient—and at this point the old rascal fairly oozed self-satisfaction—the sick man had lived only long enough to see three more suns. He was now dead.

There was a moment of silence. Then the widow uttered a long-drawn-out wail of grief, and the other relatives joined in.

Sasha had slipped away in the darkness. However, he told me that, frankly, he hadn't felt too badly about the murder. He had decided the man probably would have died anyway; the medicine man had merely cut short his agonies.

The story still was vivid in my mind, though Sasha had told it to me more than a year earlier. I thought about the Bororo child who now lay buried—temporarily—on the tribe's playground, and wondered whether this horrible medicine man had taken care of him in the same way. I turned to Sasha, who was idly digging in the soft riverbank dirt with his boot heel.

"Sasha," I said slowly. "That little boy for whom they held the ceremony this morning—do you think the medicine man murdered him?"

Sasha brushed the dusty earth off his boot.

"Well"—his tone was cynical but tolerant—"the chief told me he'd been seized by a sudden pain in his stomach."

"But that—that dreadful medicine man," I persisted, "undoubtedly attended him—don't you think?"

Sasha picked up another stone before replying and skipped it across the river. He nodded disinterestedly, then sighed wearily and rose to his feet, extending a hand to help me up. "Undoubtedly."

As we turned to leave I noticed that the little Indian boys had disappeared. But the man upstream still stood in the lengthening shadows with his bow and arrow poised, his eyes glued on the smooth-flowing water.

The next day was the one I'll remember longest of the four we spent among the Bororos.

We awakened at sunrise to find the entire village fairly throbbing with excitement, noisy with a feverish activity which far surpassed that of the previous morning. I woke up with a headache and, feeling out of sorts, wished I could sleep until noon. But I knew it was impossible, for this was the day when the all-day *bakororo,* or funeral sing, would be held for the little Indian boy.

Thin gray plumes of smoke arose into the deep blue sky from

scores of breakfast fires. The sunlit village was noisy with the rollicking shouts of youngsters; the squalling of impatient, hungry infants, the yelps of hollow-stomached curs kicked in attempting to snatch a bite of food.

The chief arrived while we were breakfasting—arrived with solemn mien, garbed in his customary towering blue, yellow, and red paracu, his armadillo-claw necklace and tiger-teeth amulet, and a fresh, glistening, head-to-toe paint job, as yet unstreaked with perspiration and unsmudged with dirt. And this time I discreetly observed that he wore "formal dress"—a ba sporting the decorative two-inch flag. As usual, he ignored me and extended his invitation only to Sasha. But Sasha, of course, overlooked this.

He had prepared me for today's program by explaining that, in accordance with the unalterable ritual, the five Indians who had acted the parts of the bope in yesterday's colorful pageant undoubtedly had secretly dug up the little boy's body during the night (well decayed after six evenings of being watered in its shallow grave by the bereaved family) and had spent the rest of the night preparing the corpse on the riverbank by scraping off all the flesh (to be disposed of by vultures) and washing and dearticulating the skeleton, and had placed the bones in a heap in the center of the village playground and then, having finished their job, had retired quietly to their several huts. The tribe always maintains the pretense that it doesn't know the identity of these bope. The village merely awakens, as it did today, to find the undertaking job done.

I was hardly prepared, however, for what I saw when the chief led us through the throng of men, women, and children standing, several deep, in a feverish-eyed circle around the playground. I was conscious at first only of the fact that I was breathing more rapidly than usual, and that I had an unpleasant sensation of "butterflies" in my stomach, and that the roof of my mouth was dry, and that I wished I were some other place—all of this undoubtedly reflecting an uncomfortable nervous tension and reluctance to face the mental ordeal I anticipated. And then I was conscious of the fact that the Indians crowded about me were even more emotionally disturbed. They were completely silent, their black eyes had a frenzied sparkle, and they were staring

with an openmouthed, avid, yet fearful fascination toward the
center of the playground.

It was a beautiful morning. The sun was bright and not yet too
warm, and the sky was a vivid, almost incredible blue. I shielded
my eyes against the brightness.

About twenty men and women were sitting cross-legged, two
deep, in a little circle in the center of the playground, the men
on the inside, the women behind them. The women's bodies were
all painted a uniform black; the men's bodies the usual Bororo
orange-red, but their faces were daubed in patterns of black and
white. I stared, then caught my breath with a sensation of shock
that made me feel momentarily panicky, even though I'd been
bracing myself. In the center of the circle, gleaming whitely in the
bright sun, was a little pile of bones—topped by a tiny skull!
I stared at it, horrified. And at that moment a man in the circle
of silent, squatting relatives (whom Sasha identified as the child's
father, because his hair had been cut close to his head to show
his bereavement) leaned forward and carefully, reverently placed
atop the skull a miniature paracu, a child's pitiful little playtime
headdress of bright yellow and orange feathers. I felt a sudden
lump in my throat.

"Oh, Sasha," I whispered. "It's so pathetic!"

Sasha clasped my hand and looked at me intently.

"Do you want to leave?" he asked quietly.

I swallowed quickly and shook my head.

"No. . . . No," I said. "Of course not!"

Then my glance happened to light on two small Indian boys,
probably about the same age as the dead child had been, who
were standing a few feet away, fascinatedly staring at the squatting
circle. One abruptly turned to the other and spoke in a low, excited tone, pointing at the heap of gleaming white bones, and I
sensed with a chill of horror that that child of five or six years was
happily recognizing the gay feathered headdress atop the little
skull as his dead playmate's. The pathos of it sent another surge
of emotion over me, and I had a difficult time holding back tears.
These two small boys looked so terribly eager and alive.

The swarms of buzzing flies hovering over the crowd, and the
smelly, elbowing Indians with their morbid, hungry staring sud-

denly repelled me almost to the point of nausea. At the same time I was conscious of a rather dreadful parallel between the atmosphere here, the attitude of these savages, and the barbarism of a so-called Christian funeral. Here, in the brilliant sunlight, in garish mourning paint, were the bereaved—and crowds of casual onlookers avidly drawing the last ounce of sensation from the little skeleton. Here, with only its veneer off, was civilization.

For a moment I was on the verge of changing my mind about staying. My lips half formed Sasha's name, but just then, as if the placing of the little feather headdress atop the child's skull had signaled the start of the bakororo, abruptly there arose from the tight double circle of grieving relatives squatting about the piled-up bones a startling concatenation of weird sounds.

Four of the men picked up huge calabash rattles and, shaking them in concert, began wailing in an eerie, off-pitch tune. Then the seven or eight women sitting behind them joined in the wailing, in a higher-pitched accompaniment, simultaneously waving palm fronds like fans, to keep the hovering clouds of flies off the male quartet. A moment later two more men in the circle each picked up a four-foot-long bass flute, and two others raised large calabash trumpets—I recognized the odd-looking musical instruments from Sasha's earlier descriptions. The grotesque sounds that harshly blurted out into that clear sunny morning as these four musicians noisily set the tempo for the wailing men and women caused a sudden feeling of shock; and then I had difficulty repressing a smile, for the sound made by the bass flutes can only be described as a hoarse snort, and that of the calabash trumpets as a bark.

And while the huge flutes snorted, the trumpets barked, and the male quartet with the female accompanists wailed and shook their rattles and swayed from side to side, keeping their eyes always on that grisly little heap of bones and the white skull with its incongruously bright feather headdress, the child's father began a loud monologue, reciting his dead son's virtues; and the mother, seated beside him, meanwhile began slashing her arms and legs with a broken, jagged mussel shell and smearing her blackened body with her own blood, while she suffered her hair to be jerked out, a few strands at a time, by the women relatives squatting behind her.

I stood there with Sasha for nearly an hour, entranced and fascinated in a morbid way, drinking in the macabre scene and grotesque sounds. The wailing and the rattling of the gourds and the snorting and barking of the big flutes and trumpets never ceased for a moment.

Then I noticed that the crowd of watching Indians was becoming restive. A few were beginning to leave unobtrusively. I myself felt limp and wilted under the brassy sun, which was now high in the cloudless blue sky, promising another broilingly hot day. I noticed that beads of perspiration were beginning to pop out from beneath the chief's gaudy urucú paint job. The smell of the rancid fish oil on him and on the other naked Indians pressed around us was heightened as they began to sweat. I didn't think I could ever eat fish again, and I began to feel really nauseated. I turned to Sasha.

"Sasha," I said, shouting to be heard over the monotonous wailing of the mourners and the rhythmic, woody braying of the primitive instruments. "Sasha, do you think—maybe——"

"You want to leave?" Sasha's eyes met mine quickly; there were beads of perspiration on his brow, too, and his khaki shirt was darkly damp about his shoulders.

I nodded. "If we can, gracefully," I added; then I smiled a bit wanly, thinking how incongruous that sounded—although there *were* amenities to be respected, I was quite sure, even at such a ceremony.

Sasha nodded and put his hand on my back, then turned to the chief.

"Archie," he boomed, "my poor wife has had about all of this that she can stand for the time being. I think we'll take a walk and get a little fresh air. Frankly"—he gave me an expressionless sidelong glance, then turned again to the chief—"frankly, Archie, you boys stink to high heaven in this hot sun. Especially when you get together in crowds!"

The chief replied solemnly in his own language, and I whimsically reflected that he, with his sonorous Bororo, might be insulting us with equal dead-pan impudence, for Sasha at no time understood everything he said—except that I didn't credit the chief with that much subtlety or humor.

We began weaving our way through the Indians still bunched around the dusty playground. I thought I recognized the medicine man watching us from the edge of the crowd as we left, though I couldn't be sure; the man was without his distinctive palm-frond cape and skirt, and his face and body were daubed only with the orange-red urucú that the non-mourners wore.

We left the playground and moved down what passed for a village street between the scattered grass huts, toward the edge of the forest where our horses and hammocks were, and immediately I began to feel better. I took some long, gulping breaths of the fresh, untainted air. The village seemed quiet and deserted, which was understandable, of course, with virtually the entire population still at the noisy bakororo—the monotonous, off-pitch sounds of which were clearly audible wherever we went. We passed a few macaws pecking and scratching in the dusty earth for insects. As they were kept plucked to satisfy the tribe's feather requirements, they were unable to fly and so were forced to find their food entirely on the ground, like domestic chickens. There were the ever-present huge swarms of flies buzzing over well-gnawed bones or other bits of refuse lying about. We passed several moth-eaten dogs, either stretched, panting, on the shady side of a hut, or warily slinking about, sniffing endlessly, in search of food. An Indian mother with a squalling infant tied to her back came out of the woods with an armload of earth-encrusted roots she had obviously just dug. Her soft black eyes met mine momentarily, but her imperturbable expression showed no whit of friendliness, or any other emotion, for that matter.

And then we came upon a young Indian woman sitting cross-legged in the shade of a hut, weaving, while beside her a naked baby played about on the ground. Her loom immediately excited my interest, and I grabbed Sasha's arm.

"Oh, I'd like to see this, Sasha!" I exclaimed eagerly. But I paused, for I was struck by the appealing way in which the little naked toddler stared trustingly up at us with his huge black eyes. "What a cute baby!" I stared fondly down, wishing I could pick him up and hold him.

Sasha smiled, too, and casually placed his arm about my shoulders as he followed my gaze.

"The mother's not bad, either," he observed mischievously.

The Indian woman looked up at our words, and her stolid eyes flicked over the two of us. She was young, and her bare breasts were pretty—not elongated like those of the older women. Her face would have been very attractive if she hadn't, in accordance with tribal custom, denuded herself of eyebrows and eyelashes. I was about to make a sarcastic retort to Sasha, when I noticed she was glancing warily from us to her child, as if fearing we might harm it. She had stopped her weaving. I looked questioningly at Sasha, and he nodded.

"She's afraid you might use your magic on the child," he cautioned. "Better not act too interested."

"How silly!"

However, I moved a step away from the baby—who was still staring, wide-eyed, from one to the other of us—and stooped to peer more closely over the mother's shoulder at her loom. From that position I was able, too, to watch the cute little baby out of the corner of my eye. The Indian mother, after another quick glance at her child, resumed her work, partially reassured.

I stared, fascinated, at her half-finished handiwork on the small, primitive wooden hand loom. I nodded at it silently.

"A feather cloak," Sasha said. "Handsome, isn't it?"

"Beautiful!" I exclaimed, adding quickly, "Do you think——"

Sasha moved closer to look, with me, over the woman's shoulder.

He had told me of the elaborate feather cloaks which the Bororos weave and had promised that during our visit he would try to get one for me. The base of the cloaks, he had explained, was a coarse, strong cloth woven from the fibrous inner bark of the caraguata, or wild-pineapple thorn bush, which they also used for their hammocks, for the shawl-like affairs in which their infants were slung, and for the two-inch aprons the females donned when they arrived at puberty. When they made their feather cloaks, Sasha had explained, they worked the short, soft breast feathers of various birds, especially macaws and toucans, into the weave so that the vivid colors made intricate and striking designs. The feathers thus overlaid formed an inch-deep, close-set, and wonderfully soft nap.

The partially finished cloak on the loom before us had a design of long-legged blue and red birds chasing each other across a white background, a red Indian shooting an arrow at a yellow deer, and various abstract geometrical designs—all of which seemed to me to indicate a high level of artistry and exquisite workmanship, since the designs were so delicately outlined in such a difficult medium.

I stood silently admiring the cloak for several minutes, while the young woman stolidly worked her pointed wooden bobbin with its strand of weft through the stretched threads of the warp, then took a handful of rainbow-hued feathers from a cane basket and deftly inserted their quills into the cloth, selecting colors to carry out the design with a practiced ease and speed which astonished me.

"That's really breath-taking, Sasha," I said finally. "I hope you can get it for me."

"I'll have to see her husband," Sasha replied. "Maybe tonight. Or tomorrow."

The Indian woman, who of course had no idea what we were saying, warily glanced up at us again at the sound of our voices; then she shot a quick, worried look at her crawling infant—all, however, without pausing in her weaving.

I nudged Sasha and smiled at her anxiety, then I glanced at the baby, who had eagerly begun to pursue a beetle on his hands and knees. The child suddenly pounced on it, and the next instant I saw him dropping back on his bare bottom and raising his chubby fist, from which part of the struggling beetle protruded, to his mouth. I heard the unmistakable crunch of the child's little teeth on the crisp shell of the large insect.

"Sasha!" I gulped, and pointed to the baby, whose little jaws were now working away rhythmically. "My God! Did you see—— That baby just ate a beetle!"

Sasha's eyebrows raised. "Really?" he murmured disinterestedly; then abruptly he frowned at me. "You shouldn't have pointed at him, Edith," he said reprovingly; he looked anxious and jerked his head toward the Indian mother.

But it was too late; the harm had been done.

The woman had dropped her weaving and rushed over to scoop up the child in her arms. The baby, startled by her rough action, began to cry. And she, holding him cradled protectively as if to shield him from me, scurried with him into her grass hut, looking at me fearfully as she did so.

Sasha quickly grasped my arm. "Come," he said in a low voice, urging me on. "That was unfortunate."

Sasha was taking long strides but obviously was attempting to appear unhurried. I suddenly felt panicky and wanted to run, but Sasha, sensing that, hissed, "Take it easy. Don't act frightened!"

"Are we—are we in danger?" I gasped. I felt a little hysterical.

Sasha slowed down, and I could feel him relax; the chief's hut was just ahead of us.

"No. No, of course not. Don't be silly," Sasha assured me; he turned and smiled warmly. "I just didn't want her to start shrieking while we were there." He squeezed my hand comfortingly. "It's all right now."

I looked up at him dubiously, not certain whether to believe him; but the sight of the chief's hut and his older wife, squatting before the fire hole scraping out ashes, who turned to look at us placidly as we approached, and, beyond, our four horses peacefully grazing on the edge of the thick forest—all familiar surroundings by now—made me feel more comfortable. We halted by the fire pit, and Sasha smiled at the Indian woman.

"Where's Archie?" he inquired.

She stared blankly for a moment, but the word "Archie," which Sasha had often used in her presence, must have had some connection in her mind with the chief. After a moment of ponderous thought she raised an arm and pointed in the direction from which we had come, toward the playground, from which still came, plainly audible, the monotonous, rhythmic sounds of the bakororo, the weird off-pitch wailing, the throbbing snorts and barks of the flutes and horns.

Sasha shrugged. "Well, let's retire to our hammocks for our siestas," he said indifferently.

I fell into step beside him. . . .

A huge yellow moon was high over the jungle that night when we ate supper at our own campfire on the edge of the clearing. The village was strangely quiet—extraordinarily quiet—for the wailing of the mourners at the bakororo, which had continued without interruption since sunrise, had finally stopped at sunset,

(*Above*) Tu-yu-yu (stork) on nest and (*below*) young white herons on nest.

by which time every one of the grieving relatives was so hoarse he could hardly whisper.

Dozens of little campfires dotted the clearing before us, and their coppery flames, in the fitful breezes that occasionally swept across the still river, sent grotesque shadows sprawling among the scattered circular huts—shadows that were quickly swallowed up by the black wall of towering jungle that crowded close on every side. Occasionally the sharp squall of a baby broke the silence, or the yelp of a kicked dog, or, from the jungle behind us, the catlike scream of a hunting animal. There seemed to be an air of suspense hanging over the village, an atmosphere of fear, in which those evil spirits, the bope, walked with the giant shadows that stalked the clearing. But maybe I only imagined it because I'd been thinking about the ceremony that would take place at midnight— the ceremony which would climax and end, finally, the extended death pageant, a ceremony so highly sacred that no woman of the tribe was ever allowed to witness it.

The chief had called on Sasha just before dark and had indicated that for a consideration (apparently he suspected Sasha had more rum) he could arrange to take him along to witness the ceremony, as he had done several years earlier when Sasha had spent two weeks with the tribe. But he had made it plain that it would be absolutely impossible to take along any woman, even a white woman. So my spouse had turned down the offer, not wanting to leave me alone in the village.

Sasha was staring thoughtfully into the fire now. Abruptly he picked up another piece of wood and threw it on the glowing embers. The flames leaped greedily upward, and for a minute or two the alive, breathing blackness all about us retreated a few feet farther. We had been silent for some time.

"I'm not afraid to stay here alone," I finally said a bit defiantly. "Why don't you go with the chief?"

Sasha looked at me enigmatically for a moment, then gave me a rueful grin.

"Don't be absurd, Edith," he retorted shortly. "Anyway, I've seen it before—and I imagine it's always the same."

"Tell me more about it, Sasha," I urged. I leaned forward,

hugging my knees, anticipating the heightened, spine-tingling effect his words would have in this setting.

And Sasha launched into an enthusiastic, detailed description of the ceremony whose counterpart would take place tonight—the ceremony for which both the symbolic pageant of the bope and the mourners' day-long wailing had been merely a prelude.

The burial Sasha had seen had been dramatic to the nth degree. It could not have been more so, Sasha said, even if its stage manager and chief actor, the medicine man, had had full control over the elements.

It had begun at midnight. One of the frequent tropic thunderstorms that come up so quickly was ripping the black sky with jagged flashes and sending rumbles of thunder over the hot jungle night, when the medicine man and his ten aides, their faces and bodies made grotesque with black and white paint, had suddenly descended on the deserted playground. Quickly scooping up in a basket the pile of bones over which the mourners had wailed all that day (the deceased was the warrior who had died of pneumonia—with the assistance of the medicine man), they jumped into five of their fast small dugouts and began swiftly and silently paddling up the night-shrouded river.

Sasha said that the chief, who had been waiting unobtrusively in the shadows with him, had quietly led him to his own dugout. They had followed at a slight distance, for the ceremony was supposed to be highly secret. Frequent flares of lightning made following easy.

The medicine man and his ten weirdly painted assistants paddled for some time, Sasha said, until they came to a narrow inlet through which they slipped into a quiet lagoon walled by impenetrable jungle. Here four dugouts were maneuvered into a rough circle surrounding the fifth, which held the medicine man. Then one man in each of the widely separated surrounding dugouts raised an *aige,* or bull-roarer, the sacred noisemaker which is used only for burials and which no woman is allowed to see.

Sasha described a bull-roarer as a thin-edged, two-foot stick attached by about six feet of rope to a longer stick which was used as a handle, a simple-looking instrument but with astonishing potentialities. Unwinding these, the Indians, at a signal from the

136

medicine man in the central dugout, simultaneously flung the bladed sticks into the air and, by means of the handle sticks, began slowly swinging them about their heads.

At first, he said, the rotating blades made a deep roaring sound; then, as they whirled faster, the roaring became high-pitched.

The Indians then took up the pattern of their ancient—perhaps ten-thousand-year-old—ceremony. While one whirled his stick so the notes were of a deep, ominously guttural bass, another achieved a higher, more angry note, a third became shrill, demanding, and the fourth, as a sort of virtuoso, altered his tempo rapidly, so the voice of his whirling blade changed rapidly from a somber bass to a shrill scream and back again.

Then the men started wailing—at first in the lamenting tone of the mourners in the earlier day-long bakororo; then their voices rose and became angry—menacing the bope whom they simultaneously feared, yet sought to control—the tempo of their chanting quickened, and the bull-throated moaning and the shrill screams of their whirling aige became more demanding, more .threatening. The almost continuous lightning, Sasha said, blazed and eerily lighted up the weird scene; thunder amplified the sound effects. In the midst of this the hideously masked medicine man suddenly stood up in his dugout. Lifting the basket containing the dead warrior's bones high in his hands, and with a final scream of defiance at the waiting bope, he hurled it into the black lagoon water.

Sasha said that the chief and he had sat in the dark in their dugout, hidden among thick underbrush which hung in an almost unbroken curtain over the lagoon's edge, until the medicine man and his assistants had paddled their dugouts swiftly and dramatically out of sight. After some minutes they, too, had silently made their way out of the lagoon and slowly, warily, had paddled down the river and back to the village.

"However, the next day," Sasha concluded, "when I tried to question the chief on the burial, he blandly pretended not to understand what I was talking about!"

Sasha's tale had taken some time, for the fire was again but a bed of glowing coals, silvered around the edges. Occasionally a spark shot up to live briefly in the thick darkness overhead. The fires in the village had all been out for some time, and only the bright jungle moon lighted up the silent, ghostly clearing, with its darkened huts grouped about the deserted broad playground. Deserted, I thought, except for that waiting, lonely little pile of bones. . . . From the river came the angry bellow of an alligator.

"Sasha," I said slowly, breaking into the silence with a sudden idea, "Sasha, isn't it odd, really inconsistent, that the Bororos are so friendly and hospitable to us, or any stranger, and yet have all these wild, gruesome burial customs—and permit a diabolical medicine man to execute their children and old people? How—how could such a peaceful tribe ever have struck on such a code?"

Sasha rubbed his cheek absently and stared into the embers. At length he turned back to me.

"Well," he began with a half grin, "they haven't always been such a peaceful lot. In fact, until recently they've been a warrior tribe—one of the most fierce and warlike in the Mato Grosso!"

"Really!" I exclaimed.

I must have looked not only astonished but even a little frightened, for Sasha began laughing.

"I said 'until recently,' Edith," he chuckled. "They're 'pacifists' now. Because of their constant warring they've been decimated—and I don't suppose there are more than two thousand left, scattered in a couple of dozen villages. Their days of glory are done, and they know it.

"But you can tell by their physiques," Sasha went on with enthusiasm, "that they must have been a superior race. In the days of the conquistadores they dominated a large part of Brazil."

I was silent for a minute, considerably impressed by this new slant on the Bororos.

Sasha rose slowly to his feet and threw back his shoulders and extended his arms in an enormous stretch. Then he crossed over to the log on which I sat and stood looking down at me.

I tilted my arm so that I could see my wrist watch in the dim glow from the coals.

"Why, Sasha," I said excitedly, with a meaningful glance toward the deserted playground, "it's nearly midnight!"

As if he had not heard, Sasha took both my hands and pulled me to my feet.

"But, Sasha," I protested anxiously, "it's—it's nearly time——"

He put his hands on my shoulders and looked down into my eyes with a fond smile.

"Yes"—he finished the sentence for me—"it's time old married people were in bed."

As we started toward our hammocks Sasha halted abruptly.

I looked back uneasily. The moon was momentarily behind a cloud, and the village was deep in shadowy darkness, but from the direction of the playground I was certain I heard the sudden eager rush of many bare feet across the hard-packed earth.

Sasha's arm tightened about my waist, but I shivered. . . .

We arose at dawn the next morning to witness a naming ceremony for a little Bororo baby. It was for a boy baby, of course, since Bororo girls aren't named.

The chief didn't appear to escort us, but he had invited Sasha to the ceremony the day before.

The sun was streaking the eastern sky with vivid hues of rose and pink and crimson; the grass was heavy with dew and the air still cool and fresh when we arrived at the playground, where the ceremony was to be held. A good part of the village already was there —men, women, and children, looking bright-eyed and alert, their odoriferousness freshly fortified with newly daubed, still gleaming coats of urucú and fish oil, their black hair glossy with more of the same stinking oil. They were laughing and talking lightheartedly among themselves, in sharp contrast to their strained, feverish manner at yesterday's bakororo.

"The usual crowd!" I observed, pretending the ennui of an habitué. I *was* beginning to feel like a veteran seat holder, or rather standee, at the tribe's ceremonials.

Sasha looked down at me with an amused expression.

"I should think they'd need a stage manager here to keep the acts from getting in each other's way," I said with my tongue in my cheek. "This is such a busy spot."

"That," Sasha said dryly, "is another of the medicine man's jobs."

"Doesn't he ever sleep?"

Sasha chuckled without comment.

The edge of the crowd burst into excited, pleased exclamations. I turned. A small procession was moving toward us. The waiting

Indians fell back to make way, and the procession headed for the center of the playground—the same place where the grisly remains of another child had fed the crowd's avid interest only twenty-four hours earlier.

The medicine man was in the lead, of course, in his usual bogey-man getup of black and white paint, towering paracu, and palm-frond cape and skirt. Behind him, heading a single file of members of the family and other relatives, came the tiny chief actor in the drama, carried in the arms of his proud father.

"Oh, Sasha!" I gasped. "Isn't he cute!"

The little boy baby, no more than a year old, looked exactly like a plump bird. I knew from what Sasha had told me that the effect was obtained by first smearing the youngster from head to foot with a resinous pitch, then covering him with the small breast feathers of egrets and macaws. But Sasha had vastly understated the effect. The little boy was so thickly coated with the soft downy feathers—the red feathers forming geometric patterns on the white—that only his small face and awed big black eyes could be seen!

The Indians crowded about the playground smiled broadly as they gazed at the wide-eyed baby, and I'll swear their ejaculations actually were coos of delight, fondly admiring—more admiring, in fact, than any gathering I'd seen summoned for a christening back home.

Just at sunrise, when the sun's first direct rays shot above the jungle's green horizon and the jungle forest seemed to awake all at once with the mingled raucous calls of thousands of gaily plumaged macaws and toucans, parrots and parakeets, the medicine man took the birdlike little toddler and sat him down facing the sun, within a circle formed by his seated parents and relatives. He pierced the little boy's lower lip with a sharp bone-pointed instrument decorated with bright feathers. The child cried briefly with the pain, but the medicine man quickly inserted a small bone plug in the opening he had made—the badge of membership in the tribe. Then he intoned softly the words Sasha translated for me:

"*Piadudu . . . Piadudu . . .* I name you Humming-bird."

The seated circle of the little boy's parents and relatives repeated after him, in a soft, gentle chant, the name the medicine man had chosen:

"Piadudu . . . Piadudu . . . Piadudu . . ."

It was such an appealing and beautiful little scene that it brought tears to my eyes. I hastily dropped my head and pretended that I had something in my eye, though when Sasha gently patted my shoulder I knew I hadn't fooled him.

The crowd was beginning to move away now, slowly—first a few, and then more. Sasha had his arm around me, and I sensed he was waiting for me to give the signal to leave; I turned reluctantly, and we drifted for a few steps with the naked, painted crowd who, strangely, didn't seem to me now to be so smelly and horrid and fearsome as they had before. I began to feel a warm surge of sympathy, almost affection, for them. We were brought to a halt by the slowness of the crowd, and I turned back, eager for another look at the cute little Indian child. Sasha understood immediately.

"Let's wait here a minute," he suggested quietly. "They'll come this way."

I nodded eagerly. "Let's."

When the odd-looking, feather-coated little youngster came past again in the arms of his father, I suddenly saw that the young woman at his side, who betrayed the fact that she was the mother by her almost adoring watchfulness over the vividly decorated little tot, was the young Indian mother whom we had watched weaving the day before—the mother who had been frightened of my "white man's magic!"

"Sasha," I said excitedly, "that's the little boy who ate the beetle! See his mother, beside him?"

"Why—so it is."

By that time the befeathered little boy and his father and mother were just a few feet from us, also momentarily blocked in their departure by the slow-moving crowd. I had a sudden crazy impulse.

"Sasha"—I clutched his arm tightly—"let's give the cute little fellow a christening gift! Please! I want to, very much!"

Sasha looked at me in a surprised manner, then shrugged. "All right. What do you want to give him?" He grinned. "A pair of pants? A wrist watch?"

In the meantime the principals in the naming ceremony began to move again, slowly.

I cast about with frantic haste for an idea, looked Sasha up and down, and took a quick mental inventory of what I, myself, was wearing. Then I thought of the red silk bandanna I had in my pocket. Quickly I pushed my way toward the youngster.

"Here, little Humming-bird." I smiled, dangling the crimson square of silk temptingly before the silent, wide-eyed little boy, who must have been, by that time, exceedingly warm and uncomfortable in his thick coat of pitch and feathers. I added, though of course he couldn't understand a word, "Here's a pretty silk handkerchief for you to chew on!"

The child's father stared at me with a surprised expression, as did the other Indians crowded about. I had a glimpse of the mother's face, reflecting alarm. The child looked solemnly first at the bright silk, then at me; slowly a wide grin spread over his face, and he reached for it. I smiled back and quickly backed away. And the father, now that he understood my action and saw the glowing face of his small son as he handled the gift, turned toward me again, and his dignified, stern-looking face relaxed into the semblance of a smile. He said something in a gruff voice which I interpreted as thanks and then, the crowd before him having thinned out, began to move on again.

I felt a hand on my shoulder and turned; Sasha had followed me. He smiled in an amused fashion.

"I feel like an autograph hound chasing after a Hollywood celebrity," I said sheepishly.

Sasha shrugged. "If you want to do it, why not?"

"Well, anyway," I said defensively and with some heat, "maybe I've made a friend for little Sashinho!"

Sasha smiled. "It may be. There won't be too much difference in their ages." He thought about this for a moment, then added with a grin, "His little Bororo brother, huh?"

Early that afternoon the chief, whom we had missed at the naming ceremony, triumphantly entered the village with a score of his warriors, who were loaded down with the dismembered parts of a big tapir. The entire village then seethed with excitement and activity, for the chief immediately announced that a feast would be held—in honor of the visiting white tiger hunter. The chief knew we were planning to leave the next day, and the feast was his farewell gesture.

The tapir, luckily, had made it possible. Sasha learned that the grotesque, rhinoceros-like animal, which must have weighed nearly half a ton, had been sighted near the village by one of the tribe's outpost guards shortly after dawn. He had hurried in to the chief with the news, and the chief had quickly gotten together the best hunters and their dogs.

The tapir had been killed, Sasha gathered, only after a chase of several miles through the jungle—ending finally at a marshy stretch of the river when the lumbering, great animal, harassed by the dogs and shot full of arrows, floundered into the water, swam a short distance, and sank and died. Two of the Indians had dived into the water and fastened vine ropes to its legs as it lay on the muddy bottom. But it had taken the full twenty Indians to drag the huge carcass out of the water.

When Sasha returned to our camp site at the edge of the clearing to tell me of the preparations for a feast in our honor, I was pleased, naturally. And I observed that the chief had turned out to be a virtually unparalleled host, for during our relatively short visit he had produced a birth, a funeral, and a christening. Now, with a feast coming up, it seemed as if we'd really hit the jackpot.

"There'll probably be nothing more happening in the village for the rest of the year." Sasha grinned.

"Of course," I mused, "we haven't seen a wedding, nor a hunt."

Sasha seated himself on a log nearby; I was sprawled lazily in my hammock, swinging one foot back and forth.

"Well, there's not much to a wedding," Sasha pointed out. "And I just told you how they killed the tapir."

"But how do they hunt tigers?" I persisted.

Sasha settled himself more comfortably on his log.

He had gone on a tiger hunt with the men of the tribe when he visited the chief several years earlier, he said. And the thing that had impressed him most was the fantastic sense of smell the

Indians demonstrated. During the several hours that they followed the tiger on foot, at first through bush forest bordering deep jungle, and then through a long stretch of thorn-infested, dried-up swampland, their dogs more than once lost the tiger's trail.

"And each time that happened," Sasha said, "one of the men dropped to his knees, sniffed around for a few minutes in the high grass, and then confidently pointed out the trail to the dogs!"

I shot a suspicious look at Sasha. "But then why bother with dogs at——" I smiled lamely. "Oh—you're joking."

Sasha shook his head emphatically. "I've seen it, Edith. So help me God, it's true."

He went on after a short pause.

The Indians had killed the tiger more through sheer power of their overwhelming numbers rather than any particular skill, he said. Their dogs had treed the big cat, and they shot arrow after arrow into him, until he looked like a porcupine—when, bleeding badly, he half fell, half leaped to the ground. Dodging back hastily, the Indians shot still more arrows into him while he made a couple of limping, halfhearted charges, swiping at the dogs that snapped at his heels. He managed to kill a half-grown bitch before the Indians rushed in with rocks and sticks and clubbed him to death.

Sasha said that the chief claimed he had killed eighteen tigers during his lifetime, a record of which he was inordinately proud.

I uttered an ejaculation of surprise, then smiled.

"I imagine, however," I said, "that each of those eighteen is also claimed by every Indian who was along!"

Sasha grinned. "Undoubtedly."

I asked Sasha why the Bororos used such extraordinarily long arrows; their six-foot arrows were as long as their bows. And he explained that although they were expert hunters with a bow, their ability was due not so much to their marksmanship as to their infinite patience in stalking game. This often enabled them to creep up within ten feet of their quarry. In such a case, Sasha pointed out, a couple of extra feet on the end of an arrow would bring them that much closer.

They used several types of arrows, Sasha said, all evidencing very fine craftsmanship—a barbed arrow for shooting fish; a needle-pointed one without a barb for big game; a saw-tooth, difficult-to-pull-out type for hunting monkeys; and a whistling arrow with a blunt point, designed only to stun, for knocking down birds. When on the warpath, Sasha added, the Bororos smeared their arrow points with well-putrefied carrion, knowing that this would cause a gangrenous wound.

"Hmmm . . ." I murmured. "Germ warfare in the jungle."

Sasha rose from the log and brushed some bits of bark from his trousers; then he moved toward his own hammock.

The feast that night was a fitting finale to our visit.

The preparations had begun in the afternoon, when a large fire was built on the playground and the women set to work barbecuing that half ton of tapir meat. They also baked an enormous quantity of cassava-root cakes and collected big heaps of palm hearts and fruits—ginipapos, goiabas, and papayas.

Just after nightfall—with the huge, leaping barbecue fire painting the playground in tones of black and red—the chief appeared at our camp site. He was attired, as ever, in his paracu, ba, nose bone, and barbaric necklaces. But tonight the whole was topped with a splendid feather cloak which swirled dramatically whenever he moved, displaying an intricate geometrical pattern in iridescent rainbow-hued feathers. We didn't leave immediately, however, as Sasha had "just happened to find" another quart of rum in a saddlebag, for which fortuitous circumstance the chief was duly appreciative.

Before we finally left for the playground I learned from him, unmistakably, that the Bororo word for "tiger" is *adugo*. I'm quite certain I won't forget it; I don't know how many times the chief proudly pointed to his tiger-teeth amulet, boomed out, "Adugo," pointed to himself, and then counted on his fingers up to eighteen.

And each time Sasha would grin widely and reply: "That-a-boy, Archie! You're okay, aroma and all!"

And then they would shake hands like a pair of reunited, long-lost brothers, while I tried vainly to hide my amusement.

When we eventually arrived at the playground I was intrigued by the effect of the scores of naked Indian women busily moving about before the leaping flames of the big barbecue fire. Their shining bodies were blood-red by firelight, and with the black jungle night as a backdrop, it looked like some fantastic scene in the feminine department of Hades.

We quickly found out that we were not the only ones who had made a pilgrimage to Bacchus. In the Indians' case, the medium was palm beer. At one edge of the clearing dozens of the usually so dignified Indian men were repeatedly "walking up" acuri palms with hollow reeds in their mouths and then sucking up the fermented sap. The traffic up and down the palms was heavy, and ludicrous as well, for each Indian climbing stiffly up a trunk looked like a giant monkey on a stick.

When I anxiously asked Sasha if they might not become so intoxicated that they would run amuck, he quickly pooh-poohed my fears.

"The Bororos have one custom," he said, "that civilized races would be wise to adopt. Before they start drinking they always appoint two men of the tribe to stay sober and take care of those who drink too much and misbehave."

"Really?" I looked at Sasha, a bit surprised. "What a sensible idea!"

He glanced about the large playground and finally pointed out a pair of stalwart, stern-looking braves in feather cloaks, standing together off to one side. "There's the temperance guard!"

I decided they certainly looked glum enough, amid all the surrounding hilarity, to be completely sober.

At that moment the chief, who had left us for some minutes, returned. His bearing was as erect and dignified as always, but there was a bright gleam in his black eyes, and he obviously was in an excellent humor. He spoke to Sasha, and then we started toward the barbecue pit. Sasha reached for his sheathed machete, since, as at our meal in the chief's hut, the custom was that each person sliced as big a hunk from the meat as he desired. The men, of course, ate first—however, as before, that rule would not affect me.

Although the Indians wolfed their food, they ate steadily for an amazingly long time. At a feast they always gorge themselves almost to the point of insensibility, then sleep it off and immediately begin eating again. Thus a feast often extends for two or three days, until the meat is entirely consumed or rotten. Then, since they never bother to convert surplus meat into charqui, the tribe eats meagerly what small game is available—or not at all—until a hunt results in the wherewithal for another feast.

As the evening wore on I was amused to note that the emaciated dogs finally had their day—they, too, ate heroically and wound up looking like balloons.

After about two hours the chief abruptly rose and stood silently looking around the large circle of his tribesmen sitting cross-legged facing the fire. Then he began speaking in a sonorous, booming voice. I had no idea, of course, what he was saying. But I was instantly impressed with his poise, his dignified, rhythmic phrases, and the magnificent picture he made. In the flickering, unreal firelight his stiff, high paracu seemed actually to become a part of him, so that he was no longer a mere six feet six inches tall but towered a godlike ten feet above the silent, seated tribe. His tone was oratorical; his unstudied gestures would have done credit to any civilized speaker I ever heard; and each gesture was emphasized by the dramatic sweep of his feather cloak. He was telling the tribe, Sasha said, that the feast was being held to honor his famous friend, the bearded white tiger hunter, who would depart after but one more *nadua,* or sleep. He gave an original, highly colored version of Sasha's travels and his prowess at killing tigers.

Then the chief spoke of today's successful hunt, when he and his warriors had killed *ki,* the big tapir; and afterward he called, successively, on the men who had been on the hunt. Each one rose and, while Sasha interpreted for me, gave his full-blown account of the affair, inflating the part he and his own dogs played, of course. The women and children stood in the background, listening meekly, naïvely awed by their men.

Finally the chief turned to Sasha and gravely indicated that he wished him to speak also. Sasha immediately arose, and I felt a certain uneasiness, as, I suppose, all wives of public speakers must feel at such a time. I was extremely glad that it was not I who had to get up and make an extemporaneous after-dinner speech to a bunch of staring, half-drunk savages.

But Sasha was poised, apparently completely at ease. He turned first to the chief.

"Archie"—he spoke, as usual, in Portuguese, but I noticed the Indians all eyed him intently—"Archie, you've been a fine host, and I appreciate it." He shifted to look about the firelit circle of stolid, painted warriors and added graciously, "And you have a well-behaved tribe here. . . . And while that's all I have to say, I'd better keep talking for a while to match your own oratory and uphold the verbosity of the white man. So here goes—remember you asked for it!"

Sasha abruptly thundered magnificently into some of the more overpowering passages of *King Lear;* his voice rolled majestically into the night, and he declaimed with a full repertoire of burlesqued stances and gestures. I tore my eyes away only long enough to note that his audience was watching absolutely motionless, with a grave approval and a vast respect.

Sasha suddenly switched to a more normal, very sincere tone.

"In conclusion, I hope all of you have many more happy years left. Many more years left, that is, before you fall into the hands of your medicine man!"

He smiled, bowed to the chief, and sat down.

This ended the dignified session. Everyone rose and hurriedly began preparations for the dance. The chief stepped closer to us, still looking pleased at Sasha's speech.

Sasha, of course, knew what was on the chief's mind.

"Let's take a little walk, Archie," he suggested with a grin; and the three of us moved a slight distance away from the bright fire. "I don't suppose you'll be satisfied until we finish this cachaça, you red-skinned barfly!"

I made no attempt to conceal my smile as Sasha handed the chief the bottle, for we were now in the dark. The chief tipped it to his lips for a long minute. Sasha had a short drink, and then he tossed away the empty bottle.

When we returned to the firelight, the musicians already had assembled—nearly a score of them—with bass flutes and calabash trumpets and also a third type of instrument, an odd-looking ocarina-like affair made of the two halves of a mussel's shell, which Sasha said they would play by blowing into it with one

148

nostril, instead of with their lips. Needless to say, I was curious to see it in action.

The opening of the dance was signaled by an astonishing and really artistic solo performance of what Sasha said was the Bororos' famous Tiger Dance. As this ordinarily celebrated a tiger's killing, Sasha gathered that tonight it was being danced in his honor.

An Indian suddenly ran into the playground from the edge of the jungle, realistically imitating the tiger's mating call on an enormous gourd trumpet. As he blasted forth his spine-prickling roar, a second Indian plunged into the firelight from the opposite side, crouching under the skin of a large tiger and wearing the tiger's head as a mask. While the trumpeteer continued roaring, the Indian in the tiger skin loped, ran in sudden breathless rushes, and wove about in sinuous, graceful movements that were an astonishingly credible imitation of a tiger. The performance was climaxed by a re-enactment of a tiger hunt, in which the man in the tiger skin repeatedly charged his invisible Indian enemies and bit at the imaginary arrows shot into him and finally "died"— dramatically.

Abruptly, then, the big bass flutes began to snort, the calabash trumpets barked, and the Indians with the mussel ocarinas bent their nostrils to their shrill-voiced shells.

Simultaneously twoscore Bororo men clad in paracus and feather cloaks nearly as colorful as the chief's, clutching gourd rattles in both hands and wearing circlets of rattling seed pods about their ankles and wrists, began a slow, rhythmic circling about the fire—stamping, moving crab-fashion from heel to toe, swaying from side to side—at the same time chanting in a weird, stirring tempo. Immediately the women, outside the circle, began dancing an accompaniment—linking arms, striding forward six steps toward the circling men, then backing up, and chanting also in a muted key. The Indian in the tiger skin, within the circle, still pranced and roared and charged in sudden plunges.

We watched for an hour or two by the eerie light of the flickering fire and the huge jungle moon overhead. I was fascinated, actually hypnotized, by the harsh, discordant music crashing against my eardrums, the monotonous, rhythmic stamping, and the weaving, repetitious pattern of the dance.

I finally sighed wearily and leaned my head against Sasha's shoulder. He turned to me.

"Well, dear," he said gently, "have you had enough excitement for today?"

I nodded, too tired even to answer.

He rose and helped me to my feet. Wearily I trudged beside him as we skirted the sweating, stamping, chanting dancers and then made our way between the long line of empty huts to our hammocks on the edge of the forest. As I pulled my mosquito netting over me it took real effort to manage a tired "Good night, darling."

I woke up momentarily near dawn. The big bass flutes were still snorting, the ocarinas were shrilling, and the barks of the calabashes were hoarsely staccato.

CHAPTER 4

LUCKILY, I THOUGHT, IT WAS PLEASANTLY COOL INSIDE THE houseboat. I raised the presser foot of my new Singer sewing machine to insert the folded edge of rough linen, then lowered it again, gave the hand wheel a shove, and began pumping hard on the treadle. The machine hummed, and under the dancing needle the neatly stitched seam marched steadily forward.

"Damn!" I put my forefinger to my mouth for an instant. I'd just pricked myself on one of the pins I had used for basting.

Having finished the seam, I sat back in my chair, brushed my tousled hair out of my eyes, and smiled contentedly to myself. I had nearly forgotten to finish the shirttail—and after spending so many hours fondly edging all those buttonholes and sewing on buttons to give the shirt an extra-fancy, really sporty look! And also, of course, to indulge my delight in using the sewing machine's clever buttonhole attachment.

I had never made a buttonhole before in my life, as it was such tedious work if you did it by hand. But in the two weeks I had had my new sewing machine I had been on a buttonhole binge, making myself some nightgowns and remodeling a dress—and putting buttons and buttonholes wherever remotely possible. The sewing machine had been waiting for me when we returned from our trip to the Bororos; Sasha had ordered it from Rio some months before and had had it freighted to Corumbá, where Rosando found it, together with our new stove, when he arrived with the countess. He had brought it and the stove back in the dugout. Sasha, however, had accused me of concentrating all my attention on the new sewing machine and neglecting the equally new stove, to the detriment of his meals.

I had been making him this dress sports shirt, using one of his old ones for a rough pattern, as a sort of consolation gift.

I scissored the last thread end and then admiringly contemplated the finished shirt as it lay on the sewing machine before me. My little scourge, Rupert, suddenly poked his head up from behind a low rosewood chest and seemed to be admiring it too. My eyes moved idly from him to the Bororo feather cloak spread fanwise on the wall above the chest. Its rainbow-colored designs added an exotic decorator's touch to our living room and served as a concrete reminder of our Bororo visit, which already seemed like a fantastic dream.

Abruptly I heard footsteps on the plank walk leading from the bank to the houseboat. I knew it was Sasha, because he and I, of course, were the only people around who wore shoes. A moment later the screen door opened and he sauntered in.

He halted just in front of me, where I still sat at the sewing machine. With his hands on his hips, he began laughing silently. I felt my welcoming smile fading; I frowned.

"All right, all right," I said irritably, knowing I was going to be kidded some more about having fallen in love with my sewing machine. I scowled up at his grinning, deeply tanned face. "What's so funny?"

Instead of replying, he laughed even more heartily.

I leaned my head on my hand in a pose of resigned patience, waiting for him to be through enjoying his little joke.

"I was just thinking, my dear," he said finally, "how much you remind me of my youthful days in the diamond fields!"

"Oh, do I?" I murmured with exaggerated politeness.

He nodded, still grinning. Drawing out his handkerchief, he wiped his damp forehead, then slumped into a chair and crossed his legs with a "Whew! It's hot out there in the sun!"

"Well, I'm waiting," I said coldly, determined not to be diverted. "What about me—and your 'youthful days in the diamond fields'?"

"Oh—oh yes," he said, blandly innocent, as if he had already forgotten his remark; then his eyes met mine and he began to grin again.

"It was the women there, my dear," he said suavely. "The camp followers, you know. Several packed battered old sewing machines into the fields with their few belongings. And I can still remember them industriously working away on their treadle sewing machines in the daytime—to supplement their earnings at night. Ah me, those unfortunate women——"

"Oh, so now I remind you of prostitutes!" I said icily. "How *very* flattering."

Sasha's grin evaporated.

"Now, Edith," he began in a conciliatory tone, "you know what I meant."

I sniffed haughtily and coldly turned my back. My eyes lit on the finished sports shirt. Picking it up, I rose from my chair and moved toward him, smiling sweetly.

"Here's a little present I made for you on my new sewing machine, dear!" The amount of saccharin with which I loaded the words was a bit appalling, even to me. "I've spent every minute of the last three days working on it when you weren't around."

Sasha's mouth gaped, and he met my eyes dubiously—as if in doubt as how to take my abrupt change of mood.

"Why—why, thank you, Edith! Thank you," he said rather awkwardly, still eying me speculatively. I could see he was struggling to decide whether or not to apologize for teasing me so much about my constant sewing. He looked down at the shirt in his hands and added cleverly, "A shirt!"

"A sports shirt," I corrected proudly, adding, "Aren't you going to try it on?"

He smiled. "Why, of course, dear!" He quickly took off the wilted one he was wearing. A moment later he had the new one on, though he hadn't yet buttoned it, and was extravagantly admiring it. "It's beautiful, sweetheart!"

I beamed. "I made it a really sporty sports shirt, with plenty of buttons," I said. "It's perfectly *lush* with buttons!"

"So I see," he observed, as with a rather disconcerted expression he began buttoning the front from the wide collar down—a marathon task, since I'd spaced those buttons only an inch apart; in fact, by actual count, I had sewed ten on the shirt, including the two on each cuff. "So I see," he repeated dryly.

For a moment I felt guilty at having let my madness for buttonhole making run wild with me, but I quickly brushed the feeling aside.

"Well"—I moved closer and looked up at him teasingly—"don't I get a reward?"

Sasha halted his buttoning and smilingly planted a vigorous kiss on my lips. We moved to one of the wide windows and stood arm in arm, looking out over the broad sunlit Upper Paraguay.

"Ah—it's a wonderful life," Sasha said expansively. "Here in our own peaceful wilderness—with tigers to hunt and a houseboat to come home to, and you and your sewing machine!"

I let this pass, for I was feeling very kindly toward him at the moment, in spite of his flippancy.

"You know," I said slowly, "if that darned slow mailman ever gets here again, maybe he'll bring those patterns I sent for."

"Yes?" Sasha said absently.

"Well"—I smiled a bit self-consciously—"then I could start making those baby clothes.

"Sasha . . ." I said. "You know I have an awful craving for some honey!"

"My dear, are you taking advantage of your condition?" He grinned.

"Don't laugh! I mean it!" I was indignant.

"I'm not laughing, darling," Sasha replied soothingly. He pursed his lips and frowned thoughtfully. "Maybe we can do something about that, dear. I believe I just happen to know where we can find a honey tree."

"Oh, you're wonderful!"

Sasha cleared his throat. "Think nothing of it, dear," he said modestly. "It's a Siemel Special Service."

There was another silence.

154

"Sasha . . ."
"Yes?"
I looked up at him with a mischievous smile.
"Would you like me to finish buttoning your shirt?"

It was not until several days later, however, that we set out to satisfy my craving. The place where Sasha had noticed the honey tree on the tail end of our return trip from the Bororos was only a few miles from home and near the river, so we decided to take the dugout with the outboard motor, instead of our horses.

Lauro and Rosando were sawing and splitting firewood into lengths that would fit our new stove, and Antonia was bent over our laundry at the edge of the river, humming some Portuguese love song, when we set out. We took along a pail in which to bring back the honey, an ax, and a couple of gourd scoops. And when our outboard motor settled down to a steady putt-putt-putt we looked at each other and smiled, for the sun was bright but not unbearably hot, the river was smooth, shimmering glass, and the jungle was bright with color.

It was September, and south of the equator it was spring. For miles around our houseboat, where piuva trees composed two thirds of the jungle forest, the entire landscape seemed purple from the huge, waxy blossoms with which these trees were covered. The paratudo trees, which punctuated the purple with their prodigally massed smaller yellow flowers, and the many wild fruit trees, with their various flamboyant blossoms, contributed to the vivid jungle scene.

The honey tree would be easy to find, Sasha said, because it was a twisted old piuva standing alone in the high brown grass of the largo near a stretch of dried-up swampland. There was no other tree within two hundred yards.

A couple of hours later we were triumphantly grinning into each other's dirt-smudged and perspiring face, admiring the results of our work. The acrid odor of smoke hung about us, and a thin plume of gray still rose from the half-burnt swamp grass at the base of the tree with which Sasha had smoked out and stupefied the wild bees. The honeycomb, luckily, had been only about five feet above the ground inside the hollow trunk, and after Sasha had chopped away enough of the soft bark and the rotting wood to expose it, we easily scooped out most of the crisp comb, filled nearly to overflowing with dark honey, and dropped it into our pail.

Sasha had just peered into the hollow again to be sure we had all of the honeycomb, when a lone bee left inside, which must have revived from our smoke barrage, suddenly darted out, spiraled groggily around my head a couple of times, and lit on my bare arm.

"Eeeek! Get away!" I shrieked, brushing at it frantically.

The poor bee tumbled off, recovered in mid-air, and erratically zoomed away.

Sasha started to laugh. Then he became serious again and held up his hand. "Listen!" he said. "I thought I heard——"

Abruptly intent, he didn't finish. I turned quickly and stared, too, into the bright sun, out over the brown waist-high marsh grass that stretched on three sides of us to the vast, open marsh more than a mile away. But at first I heard nothing. Then . . .

"Look!" Sasha pointed, excitement in his voice.

About four hundred yards away, atop a slight rise in the otherwise flat largo, the calm sea of high marsh grass seemed suddenly struck by a tornado, for it bowed and swayed and shook tortuously—a tornado that was moving straight toward us. I heard eager little squeals—dozens of impatient, eager little squeals—and the thudding of hundreds of feet. The pitching and swaying marsh grass was now less than a hundred yards away.

"Peccaries!" Sasha exclaimed. "A drove of peccaries!"

"What—what'll we do?" I gasped.

"Quick!" Sasha pulled my arm. "Up in the tree, Edith. I'll boost you!"

"Oooh!" I wailed as he hurriedly pushed me over to the gnarled and leaning piuva. He grasped my legs and roughly hoisted me up. I scrambled to reach a jutting limb above me and looked down worriedly. "Aren't—aren't you coming too?"

I could hear the squealing louder now. The peccaries sounded vicious, ravenous. I was frightened, for I knew what a drove of peccaries could do, and I trembled as I pulled myself up by that first limb and reached for another. I glanced over my shoulder,

156

and the sight momentarily paralyzed me, for I saw the dark shapes of the foremost animals in the swaying, bending grass—an enormous number of them—not more than thirty yards away. Their racing over the sun-baked ground sounded like thunder.

"Oooh, Sasha! Hurry!" I cried out, for I could see, as if in a horrible nightmare, that he was still on the ground.

"Climb! Climb!" Sasha roared, to make himself heard above the squealing din. "I'm coming!"

Trembling so hard I was afraid I would shake myself loose, I reached for a still higher limb and drew myself up; and then I glimpsed Sasha, with a sudden leap, grabbing the lowest limb of the tree just as an enormous horde of the bloodthirsty wild pigs pounded up and swarmed about in a noisy, tightly packed, shoving mass of bristly black backs, mean little red eyes, and foam-flecked red mouths with huge, jutting white tusks. Several of them, champing their tusks with an angry staccato clicking, leaped up at the base of the tree to grab Sasha's dangling feet.

I gave a shout of horror and closed my eyes, shuddering, as I pictured one of those wickedly tusked mouths closing on Sasha's leg, but my shout was drowned in the other noises—the banging and clattering of the tin pail, and the peccaries' angry squealing and grunting and champing as they fought over the honey we had collected.

Then I dared to open my eyes, and there was Sasha—safe—his legs locked high around the tree trunk, climbing easily and quickly just beneath me. He grinned reassuringly.

"My God, Sasha!" I exclaimed, mustering a weak smile, though my voice shook. "For a moment I thought——"

I stopped, alarmed, for at that moment there was a hard blow against the base of the tree, so hard that it actually shook the tree—and then another, and another. I hastily wrapped my arms tighter around the shuddering tree trunk; immediately I felt Sasha's hand on my elbow, and from where he sat, comfortably straddling a limb on the opposite side of the trunk, he met my eyes with a cool, faintly amused smile.

"Don't be afraid, dear," he said reassuringly. "Just hold tight!" He grinned. "The little devils are trying to shake us down."

I gulped as the tree shivered under still more vigorous blows.

"Oh, is that all?" I replied with what was meant to be a tone of sarcasm, though the shaking tree caused me to hold on even tighter just then and somewhat spoiled the effect. "I hope," I added with a worried frown as we swayed ludicrously back and forth with each battering, rocking blow, "I hope there isn't any chance of their succeeding."

Sasha shook his head emphatically. "Not if we stay awake."

He peered down, and I followed his gaze. Through the thickly clustered purple blossoms on the lower limbs of the tree I could see the crowding, constantly moving black backs of the animals as they angrily charged at the trunk and rooted at it with their big tusks. The tin honey pail still rattled and banged as they kicked it about, and their angry grunts and squeals continued unabated.

As I met Sasha's eyes again he grinned.

"Of course," he drawled, "this tree is partly hollow and undoubtedly not as strong as it once was."

"Sasha!" I looked at him, startled. "You don't really think——"

Then I saw the glint in his eyes.

"You—*you*——" I sputtered indignantly. "As if this weren't bad enough as it is. Trying to scare me more!"

There was a silence while we rocked and swayed, for the peccaries, though frustrated in their attempt at overtaking us on the ground, continued angrily and hopefully rooting at the base of the tree. Occasionally there would be a louder squealing, as if there was fighting among them, and then the tree shaking would stop for a minute or two, only to be resumed again with redoubled, wrathful vigor.

"Why don't you shoot at them?" I demanded finally, eying the heavy Magnum revolver Sasha wore.

"My dear," he said dryly, "there must be between three hundred and four hundred peccaries down there. I don't have over twenty-five bullets on me."

"But if you shot a few," I persisted, "wouldn't that scare the rest away?"

Sasha shook his head. "It would just anger the rest that much more! They'll give up and leave sooner if I don't."

"And how soon will that be?" I said irritably, for my derrière was beginning to tire of that hard perch on the narrow limb.

Sasha shrugged, as if it was a matter of no importance. "Oh, possibly an hour—or two—or three."

"How nice!" I returned sarcastically.

There was another silence while we continued rocking, then the peccaries below squealed and grunted, and we recurrently heard the tin pail being banged about, although it must have been emptied long before now. This really was a maddening predicament, I thought moodily. Several hours to kill and nothing to do— nothing to read, nothing to eat or drink, and all my muscles beginning to feel cramped from not being able to move. Sasha wasn't even trying to be amusing, I told myself resentfully. The tree shuddered and rocked again under a new attack below, and the noisy peccaries sounded even more impatient and angry.

"Well, anyway," I said, "if we have to be flagpole sitters, we at least have a beautiful setting."

I broke off one of the big purple blossoms with which the tree was weighted down—an exotic blossom as large as a good-sized rose—and absently lifted it to my nose. It had almost no fragrance, like most of the jungle's oversize blooms whose development seems to run to size and color rather than scent. A tiny ruby-throated green hummingbird was poised in the air before a blossom near my head, completely motionless except for its rapidly beating, almost invisible wings. Huge brilliant butterflies hovered like drifting mosaics of color over other blossoms.

But being besieged in a tree, I thought bitterly, was a stupid way to spend a lovely spring day.

Sasha broke into my thoughts by loudly clearing his throat.

"These peccaries," he said slowly, "can really be dangerous, because they always travel in big droves—droves of as many as three or four hundred."

He went on to explain that peccaries will savagely turn on any creature, even a full-grown tiger, if one of their number is attacked, and that, amazingly, they bring down their prey by using a classic military maneuver. Ordinarily a drove travels over the marshlands in a compact mass. But when they sight any prey they quickly re-form into a U shape, with the open end of the U pointed at the quarry.

"And then," Sasha concluded, "they race to bring down their prey by outflanking and enveloping it!"

"Really?" I mused, idly stroking my chin with the big purple piuva blossom.

Sasha nodded and continued after a short pause:

"When I was in the diamond fields, a prospector I knew, a city-bred man who knew little of the jungle, was killed by a drove. He'd ridden out with a hunting party to get meat. They ran onto a large drove out on the marshland, and this man shot one of them. Then, very foolishly, he jumped off his horse and ran over to the dead peccary. The drove immediately turned on him, cut him off from his horse, and in a few minutes they'd torn him to bits!"

"How horrible!" I shuddered. Then I peered down through the massed purple blossoms at the heaving, crowding, bristly backs of the peccaries just a few feet beneath us, for they hadn't shaken the tree for some minutes. I let my imagination dwell morbidly for a moment on what our fate would have been if we had been a minute slower in scrambling up.

And just then, as if to reassure us that they still were patiently waiting, the drove began moving about more nervously—squealing and grunting with renewed vigor, and champing and clicking their sharp tusks. They began savagely rooting again at the base of the tree, and the tree shuddered and jerked, and petals from some of the purple blossoms high above us drifted down onto my hair and shoulders. I warily shifted my position a trifle and found a better hold on the rough tree trunk. I turned back to Sasha with a weary expression.

"Don't they ever give up?" I demanded petulantly.

"They're wild pigs, my dear"—Sasha smiled—"and pigheaded."

I made a face at him.

He cleared his throat again.

"But when I was in the diamond fields," he drawled, resuming his reminiscences, "I developed a special technique for hunting them. I had an intelligent little dog who co-operated with me. I'd trained him to howl on command."

"How cute!"

Sasha ignored the remark. "When I reached the marshland frequented by the peccaries, I'd climb an isolated tree like this one, carrying the dog and my rifle. The dog knew what was coming, and he'd be trembling with excitement, but game.

" 'All right, Tupi,' I'd say after I got settled high in the tree. 'Bark now! Loud!' And Tupi would cry out mournfully: 'Ow-woooh! Ow-woooh!' "

Sasha's imitation of the dog's mournful howls was so realistic that it brought a sudden startling silence among the noisy horde beneath us. And then, as if the apparent disclosure of still another potential tidbit among the prey just out of their reach infuriated them, they started battering at the tree with an insane fury.

As I clutched the tree trunk and swayed jerkily back and forth with its crazy rocking I gave Sasha a woebegone look and sighed wearily.

"Good lord!" I said. "Don't they have a home to go to?"

Sasha merely grinned and resumed his story in a half shout.

"Invariably," he said, "after Tupi had howled for a few minutes I'd hear the grunts and impatient squeals of the peccaries as they hurried through the high grass, eager to catch what sounded like a dog lost on the marshlands. And as soon as they got close enough I'd shoot one. After that it was easy to kill as many as I wanted. For the enraged peccaries, instead of fleeing, would surge about the base of the tree, rooting and slashing at it to try to shake me out."

I smiled. "Even as now?"

Sasha nodded.

"But they eventually left?" I asked dubiously.

"After an hour or two."

"What's become of Tupi now?" I asked finally. "He'd probably enjoy this."

"I never found out," Sasha replied. "He just disappeared one day. But something undoubtedly killed him. He wasn't the kind of dog who would wander off."

"Oh, that's a pity," I said. Then I smiled. "Maybe the peccaries finally got revenge."

Sasha was peering down through the blossom-loaded lower limbs of the tree.

"Our friends have left!" he exclaimed abruptly.

"No! I don't believe it!" I said incredulously. I hastily bent to look too. But it seemed to be true. I could see the bare ground beneath the tree; there were no bristly black backs in the way, and it was perfectly quiet below.

Sasha started climbing down the trunk of the tree.

"Be careful!" I warned. "They may still be near!"

"Don't worry," he said. "I'm just going lower for a better view."

He climbed down to within a few feet of the ground and remained there for some minutes, peering out over the dried-up marshlands. Then he called to me that it was safe; he had just spotted the high marsh grass moving over the rapidly traveling drove a half mile to the west. With a sigh I began stiffly descending the tree, fairly creaking in every joint from my long cramped position. Sasha gave me a hand for the last few feet.

When I finally reached the ground with a thump, I eased my numbed muscles by stretching—wonderful-feeling stretches—for a good three minutes.

Sasha called my attention to the base of the tree. I stared at it. The bark was completely scored away to a height of nearly five feet; and huge gashes, as deeply and cleanly made as if with an ax, had been cut by those razor-sharp tusks into the live wood itself. A short distance away, battered and flattened nearly past recognition and half buried in the red dust, was our honey pail. The ax handle was broken and splintered.

Sasha was looking at his wrist watch.

"Two hours they held us at bay!" he said, with as pleased an expression as a horse breeder who has just clocked a potential Derby winner. "Two hours always seems the limit of their patience."

"And mine," I observed wryly.

We started out rather lamely toward the riverbank a quarter of a mile away where we had beached our dugout.

"What a completely wasted day," I said disgustedly. "I don't suppose you know where we can find any more honey trees?"

Sasha shook his head. "Unfortunately, no."

"Darn it, Sasha," I sighed. "I have such a *dreadful* craving for some honey."

Early in the morning, during a heavy storm with dramatic thunder and lightning effects, we started out with our dugout loaded with a week's supply of food and camping equipment.

The torrential rains were still continuing—with each dark, dripping, steaming day a dreary repetition of the one before—when, in February, Sasha and I decided we'd better not wait any longer to make the long trip down-river to the small Catholic hospital in Corumbá for the advent of little Sasha.

It was high time we started, for by now I was nearly eight and a half months pregnant, although there was a certain amount of guesswork involved, as I naturally hadn't been able to consult a doctor and had arrived at this conclusion only by approximation and arduous application to a fat mail-order volume, *The Expectant Mother.*

The Expectant Mother had given me all sorts of advice on diets and exercise, and I had followed its countless admonitions religiously—to a point where Sasha teased me about not putting salt in the soup without consulting my book (as a matter of fact, *The Expectant Mother* actually frowned on salt and warned that it would make my feet swell) and began referring to it alternately as "The *Holy* Mother" and "The Baby Bible."

I had also tried to supplement my original hazy information on the subject through a few conversations with Cenaria—who, having had six children herself, should have been an expert. But she had been disappointing. When I asked her how much time she thought I had, she ran her eyes expertly over me, then shrugged and said maddeningly, "God alone knows, but why worry? When they are ready, they always come. Nothing can stop them." When I expressed a certain anxiety about the difficulties of childbirth she shrugged again and said, "There is nothing to it, senhora. The senhor himself said once, 'Making babies is the Brazilian national industry.' That which everyone can do cannot be hard." And when I casually mentioned my reference book she rolled her eyes upward and, after a shocked silence, said, "Senhora, is it possible that you must read a book to have this baby?" She hesitated, then went on earnestly, "Senhora, I would burn the book and forget all about it. The baby cannot read the book, and yet he will get himself here without it." And that was all the advice I got from her.

But whether my figuring was guesswork or no, my figure certainly bore it out. Although I didn't know how much I weighed, I was glad we didn't have a scale. My weight and my waistline had advanced by leaps and bounds to a point where any further increase was obviously a physical impossibility.

So our margin of safety couldn't be much more than two weeks, and that was little enough at best. I knew that babies are unpredictable and quite often come a couple of weeks early.

On the day we set out we hadn't seen the sun in weeks. And the murky, pouring morning—with its recurrent zigzag flashes of lightning and their obbligato of almost constant, distantly rumbling thunder—wasn't calculated to inspire one happily. I considered this rather morbidly as our houseboat finally was blotted from sight when we rounded a broad bend of the enormously swollen and turbulent Upper Paraguay on our first lap of the five-hundred-mile journey to Corumbá.

But it was intimate and cozy beneath the tarpaulin Sasha had spread to protect us from the pelting rain, and the laboring, regular putt-putt-putt of the outboard motor was a homely, comforting sound in that vast expanse of floodwaters, of never-ceasing downpour and distant, hazy jungle only vaguely visible through the screen of heavy rain and the steamy mist that hung over the far reaches of the river—distant jungle that during the dry season had marked the banks of the then mile-wide river, but which now was broken into tens of thousands of little islands by the flood.

Our food and camping equipment were stowed away in front of me. Sasha had bundled in plenty of blankets to keep me safe and warm, though as usual during the rainy season, the Mato Grosso "summer," the temperature hung around one hundred degrees; and this, together with the excessive humidity caused by the never-ending downpour, made the air almost stifling. However, it occasionally did get cool at night, even in the rainy season.

We had been silent for more than an hour. . . .

Sasha sat upright in the stern under the sagging, dripping tarpaulin, his hand on the throbbing steering rod, his eyes glued on the broad expanse of river unfolding before us, peering through the pelting, driving rain which greatly reduced visibility and thus greatly increased the danger of our striking a drifting log or partially submerged alligator and capsizing.

I shuddered as I thought of that possibility. It would mean almost certain death—if not from drowning in those treacherous floodwaters, from attack by the now swarming, bloodthirsty piranhas.

An unusually bright flash of lightning split the eastern sky, and an instant later a crackling explosion of thunder cascaded in tumbling reverberations. I shivered again, then hastily lowered my eyelids as though I were dozing, for I caught Sasha looking at me with an anxious expression. I huddled deeper into the blankets in which I half lay, half sat, facing him. The rain drummed unceasingly on the tarpaulin overhead. Would it never stop? I asked myself, feeling suddenly frantic. I turned my head slightly to look out over the enormous expanse of muddy water, seething and needled by the bouncing raindrops. We passed a half-submerged huge tree, torn up and rolling along in the flood, its crown of leaves still green.

Would we ever reach Corumbá? I asked myself. I felt as though we had been traveling through the rain for years, though it was still the first day of our trip. Would this never end? What if our baby decided to be born before we got to Corumbá? What would we do? What could we do, here in this little dugout out on the middle of the river, in the rain? I felt a sudden frenzied surge of fear at the thought, and I caught my breath. Then I pressed my lips together grimly and tried to force myself to be calm. I became conscious of the pounding of my heart, and I concentrated on it. I tried to synchronize it with the steady putt-putt-putt of the outboard motor to circumvent any thinking. But then a new black thought struck me: What if . . . ? I recalled the many stories I'd heard of women dying in childbirth. What if that happened to me? Who would Sasha get for a stepmother for Sashinho? A wave of despair and self-pity surged over me, and I felt the tears swelling in my eyes. I determinedly tried to blink them back.

"Oh, Sasha——" I suddenly choked. "What—what if something terrible happens?"

Sasha turned startled eyes on me. Then he leaned forward

quickly, keeping one hand on the steering rod, and—apparently taking in my mood at a glance—reached for my hand and pressed it.

"Everything will be all right, sweetheart," he said gently. "You're tired. Try to get a little sleep."

I shook my head. "I can't sleep," I whimpered.

His eyes left my face momentarily to peer ahead at the river, then he turned back to me.

"I'll make you a birth charm"—he grinned—"that'll guarantee everything'll be all right!"

I attempted a smile. "I don't believe in charms."

He again glanced at the river.

"I saw one work years ago," he said with a slow smile. "It was one hundred per cent effective."

"I don't believe it."

He nodded emphatically. "About ten years ago. I was traveling alone through the jungle, eating what game I could kill. I came upon a little backwoods ranch, and naturally, after weeks of living off the woods, I welcomed the opportunity for a well-cooked meal."

I smiled.

"I found I wasn't alone in this," Sasha continued with a reminiscent gleam in his eye. "An Englishman was there ahead of me. He'd dropped in on the ranch house several hours before, and he was even hungrier than I was. He hadn't been fed yet. The difficulty, I soon found out, was that the rancher's wife had been having labor pains since the previous midnight, and the entire household, including the cook and the woman's mother and sisters, were all too busy worrying over the child's slowness in being born to prepare a meal."

Sasha looked sharply through the driving rain and edged the steering rod a bit to the right. There was a bright flash of lightning and another crackling explosion of thunder.

"The Englishman was so hungry he was stalking up and down outside the ranch house, cursing to himself. Finally he turned to me"—Sasha grinned—"and said, 'I'll fix that damned procrastinating woman! If I don't, we'll starve to death!' He took out a notebook, scrawled something hurriedly on a page, tore it out and folded it, and stuffed it into a woman's locket which he'd carried in his pocket. Then he called the woman's husband out and said he

(*Above, left*) Boa constrictor battles young alligator;
(*above, right*) wild capibara near camp and
(*below*) alligators in jungle creek.

had a magic charm to hurry up births which he'd lend him. He told the rancher to put it beneath his wife's pillow."

I smiled. "I suppose the baby was born immediately."

Sasha chuckled. "As a matter of fact," he drawled, "the baby was born a half-hour later. And in a short time the other women had a big dinner fixed, by way of celebration! The Englishman was the guest of honor. They figured he'd saved the mother's life."

I looked dubious. "Just what was his magic charm?"

Sasha cleared his throat and his mouth twitched.

"After dinner I asked the Englishman that same question. By way of answer he drew out the locket, which had been returned to him, and let me read the paper he'd stuffed inside." Sasha paused, then added dryly, "On it he'd written, 'Accursed woman, either have your brat at once or hurry up and die, so we can eat.'"

I was somewhat taken aback.

Sasha chuckled quietly at the memory.

I was silent for a minute, then spoke up.

"Sasha," I said earnestly, pretending considerable concern, "that little hotel in Corumbá is still serving meals, isn't it?"

Sasha smiled. And I smiled back at him and settled myself comfortably among my blankets and listened contentedly to the drumming rain on the tarpaulin. The lightning ripped the sky, and the rumbling of thunder continued. Then I began to doze under the mesmerizing, monotonous chugging of the motor, and the last thing I remembered was the sight of Sasha sitting upright in the stern, his eyes peering steadily into that thick curtain of driving rain, a faint smile on his lips.

We made camp that night on a little tree-clad island which during the dry season had been a bluff, the highest point on the western bank of the Upper Paraguay for many miles. It was still raining, of course, but the thickly massed tall trees sheltered us considerably although the ground was soaked. Sasha made a tent of our tarpaulin, and we slung our hammocks beneath it. We prepared our evening meal over our portable two-burner kerosene stove. . . .

On the evening of the fifth day the rains let up for a few hours, the dark clouds drew away briefly from the moon, and we saw a moon rainbow—a beautiful and rare phenomenon of the jungle skies.

"It is the natives' omen of good luck, dear!" Sasha smiled meaningfully.

But the rain started again soon, of course, and it was pouring heavily in a steady, matter-of-fact manner, as if it had no intention of ever stopping, when on the following afternoon we reached Corumbá. When Sasha helped me onto the slippery dock after making the dugout fast, I stood there, while he loaded himself with our belongings, and stared uncertainly down the deserted muddy street of the town where I was to have our baby. Under the dark, sagging skies of that rainy late afternoon it should have looked even more lonely and forlorn than on the previous times I had been there. But at that moment it seemed the equal of any metropolis in the world.

Lightning splintered the sky twice as we stepped off the gleaming wet dock and started splashing through the puddles of the street. Thunder rumbled heavily for several seconds. A miserable wet-looking dog with his tail between his legs stepped gingerly aside to let us pass and stared suspiciously at us. I pulled my sombrero lower on my forehead and wrapped my voluminous red poncho closer about my gourdlike figure. Then I turned my face up against the pelting rain to look at Sasha bowed under the weight of our considerable baggage.

"Well"—I gave a sigh of relief—"I didn't see any tired-looking stork hanging around at the dock, so I guess we beat Sashinho here, after all!"

Sasha smiled indulgently.

The next morning, after breakfasting in the hotel's small dining room, which we shared with a couple of loudly dressed "drummers" from Rio, we set out in the rain again toward the hospital.

The hotel—by virtue of its three brick-faced stories the tallest and most imposing building in Corumbá—like most of the town's buildings, faced the plaza, a small park of ragged shrubs and grass crisscrossed by unkempt gravel paths, which looked neglected and uninviting in the wet, gray morning.

The plaza, of course, as in most small Brazilian towns, was Corumbá's "front lawn." The mostly one-story, whitewashed adobe business and residential buildings, with their roofs of tiles or ugly-looking corrugated iron. were all built flush with the street which

168

bounded the plaza and jammed tightly against each other, with no room left for front or side lawns of their own.

And this morning, since it was Corumbá's weekly market day, the stone street between the hotel and the little park was cluttered with the lurching oxcarts and the basket-laden mules of mestizos from small backwoods farms bringing their produce to town. A Negro youth shambled across our path, driving a half dozen blatting sheep.

As we trudged through the rain we threaded our way through the mestizos crowded at the market place. Most, though barefoot, were dressed as we were in bright ponchos and huge felt or straw sombreros. Some leaned stolidly against the solid-wood wheels of their carts, which were piled high with melons and fruits. Others lounged beside wicker crates of soaked, bedraggled chickens. All were apparently as oblivious of the downpour as the longhorn bullocks placidly chewing their cuds while the water coursed down their bony flanks.

Barefoot black or brown women, wearing bright kerchiefs and ponchos, stood impassively beside forlorn-looking mules that were weighted down on either side with reed panniers stuffed with cassava roots, baskets of eggs, or fat pottery jars. Only when haggling with a customer did any of these people become animated, and then their eyes lit up and they plunged eagerly into noisy, voluble argument. Lean, dripping dogs, impartially sniffing everything, mingled with barelegged youngsters who stared unblinkingly at us with the hostile, tongue-tied diffidence of backwoods children.

We moved out of the crowd and continued down the street. Reaching the far edge of the plaza finally, we started splashing through the shallow pools of water that lay like a chain of lakes along the cobbled path that led to the hospital. The rain still was falling heavily, noisily, and without any hint of a respite.

The hospital was located a short distance beyond the plaza, on the edge of the town.

We walked on through the rain to the trim little building that was the hospital and mounted the steps. A receptionist behind the desk inside replied to Sasha's question that the Sister Superior was in. She would take our names to her.

Two minutes later the Sister Superior strode out of her office, a smile on her face.

"My good friend, Senhor Siemel, the tiger hunter!" she said, extending her hand. She had met Sasha ten years before when he had been in this same hospital with an alligator bite on his foot.

After introductions were over, the Sister Superior showed us around the hospital, which had about ten private rooms, each with a cot with a straw mattress and one straight chair. There were two wards of about thirty beds, and one really hospital-like room with the only hospital bed, which I was to have.

It was arranged that I would remain at the hotel until I began feeling labor pains, and that, since I wished it, a cot would be moved into my hospital room so Sasha could stay with me there. The Sister Superior also assured me that Dr. Luis Fragelli, whom she recommended highly, would attend me.

By the following week I had memorized every crack in the plaster walls of the hotel room. The downpour had continued without letup; Corumbá had little to offer in the way of entertainment, anyway, and consequently I had spent all of my time in our room except when I went downstairs with Sasha for meals.

As day after day passed with no new symptoms on my part, I could see Sasha was getting restless with so little to do. And, although he was very kind and considerate, I suspected he secretly felt that I was deliberately prolonging my pregnancy.

One morning, when I had been watching him for some time pacing around the room, exactly like a tiger cub in its cage—and pausing every now and then to cast anxious, weighing looks at me —I suddenly began laughing at him. He looked so discomfited that I chased him downstairs to the bar, where I hoped he would find some local boys who would prove more diverting than I was at the moment.

After he had gone I stretched myself lazily and reached for another wonderful, real chocolate from the large box beside me on the bed. Then, stretching and kicking the rumpled sheets down around my legs, I returned to the pages of *Oliver Wiswell,* balanced precariously on my chest. My bulging stomach propped it up at just the right angle.

I read for a while and continued munching chocolates.

I finished the book (although I had brought it along to read in the hospital) before Sasha returned. I got out of bed aimlessly and stood for a while at the window, looking down on the plaza, deserted and dreary in the rain. Then I wandered to the spotty wall mirror above the washstand. I looked rather dreary myself without lipstick. I remedied this and brushed my hair as well. I looked at my nails critically and decided I didn't need another manicure.

I sat down on the edge of the bed, yawned, and took another chocolate. . . . I dropped it back in the box, deciding that perhaps I had been eating too many, for I felt a slight uneasiness in the region of my stomach. The box was almost half empty, but it had been so long since I had had any candy.

I stretched out on the bed again. Then I grinned to myself, although the cramped, unpleasant feeling in my stomach persisted. *Was* it the chocolates—or was it the considerable weight of *Oliver Wiswell* and his 800-odd pages?

I decided that it was the chocolates after all, and I deplored my greediness. I lay quite motionless, staring at the ceiling, concentrating on two maplike water stains, and my back began a dull aching. Perhaps I was coming down with the flu. . . .

It must be nearly noon. Where in the dickens was Sasha? Had he abandoned me forever? This would be a fine time for the flu, a perfect time, I thought dejectedly. With little Sasha due any day . . .

I sat bolt upright in bed as another cramp—and a sudden thought —shot through me.

"Edith, you idiot! *This is it!*" I said aloud.

I sat for a minute hugging my knees, savouring the waning cramp with a detached, impersonal curiosity. It didn't feel in the least as I had expected it would; it was hardly a pain at all, although it did recur at regular intervals—at intervals of about five minutes, in fact.

Ye Gods! If it was coming that fast already . . .

I heaved myself out of bed and pulled my huge nightgown up over my head and began dressing hurriedly. I felt unusually clumsy and slow, but I managed all right despite two more cramps that left me cold and perspiring.

"Slow down, Sashinho," I said sternly, "you little demon! Don't you *dare*——"

Not in this hotel room, please God.

I pulled on my shoes—which was quite a feat by now—muttering crossly: "So help me, Sashinho, I'll paddle your little bottom!"

I was struggling in a rage of frustration, hopelessly engulfed in the heavy folds of my poncho, when Sasha, at long last, sauntered in, magnificently unprepared.

Despite Sasha's horrified protests I insisted I could walk to the hospital. After all, it was only a short distance away, and there was no time to get a taxi.

We started immediately.

I took the stairs slowly, leaning on Sasha's arm, and we crossed the small lobby. I felt like a fool at Sasha's hovering concern and was annoyed that he should make me so conspicuous. We passed the desk and moved on through the doorway.

I gasped as the cold rain slapped against my face, but it served as a bracer. We started across the plaza. . . .

The gray, sheeting rain was everywhere around us, sluicing into my eyes and blurring them, actually blinding me. Or was it only the pain coming again, and this time with a real insistence? I clenched my hands and tried to walk faster through the mud.

The pain receded, and I drew a deep, grateful breath of the heavy, damp air. Sasha patted my hand with wordless sympathy.

"Sasha, you didn't wear your poncho!" I said accusingly. "Oh, Sasha," I wailed, "you'll get pneumonia."

We went on silently. The rain drummed noisily, and the water made sloshing sounds beneath our feet. Then I stopped short, unable to move, grinding my fingers into Sasha's arm. I swayed a little, and the plaza reeled dizzily before me. I glimpsed a red-tiled roof scalloped against the leaden sky.

Sasha had me in his arms, holding me tightly and saying something that I couldn't understand and that was completely unimportant, anyway. I didn't care what Sasha said or felt.

"For God's sake, let me carry you!"

The pain must be leaving, if I could hear him. I gritted my teeth

172

and shook my head stubbornly. The plaza swung back into place, and I wrenched myself loose from Sasha and began walking again, a little doubled up. But from there on, despite my indignant protests, Sasha had his arm around me in such a way that he half carried me.

Up the steps of the hospital, with each step of his jolting through me . . . There were words between Sasha and the receptionist at the desk, and then to the delivery room.

A harsh light blazed down. A familiar face hung momentarily above me: the doctor. Voices jumbled around me. . . . Seven hours later my baby was born.

Sasha's face was still white and strained. He took my hands in his. "Thank God you came through all right!"

I tried to sit up and found that I couldn't. I saw there was someone else in the room, a woman. She bent over with her back toward me and then turned with a white bundle in her arms. Grinning broadly, she held it beside the bed for me to see.

I looked curiously at it, but still in a detached, impersonal way. And I saw a tiny face and one infinitely tiny curled-up hand in the nest of blankets cradled on her arm. A little pinched-looking face, with its eyes tightly shut, with a flat pug nose and a wide mouth, completely bald, with the reddish skin peeling away in patches all over it!

I gulped. So this was what we had to show for all our months of waiting. I looked up at Sasha reluctantly.

"Sort of ugly, isn't it?" I said dispiritedly.

"It is a beautiful *criança!*" The nurse spoke almost belligerently.

I looked back at our child, half hoping it would have changed. But it hadn't. Well, I supposed I would get used to it. . . .

It looked helpless and pathetic—and strangely appealing.

I smiled down at it. "Well—hello, little Sasha."

"Edith"—Sasha spoke slowly, with an odd gleam in his eyes— "that isn't little Sasha. It's a little girl!"

The tiny head twisted in its blankets, the face screwed up, the mouth opened enormously, and the baby began a lusty, indignant wail.

CHAPTER 5

WE HAD BEEN OUT AT OUR BASE HUNTING CAMP ABOUT ten days.

Our sportsman guest this time was another member of the European nobility—Prince Olgierd Czartoryski of Poland. But he wasn't at all like Sasha's last titled client, the disagreeable countess. The prince, in fact, was so amiable and unassuming, so completely the opposite of the countess in his consideration for others, that I rather fondly dubbed him, behind his back, "Prince Charming."

Prince Olgierd had had some harrowing experiences. A man in his fifties, he had been sent to a Nazi concentration camp at the beginning of the war but had escaped; his Polish estates had been ruined and confiscated, and he had given them up as permanently lost. Now he was trying to build a new life for his family and himself in Rio as a member of the growing colony of war refugees there. The prince had learned of Sasha through his old friend, Armin Baltzer, and had written to make arrangements to go on a month's hunt. However, he had come to the Mato Grosso jungles as much to relax as to kill tigers.

This was the first hunt I'd gone on in a year. I'd been champing at the bit for some time, and now that Sandra was five months old we saw no reason why she shouldn't be initiated into her tiger-hunting future—at least to the extent of coming with us to the base camp.

Altogether we made a rather large party. Besides the prince and Sasha and me, and the baby and Floridad, who was Cenaria's sister and Sandra's nursemaid, there were Lauro and his wife Cenaria, who did the cooking, and their two daughters—Florenzia, eight years old, and Denizia, seven. Their other four children had been left with Antonia and her brood; Rosando, too, had remained at home to care for our livestock and wild pets. But Sasha had taken along José, the cowboy from the Descalvados Estancia who had been with us on the countess's hunt, and Bernardo, another Descalvados vaqueiro.

The prince liked to shoot waterfowl and, though he was near-sighted and wore thick glasses, he was an expert shot on the wing. The first day in camp he'd gone out with Lauro on the nearby marsh and had returned in two hours with enough ducks to feed our entire party that night, and the eighteen dogs as well.

The prince also enjoyed fishing. So—since there was considerable work to be done in building a new grass hut, rethatching the old ones, repairing the stockade, and fixing up the site generally—Sasha had remained in camp the first few days supervising José and Bernardo, and the prince, with Lauro, had spent most of his time either fishing from a dugout in the nearby stream or duck hunting on the marsh. He proved to be equally skillful at both, and he and Lauro kept us supplied with game.

However, the prince apparently enjoyed most of all just leaning back in the dugout as Lauro paddled him downstream and watching the jungle unfold around him—or merely drifting among the luxuriant beds of water lilies while Lauro poled only enough to keep the dugout from running afoul of the tangled water vegetation or dozing alligators. While the prince had spent days with no more entertainment than this, he obviously was thoroughly enjoying himself.

"It's so peaceful here," he had sighed blissfully as he returned late one afternoon from a day spent loafing on the river. "It's so peaceful—just to be where nothing has changed in thousands of years!"

"Peaceful" was the last word most visitors would have applied to our teeming jungles, but it was obvious why the prince dwelt on this aspect.

He was reluctant to talk about his unhappy experiences in the war, so we naturally avoided the subject, though I, at least, had difficulty in repressing my desire to hear a firsthand account. He much preferred talking about the jungle and asked Sasha and me innumerable questions about the animals and birds he saw each day. (A practiced linguist, he spoke English when I was about, though he and Sasha used German when they were alone. In speaking to the natives, he of course used Portuguese, in which he was less fluent.)

The prince had immediately endeared himself to the feminine members of our party, including myself, by arriving with gifts of boxes of candy. And every day he would spend an hour or more holding and playing with little Sandra, who, despite her tender age, already was highly appreciative of male attention; or he would cut fishing poles for Lauro's two small daughters and bait their hooks while they fished from the riverbank.

I was watching him from a distance one day as he brought peals of excited laughter from the little girls with his boyish actions and jovial comments on a very small fish one of them had caught with his assistance. And I reflected that, although he wasn't really handsome—he was tall, but gray and stooped—he was truly a prince, in nearly all the meanings I'd put into that word in the days when I was an avid reader of Sir Walter Scott. He had salvaged most of my girlish, romantic ideas of the European aristocracy, which had taken an awful beating during the countess's visit. As I mused over this, standing in the shade of a quebracho tree, the prince turned and saw me.

"Ah, Senhora Siemel." He smiled, then looked fondly down at the heads of the children and sighed. "It is good to be with the very youthful! One remembers how much one enjoyed life at that age."

Before I could reply little Denizia spoke up.

"Senhor Prince," she complained, drawing a doleful face, "that fish took all my bait! Will you fix me another bait, please?"

"Your pardon, senhora." The prince bowed and smiled at me as he took the child's pole. "I have my duties to attend!"

The prince had occupied himself like this for nearly a week, while Sasha and his two helpers had finished reconditioning the camp. Sasha had assigned the new grass hut to the prince; we three Siemels had one of the old ones, Lauro's family and Floridad had another, and the two extra men had the third. With four huts in all, our camp had taken on the aspects of a small village.

Then finally we had been ready to begin hunting.

The prince had shot his tiger the first day we had ridden out! It had been a good-sized male, an old-timer.

We had practically stumbled over him early in the morning. The dogs had picked up a trail, but we hadn't suspected we were within miles of our quarry yet. Then Lauro had pointed to a wave rippling through the thick marsh grass a half mile ahead.

"There he goes, patrão!" he shouted excitedly. "He must have been dozing under those piuvas!"

The animal was heading away from a clump of trees beside the creek, no doubt trying to sneak unseen to the big open marsh on our right before the dogs overtook him. If he once reached it he could quickly lose his pursuers among its vast reed beds and thickly forested islands.

Lauro rode out to cut him off. And when the big cat heard the pounding of the horse's hoofs in front of him he turned and loped back to the little grove he had just left.

We found him crouched defiantly on the limb of a tree. He snarled as we approached and swung his head from side to side, angrily eying each of us. I thought he looked ready to spring into our midst.

Prince Olgierd had Sasha's Mannlicher. He and Sasha dismounted and moved in closer. And Sasha said hurriedly that, as the tiger's moving head was a poor target, he would suggest the prince shoot for the shoulder.

The prince coolly took aim and fired. The tiger tumbled heavily from the tree and lay still—shot through the heart.

The prince let out a whoop.

"Sasha, I did it! I've killed a tiger!" he shouted with wild enthusiasm.

I smiled a little, for I wondered why, with his invariably excellent marksmanship, he should be so amazed at this.

178

Then with a beatific smile he rushed at Sasha, flung his arms about him violently, and planted an exuberant kiss on his be-whiskered cheek!

That had been four days ago. . . .

The prince had been satisfied with getting one tiger, to prove that he could. But he had arranged to be with us for a full month, of which there were then still more than three weeks left, and Sasha had urged him to try for another.

"Sasha, my good friend," the prince had replied with an amused smile, "you love to hunt. Why do you need me as an excuse?"

Sasha had grinned at the good-natured gibe.

"As for me"—the prince had shrugged tolerantly—"I am perfectly happy—just loafing and admiring your beautiful scenery."

So while Sasha and I rode out each day behind the pack, only once did the prince leave his "communing with nature"—with Lauro and the dugout—to come with us. And he came that time, I suspected, only to alleviate Sasha's feelings of guilt at enjoying himself on a hunt while his guest remained in camp.

Today Sasha and I and José had returned with the weary hounds late in the afternoon, still without having sighted another tiger. We found Prince Olgierd stretched lazily on the grass under a paratudo tree, telling the story of Rumpelstilzchen, in his rather halting Portuguese, to little Florenzia and Denizia, who squatted nearby, listening wide-eyed. Lauro was sleeping under the same tree with his sombrero over his face. And close by, sitting cross-legged on the grass and apparently as entranced at the tale as the children, was Floridad with Sandra on her lap. Sandra, to my surprise, was wearing a bright red woolen cap that looked as though it had been cut from the heavy wool of a poncho.

Sasha and I halted silently a short distance to one side, not wishing to interrupt the prince's storytelling.

". . . And when the queen, on the third guess, correctly gave the name of the little dwarf," Prince Olgierd said impressively, "he screamed with rage and stamped so hard his foot sank into the ground. Then he pulled so hard on his leg with both hands that he tore himself in two!"

The two small girls caught their breaths; even from where we stood I could see their eyes shine.

"What happened to the little baby?" Florenzia demanded eagerly.

"Why—he grew up into a handsome prince, married a beautiful princess, and in time they had a baby of their own. And they all lived happily ever after!" Prince Olgierd dramatically concluded, sitting up to beam on his popeyed young audience. He reached over to chuck sober little Sandra under her fat double chin. "And their baby was just as cute as this infant is here and now!"

The children sighed rapturously.

At the prince's abrupt action Sandra had comically drawn down the corners of her mouth, as if about to cry, but she settled for a scowl when Floridad quickly bent over her, crooning fondly, to forestall the threatening tears.

The prince turned and saw Sasha and me.

"Ho! The hunters return," he exclaimed heartily; he scrutinized our faces with pretended concern, then concluded gravely, "And I can see by your expressions that your luck has continued—bad!"

Sasha nodded, grinning. "All we got today was exercise."

The prince smiled. "Perhaps my plan is best—no?"

I could no longer contain my curiosity about Sandra's new adornment. After all, a heavy woolen cap is a little inappropriate for a sunny August day in the Mato Grosso jungle, where the temperature hangs steadily around one hundred degrees. Sandra looked hot and uncomfortable, even though she had no hair as yet to keep her head warm. The poor child had been born bald and, to my considerable chagrin, still was as hairless as the proverbial billiard ball. Was that it? I wondered. Was Floridad embarrassed by her little charge's lack of hair, and had she made the cap to cover the defect in the presence of Prince Olgierd? Then I abruptly had another thought, but I discarded it as absurd.

"Sandra"—I stooped to address my frozen-faced baby, who now sat scowling like an unhappy fat little cherub, with the woolen cap reaching down to her eyebrows and resting ludicrously on her ears—"Sandra darling, where did you get that pretty red cap? Did Floridad make it for you?"

Sandra, of course, made no reply. But Floridad smiled, as if expecting praise.

"Sim, senhora," she beamed, tightening her arms fondly about my child and rocking gently back and forth on her heels, like a human cradle. "Sim, senhora. Floridad made it to ward off the evil eye!"

"The 'evil eye'!" I echoed, aghast.

No one else said a word.

"Sim, senhora." Floridad's big black eyes shone brightly as she looked up at me with a half-fearful, half-challenging expression. "It is needed for the small baby, senhora! All my sisters and brothers wore the red cap until they were more than a year old. My nieces, here, too! If the little one continues going without it, the evil eye will not wait much longer! And the evil eye"—an expression of horror crossed her pretty bronze face—"the evil eye is very, very bad, senhora!"

I gulped and glanced at Sasha. He had a dead-pan look; only his eyes betrayed his cynical amusement—apparently he had no intention of helping me out. I turned to Prince Olgierd. He seemed elaborately interested in a pair of parakeets quarreling in a nearby tree. I turned back to Floridad, who looked on the verge of tears.

I didn't have the heart to scold her, but still I wanted to retain supervision over my own child. I knew that not only Floridad, but Antonia and Cenaria as well, thought it scandalous that I allowed Sandra to risk the dangers of growing up without the customary jungle safeguards of charms, amulets, and other mumbo-jumbo devices—derived, undoubtedly, from their savage African and Indian ancestors. But I objected to having Sandra brought up under a lot of native superstitions and taboos. I objected not only on general principles but because I'd seen the effect these things had on native children: most were timid and nervous, and all were deathly afraid of the dark. A short time after Sandra was born I had interfered when Floridad wanted to tie a "magic dust" charm around her neck to ward off jungle fever, a type of dysentery. I had ridiculed the idea and delivered a long lecture to Floridad on superstitions, which at the time I had thought had been effective. But now this "evil eye" thing. I had a suspicion who was responsible.

"Floridad," I said evenly, "who really made that cap? You or Cenaria?"

Floridad swallowed. "Cenaria—Cenaria made it, senhora," she said earnestly. "She said that—that the poor little one——"

"I thought so!" I retorted curtly; I was annoyed.

"But Cenaria said the evil eye is much more powerful here in the jungle!" Floridad protested loyally.

"Floridad," I reported, exasperated, "that's silly talk, and you know it! Take that hot cap off the poor child immediately!"

"Sim, senhora." Floridad sounded almost brokenhearted, though she meekly bowed her dark head over Sandra's scowling little visage and reluctantly began removing the heavy woolen cap.

But at that Sandra let out a wail and grabbed with both chubby little fists at it; she didn't want to part with it.

Sasha laughed, and Floridad looked up at me with a pathetic half-smile.

"Senhora," she said gently, "the little one herself realizes——"

Sasha guffawed again. "I'm afraid Sandra has gone native, Edith," he chuckled.

Prince Olgierd turned to me with an amused smile. "She is a true diplomat. When in Rome, she does as the Romans."

Sandra was still clutching her red cap.

"What should I do, senhora?" Floridad asked hopefully.

"Maybe," Sasha interjected, "Sandra would settle for a toupee!"

I decided to accept defeat. Temporarily.

"Oh, let her keep it on then," I retorted ill-humoredly; I turned to Sasha and added, "I should have expected my children would go native, I suppose, when I came down to this jungle!"

Sasha merely continued chuckling.

And Floridad, eager for an excuse to leave now that she had won, spoke up brightly:

"Senhora"—she leaned toward me and lowered her voice, in deference, I supposed, to the presence of the prince—"the little one, I think, requires a——"

"All right, Floridad," I interrupted brusquely, "go change the little dope's diapers!"

Floridad looked at me in a shocked manner for a moment.

"Sim, senhora."

She rose and, cuddling Sandra fondly in her arms, moved quickly away toward our hut. Sandra was still holding tightly to her precious red cap, and she looked at me indignantly over her nursemaid's shoulder.

Sasha was still chuckling maddeningly.

Lauro, who hadn't stirred when we returned, now awoke with a start and climbed to his feet, looking as though he suspected he had just been the butt of a joke.

"Patrão," he said unhappily, "you are laughing. Does that mean you met up with a fine tiger while I fell asleep listening to tales for children?"

Sasha shook his head, laughing harder, and Lauro looked even more chagrined.

"Never mind, Lauro," I said shortly. "The patrão has a warped sense of humor. And he's laughing at me, not you."

Dinner was late that night. We were out of fresh meat and so Sasha sent Lauro off to shoot a marsh deer, whose tracks we had run across a couple of miles from camp on our way back from the fruitless tiger hunt. Lauro didn't return until after nightfall. He had tracked down and shot the deer, but he came back with only a small chunk of meat and the odd excuse that it was too dark to skin the deer; he would finish in the morning. Sasha, I could tell, was somewhat surprised at this, but he said nothing. And when I remarked that Lauro had acted as if something were wrong, Sasha merely shrugged.

"Possibly," he returned enigmatically. "We shall see."

The next morning, a short time after sunrise, Lauro cantered excitedly into camp, driving our horses before him. He had gotten up before anyone else to return for the deer carcass. Nevertheless, he was now empty-handed.

"I was right, patrão!" he shouted as soon as he came within hailing distance. "I knew it was him!"

He was eager to explain. Immediately after shooting the deer the night before, he had discovered fresh tracks of a tiger that apparently had been stalking the same quarry. And when he had started skinning the deer in the fast-gathering darkness he heard the sound of some big animal stalking him in the high marsh grass.

Afraid the tiger would pounce on his back while he was bent over the deer, he had hastily hacked off a small piece of meat and jumped on his horse and fled. Then he had been ashamed to admit his timidity, not being certain his fears were well grounded. But his investigation this morning had revealed the tiger had been there, eaten most of the deer, and dragged the remainder into deep cover two hundred yards away. Knowing Sasha would be eager to start the dogs on the trail, Lauro had rounded up our horses as he neared camp.

We gulped breakfast—Sasha and Lauro and I, that is, for Prince Olgierd refused to be roused from his hammock.

"You don't need me to get that tiger, Sasha," he drawled. "Besides, it's so damned early. I think I'd enjoy a little more sleep. And I have a date with some fish this afternoon."

"We'll be back long before that!" Sasha predicted rashly with a grin.

The truth was, I think, that the prince saw how eager Sasha was to go and, in his usual considerate fashion, begged off merely so Sasha could hunt down the tiger in his own way, unencumbered by his sportsman guest.

Sasha and Lauro were ready and impatiently waiting, and the dogs were straining at their leashes, when I finally cut short Sandra's breakfast—not without an indignant protest from that surprised young lady—and turned her over to Floridad. I buttoned up my shirt, gave Sandra an apologetic, hasty kiss, and rushed out of the hut. Lauro handed me my gun as I mounted, and we were off.

(On the days when I was out hunting, Sandra's morning and evening breast feedings were supplemented by milk from the longhorn cows we had brought along. Since we had no baby bottles, it was fortunate that at only five months she could drink from a glass. Floridad held it, of course, but being an independent little tyke, Sandra insisted on helping with both chubby fists, sometimes spilling the precious milk all over.)

The sun was a glowing ball of molten orange just clear of the horizon, and the eastern sky was afire with brilliant pinks and reds and lavenders.

It was only a short ride to the remains of the deer.

Lauro unleashed the dogs. They took one whiff of the carcass, which had been dragged about ten feet inside a caraguata thorn thicket, and immediately they gave the quick, excited double barks followed by half-angry, half-fearful growls that meant it was a tiger and the trail was fresh. The hair on the back of the older dogs' necks stood up. In an instant they were all off, wildly barking, with the three of us following closely, our horses straining at their bits.

Sasha leaned forward over his mount's withers and shouted an encouraging, resounding "Ai-iiii-eeee!"

Lauro, grinning widely, stood up in his stirrups and loosed a bloodcurdling Indian yell.

As always, I felt my spine prickling with the thrill of the chase. Smiling, I dug my spurs into my horse's flanks.

Cantering after the pack through the high brown marsh grass, we trailed the tiger in the coolness of the dawn for about a mile. When the dogs found the trampled grass where it had bedded for the night, sleeping with its belly full of deer, they almost went insane with excitement, barking, yipping, and yelping wildly.

The eager, noisy pack trailed the tiger for another half mile. Then, in a large patch of unusually thick and high grass, in which there were a couple of trees, they lost the scent. The tiger obviously had doubled back, crossing and recrossing its trail to confuse any possible pursuers. The dogs were baffled. With noses to the ground, completely invisible in the high grass which reached to the horses' backs, they ran this way and that, trying frantically to work out the maze.

For a half-hour, while the blazing sun climbed and kept getting hotter, we impatiently sat our horses, waiting for the pack to solve the puzzle.

Finally Sasha motioned to Lauro and me to follow and called the dogs. With as many as would come (there are always a few loath to leave a trail; you have to use force to get them to quit it), we rode about three hundred yards from the center of the maze and then began riding around it. For if, after describing a complete circle, we hadn't cut across a fresh tiger trail, we would know the big cat was still there.

Before we had completed the maneuver Sasha chanced to glance at the two isolated trees in that sea of tall marsh grass. He reined up his horse sharply.

"Look—that tree!" he exclaimed. "There he is!"

I drew up my own mount and turned. As both trees were heavily foliaged paratudos and Sasha hadn't indicated which he meant, I did not at once distinguish the tawny, dappled coat of our quarry among the thick leaf shadows. Then . . .

"Oh, oh," I said. "How right you are!"

For at that moment the tiger started down the tree—backing carefully, just as a house cat does. About fifteen feet from the ground it jumped down and disappeared in the high grass.

Sasha shouted to the dogs: *"Busca! Busca!* Get him! Get him!"

Then, waving to Lauro and me to follow, he spurred his horse forward.

However, the dogs didn't obey immediately. They hadn't seen the tiger (a good hound relies almost entirely on scent; his eyesight is none too good), and after a half-hour of trying to puzzle out the trail they had lost much of their enthusiasm and were discouraged. They finally came, but disinterestedly.

In the meantime we saw the tiger twice more as it leaped through the high brown grass and disappeared into a big thorn thicket. Sasha and Lauro, a couple of lengths ahead of me and about thirty feet apart, rode directly up to the thicket and got to within ten feet of it.

What happened next, I saw with all the startling clarity a tensely exciting moment imparts.

Suddenly there was an angry roar from the depths of the bushes, and the big cat came sailing out and onto Lauro's horse, landing with his right paw on the animal's neck, his left paw on its face. But his weight ripped the bridle from the horse's head, and the tiger fell to the ground—his claws raking deep grooves in the horse's face and neck. Panic-stricken, the horse screamed with pain, reared, and wheeled about, with Lauro hanging on desperately.

My own horse reared, catching me off guard, and I hung onto the reins with all my strength.

Again the tiger leaped—landing this time on the haunches of Lauro's horse, missing Lauro's back by an inch or two—and again he slid off the bucking, rearing, screaming horse because his claws ripped through, rather than held, in the soft hide. Lauro was helpless; he was too busy trying to keep his seat to reach the gun in his saddle boot.

By this time both my horse and Sasha's had whirled and fled. I finally got my trembling mount stopped and turned a couple of hundred yards away. I saw that Sasha, to my right and closer to Lauro, was spurring his horse frantically in an attempt to go to Lauro's rescue. His horse made two panicky jumps in the tiger's direction, just as the big cat was recovering from its second leap at Lauro. Then the tiger came toward Sasha.

Sasha's terrorized horse wheeled and, out of control, started off with the tiger after it in great, galloping bounds—each leap, a jump of from twelve to fifteen feet—missing it by inches.

My own horse began plunging again and started to run in a frenzy of panic, even though we were a considerable distance away; and I was so busy trying to keep my seat and regain control of my mount that I didn't have time to be frightened for Sasha.

But, as Sasha afterward frankly admitted, while the tiger was chasing him he felt as though his horse was standing still, and he was deeply alarmed because he had only his spear with him and it was still sheathed. A sheathed spear, of course, is of less use than a club.

Luckily, after chasing Sasha for about two hundred yards, the tiger fell behind. Realizing it couldn't catch Sasha's horse, it slowed down, then turned aside and disappeared into another thorn thicket.

By this time the dogs had come up. They surrounded the thicket, racing around it with a bedlam of excited barking and baying. Sasha, with some difficulty, finally turned his trembling, lathered horse and rode to where they were holding the tiger at bay.

Lauro was still some distance away, trying to quiet his badly wounded horse. And as I was having trouble getting mine back under control, I, too, was almost as far away from the thicket.

I saw Sasha dismount and move through the dogs, who were making an earsplitting hullabaloo, jumping excitedly about—though at a respectful distance. I got my reluctant horse to move forward a few yards. I saw Sasha, keeping his eyes intently on the thicket, unsheathing his spear and advancing warily.

He was within eight feet of its edge, when suddenly there was a loud, coughing roar and a tawny, black-spotted streak charged out and made a running leap at him.

I watched, petrified.

As Sasha afterward described it, he had but a thin fraction of a second to judge whether the tiger was leaping for his head or his legs. The tiger leaped high. Sasha raised his spear, aiming at the throat, but not quickly enough. It impaled the tiger in the chest, right up to the crossbar at the end of the blade. At the same time Sasha lunged forward, hoping that with the momentum of the animal's leap and his own thrust he could heave the big cat backward and over onto its back. But Sasha's foot slipped, his spear wavered; and the tiger slipped off the blade, scrambled to its feet snarling, and withdrew with a rush to get behind Sasha.

At this my own horse reared again and ran for a hundred yards before I could regain control.

Sasha barely was able to recover his balance and spin around when the tiger leaped again. In turning, Sasha didn't have time to aim his spear, and it caught the animal only a glancing blow on the jaw. The tiger whirled about before Sasha could get set again, and with a roar made another leap at his throat. Sasha quickly jabbed upward, and the spear again struck in the tiger's chest. With a great heave Sasha threw the tiger onto its back and, pinning it firmly to the ground with the spear, quickly side-stepped to get back of the tiger's head, where he would be out of reach of its knifelike claws. The tiger lunged violently about, raking at Sasha and frantically trying to wrench loose from the impaling blade; but Sasha, keeping just beyond its flashing claws, see-sawed the blade in its chest, working toward the heart.

There was a frantic struggle lasting nearly a minute—a climax of flailing claws and snarls and desperate attempts to throw Sasha off; then the tiger collapsed in a sudden gush of blood from the heart. . . .

By the time I finally managed to get my shivering horse turned and cantered up to rejoin Sasha, he already had withdrawn his spear, and the frenziedly barking dogs had rushed in to bite and slash ferociously at the hide of the dead animal. I dismounted and walked up to Sasha, who was sweating profusely but grinning.

"Well"—I smiled a bit unsteadily as I thrust out my hand—"for a while I wasn't certain who was going to win this bout! Congratulations, dear—and thank God."

Sasha ran the back of his hand across his forehead and smiled. "Thank you, Edith."

He looked down at the limp carcass, which the dogs were still worrying, and with a shout swung his spear to chase them away. They retreated reluctantly. I stepped up closer to look at the dead tiger with him. It was a huge animal—ten feet from nose to tip of tail. Sasha said it must have weighed easily 350 pounds and was one of the largest he had seen in all his years as a professional tiger hunter.

"This was one of the finest fights I've ever had!" Sasha said enthusiastically after a minute of silent contemplation. He gave a deep sigh of contentment, then turned to me, once more mopping his brow. "In fact"—he grinned—"if it had been any finer, I don't think I could have stood it!"

Lauro came up then, leading his bleeding and still frightened horse. He smiled rather sheepishly at Sasha, then held out his hand.

"You are a brave man, patrão," he said admiringly. "I have never seen such a tiger!"

He turned to look down at the carcass on the bloodied grass; he stared at it respectfully, then turned back to us and shook his head with a slow grin.

"For a few minutes, patrão," he said earnestly, "I could *feel* that devil's wicked claws tearing through my back!"

Sasha and I laughed. Then we both shook Lauro's hand, for he certainly had had a narrow escape. . . .

We celebrated the successful hunt with a big dinner at camp that night. We started with fish and roast duck, which the prince and Bernardo had bagged, and then we dined heartily on barbecued tiger ribs and steaks. Sasha dug out a bottle of scotch from the oxcart and supplemented that by tapping the barrel of cachaça we had brought along for the natives.

After dinner, while we lounged around the campfire feeling too full to move, Sasha, at Prince Olgierd's urging, went into the details of the hunt.

The prince, I suspected, was a little bit sorry he hadn't gone along, since it had proved so exciting. He listened, fascinated, while Sasha described the tiger's attacks, and his eyes gleamed appreciatively whenever Lauro impulsively interjected more vivid adjectives for parts of the narrative which he thought Sasha, in his calm, modest recital, was understating.

Then Lauro brought a tray of fresh drinks, which he served to the three of us. The scotch was mixed with plain river water, of course, and none too cold; but after more than two years in the jungle I had virtually forgotten the sound of tinkling ice cubes in a tall glass.

Lauro tossed his tray to the ground—it was really no-more than the end of a hardwood barrel which I had once flippantly suggested be used for this elegant purpose—and again seated himself on the far side of the fire, beside José and Bernardo. He picked up the gallon jug which he had foresightedly refilled with cachaça and, drawing the wooden plug, raised it for a long minute to his lips. Then he passed it to Bernardo.

The women had retired to their hut immediately after the meal: Cenaria presumably because she was tired from her day's work and, besides, had to put her two small daughters to bed—though actually because among the natives it is only the men who mix socially with the patrão and his family. Floridad had long ago put Sandra into her ridiculously small hammock, under her own little mosquito netting, and had herself retired.

Sasha put down his drink and leaned forward to toss another stick of wood on the fire. The flames crackled upward, and for a few minutes the tall, crowding trees surrounding our little clearing were weirdly outlined by the heightened ruddy light. A shower of sparks shot upward like a miniature fireworks display and then vanished into the blackness.

"Sasha"—Prince Olgierd abruptly broke off his steady contemplation of the fire and turned to my spouse—"when you go on a tiger hunt alone—I mean, without having a sportsman like me along—you prefer using a spear or bow and arrows to a gun, don't you? Because it's more sporting, of course?"

Sasha smiled. "Yes. It gives the tiger a more equal chance." He added quickly, as if afraid that what he had said cast an unfavorable reflection on sportsmen who used guns, "You must remember that I've made my living as a professional tiger hunter for over twenty years!"

190

Prince Olgierd smiled. "And just *shooting* tigers has become too easy?"

Sasha merely grinned.

The prince gazed at him with admiration and sipped his drink. Then he asked thoughtfully: "How did you learn to use the spear, Sasha?"

Sasha stood up to throw another chunk of wood on the fire before replying. As the flames shot up again into the dark night sky he dropped back full length on the grass, leaning on his elbow.

Momentarily meeting the prince's glance, I jerked my head toward Sasha and smiled. "The raconteur's pose!"

Prince Olgierd smiled.

"I learned the technique many years ago," Sasha said with a nostalgic sigh. "What inspired me was a youthful desire to prove to myself I could do anything anyone else could. You see, I ran across an Indian hunter who'd killed tigers for years with nothing more than a spear. I'd hunted tigers for some time myself, but of course only with a rifle."

"Ah-h-h-h—reckless youth!" the prince mused whimsically.

I had heard the story before, of course, so I sipped my drink and stared idly across the fire at Lauro and his two comrades. José was lying flat on his back, apparently asleep. Lauro had just wrenched the cachaça jug from Bernardo's hands and was raising it to his lips a bit unsteadily.

"His name was Joaquim Guato," Sasha was saying, "and he was legendary for his skill with the spear. I found the old hunter deep in the jungle, and he willingly agreed to teach me. However"—Sasha chuckled—"my first lesson nearly was my last!"

"In that case, I'm afraid it *would* have been my last," the prince exclaimed. "I think I'd have abandoned the study at once."

"I doubt it." Sasha smiled. "You'd have found it just as fascinating as I did."

He went on: "Joaquim explained the principles of spear fighting and then lent me an extra spear and took me out on a hunt with his dogs. The dogs, racing ahead, soon brought a tiger to bay for us."

When Joaquim and he came up, Sasha said, the tiger was chasing the dogs all over the place. And as soon as it saw the two

men it had turned on them and charged. Sasha had held his spear
poised, waiting until from a distance of a few feet the tiger would
leap for his head—planning at that instant to jerk up the spear
and let the animal impale itself in mid-air, as Joaquim had instructed. But the tiger had not leaped. Instead, as the big cats
infrequently do, it had gone straight for his legs. Almost too late,
Sasha had jerked his spear down; in his haste he had dropped it
too low, missed the tiger altogether, and with the force of his lunge
lost his balance.

"For a moment I was paralyzed!" There was an excited gleam
in Sasha's eyes as he relived that moment of many years ago. "I'd
never been so close to a charging tiger. I could see nothing but that
huge mouth. But before those fangs could touch me, Joaquim's
spear plunged into the tiger's mouth! Joaquim was really mar-
velous."

Sasha described how he had raised himself up and stabbed his
own spear into the tiger's chest, and in a minute the tiger was dead.

Prince Olgierd shook his head slowly. "Sasha, it's a wonder your
hair isn't white!" he said after a moment.

"That's my husband!" I said proudly, with a teasing smile.

Sasha grinned, a little embarrassed.

"But Joaquim eventually met his match," he added with a sigh.

The veteran Indian hunter had been stalking "Old Three Toes,"
a notorious big cat lacking a toe on one front paw. The tiger's
forays on cattle herds long had been the despair of ranchers, and
Joaquim had stalked him for weeks. But he never found the tiger;
the tiger got to him first while he was dragging his dugout ashore
on the thickly wooded bank of a jungle river. Sasha described how
he had pieced the story together much later when he had found
Joaquim's bones and spear beside his half-rotted dugout.

Sasha cleared his throat.

"However," he concluded, "when, still later, I killed an old
male tiger in the region and discovered he was short a toe, I knew
that I had unwittingly avenged my old teacher."

"That is good!" Prince Olgierd asserted emphatically. He lit a
cigarette, then added with a philosophic smile, "At least in the
jungle there is justice!"

"Sometimes," Sasha interjected wryly.

There was a long silence during which we all gazed into the flickering flames, now almost died down to a bed of ruddy coals, graying around the edge. Lauro, José, and Bernardo were already asleep. Lauro was half sitting, half lying, with his head propped against Bernardo. José was stretched out behind the other two. I turned toward Prince Olgierd and Sasha. Sasha looked sleepy. The prince wore a deeply brooding expression as he stared into the embers, as if he were thinking of his friends and relatives who had been killed, his own close brush with death in the war, and his lost estates in Poland—perhaps, also, of his present exile in a foreign land.

"Well, gentlemen," I said lightly, "don't you think it's time we retire to our hammocks? Remember, there may be another tiger waiting for us tomorrow!"

However, there was no tiger waiting for us the next day, nor the next; and during the remainder of our stay at the camp we saw no trace of one—though Sasha and I rode out with the dogs religiously, even persuading Prince Olgierd to accompany us a few times.

But we had other excitement during those last two weeks the prince was with us.

Sasha and I had retired early, shortly after nightfall, as we had been more than ordinarily weary from a long and unusually hot day spent in the saddle following the dogs out on the largos in a fruitless cruising about for fresh tiger signs. Sandra, of course, was already asleep in her miniature hammock between our two when we joined her.

Some time after midnight, when we had been sleeping for hours, I suddenly awoke, soaked with cold perspiration and taut with apprehension. I felt that there was something wrong, a threatening, imminent danger near at hand, something invisible and repulsive. And then I realized that my mosquito netting, which should have hung lightly and weightlessly above me, was sagging and drooping close to my face and bare arms; and, although in the heavy darkness I could see nothing, I sensed, more than heard, a faint, close rustling, as from some crawling thing.

At that moment the moon broke out from behind the thick cloud bank which had hidden it and shone brightly into the hut, over the grass-thatched wall which rose only a sketchy two thirds of the distance to the palm-frond roof. And in that sudden broad stream of moonlight I saw that my mosquito netting had moving across it a long black thing as thick as my arm—something I would have thought was a snake except that it advanced without bending or coiling, in a perfectly stiff, rigid fashion. And then the moon was blotted out by clouds again.

I lay completely motionless a moment, gathering my resources, and then I realized that what I had seen wasn't one thing but thousands—a column of crawling insects!

"Sasha!" I shouted into the blackness—with a sudden numbing terror of what those myriads of insects, whatever they were, might do to our baby sleeping in her own little hammock between us. "Sasha! Wake up!"

"What—— *Yes,* Edith?" Sasha, who slept as lightly as a cat, was quickly aroused; I could hear his hammock creaking as he sat up.

And then Sandra let out a wail. . . .

"Ooohh! They must be on her already!" I moaned. Blindly I tore the insect-laden mosquito netting from about me and swung my legs out of my hammock, wanting only to rescue my baby. Some of the insects must have spilled onto me, for immediately I felt a sharp, smarting pain, like the sting of a hornet, between my shoulder blades; then another on my derrière. I stood up, groped my way in the dark to the side of Sandra's small hammock, and scooped her up—while she continued to cry with great choking, gasping sobs, as if she were terrorized or suffering dreadfully.

"Sasha!" I repeated frantically as, with Sandra in my arms, I hastily ducked under her hammock and stumbled in the darkness to the side of Sasha's. "Sasha! There are millions of little bugs crawling over my hammock! One of them bit me! They must have bitten Sandra frightfully, the way she's crying!"

I was acutely conscious that the two bites I had received burned as if I'd been seared with a hot iron.

"Yes, yes, Edith," Sasha replied in a tense, though unhurried, voice. He added placatingly, "Just a minute! Don't get excited." I felt his reassuring hand on my arm.

Then there was a sudden burst of light and I was momentarily blinded as he held the bright flare of a match between us. It required only a moment for our eyes to become accustomed to the glare, and then we both anxiously searched our wailing, frightened child. Sure enough, there was a large red swelling spot on the back of her fat little right hand. No wonder the poor baby was crying so! We quickly brushed her pajamas and our own sleeping clothes but failed to dislodge any crawling thing. As the match died out Sasha struck another and stepped forward to hold it first over my hammock and then above the hard-packed earth beneath. He muttered an exclamation, as if his unspoken guess had been correct. I edged hesitantly behind him, with Sandra still crying unabatedly, and peered down at the bare ground.

Racing along beneath my hammock and Sandra's, all going undeviatingly in the same direction and at the same hurrying speed, was a stream—a wide column—of large wingless insects—ants!

"Army ants?" I asked in a faint, shaken voice; impulsively I hugged Sandra closer as I visualized with a feeling of horror what could have happened to her.

Sasha nodded. "Yes—and coyapos at that!" He continued to stare at them, almost admiringly; and the large ants continued to race past in regular armylike formation, about twenty abreast—swerving not a fraction of an inch from the line of march laid out by those in the vanguard of the column, completely ignoring the flaring match in Sasha's hand.

"Coyapos!" I echoed with alarm. "Heavens!"

Sasha had told me much about army ants, and I had witnessed the smaller and less vicious species of them, the *correçãos*, on the march; but I had never seen the feared coyapos before, even though they are not uncommon. One reason probably was that, unlike the species of jungle ants which build the obelisk-like ant-hills, some of them twenty feet high, the army ants live more secretly; their dwellings are a complicated series of tunnels and subterranean chambers dug out beneath the roots of a large tree. Another reason was that while the correçãos frequently march by day, the larger coyapos almost always do their dreaded marching exclusively in the night.

I knew the coyapos' reputation for savageness. The smaller correçãos can inflict a painful bite with their pincers. But the larger coyapos (over three quarters of an inch long and over twice as large) not only have more powerful pincers; in addition, they can sting as savagely as a hornet. In fact, they are so vicious when aroused that even the anteaters avoid them. Sasha had told me that, if forced by hunger, an anteater will make a meal from the correçãos, but it avoids the coyapos as it would a full-grown tiger.

I had learned that the smaller army ants can be welcome visitors at times in the jungle, especially after you have been living in a camp long enough to have attracted a considerable number of annoying beetles and cockroaches. A visit from the correçãos will, in a surprisingly short while, rid your camp completely of all such pests. Of course, while they are cleaning up, you are well advised to leave camp, for the little ants aren't too discriminating in their choice of victims.

However, when the coyapos and even the smaller correçãos are on the march, they are really awe-inspiring. They hurry along, from ten to twenty abreast, in a column which lays a more or less straight course to whatever distant objective their leaders are aiming for. And they maintain this straight course no matter what effort it costs them, turning aside only for a body of water. They not only attack every insect or small animal in their path; they even climb fifteen feet up into a tree to raid a hornets' nest or birds' nest and eat the young hornets or birds. If their small prey attempts to escape, they will use military strategy, split their column, and quickly outflank their victim.

When on the march, Sasha had said, army ants would climb right over a horse or a human being who happened to be in the way; if he lay perfectly still he might escape hurt. However, this would be somewhat difficult, as a single army of either species frequently takes two or three hours to pass a given point, even at its rapid pace. But if the horse or person nervously moved while they were using him for a highway, he immediately would be attacked viciously. And if for some reason he were unable to flee quickly enough, the thousands of ferocious little insects would swarm over him and speedily bite and sting him to death.

And this was why—remembering everything Sasha had told me about army ants and what I myself had observed—I was momentarily horrified when he said our midnight invaders were the vicious coyapos. For I knew what might have happened if those hurrying, hair-trigger-tempered coyapos had gotten inside our baby's mosquito netting in large numbers before we had awakened. If—and I shuddered as I thought of this—they had attacked Sandra's face, or eyes, while Sasha and I slept!

The match died, and Sasha lit another and held it high over my hammock again. With my free hand I rubbed gingerly at the more available of my two smarting bites. Then Sasha turned and announced with a wry grin that my bed apparently was still on the line of march, for a steady, though considerably narrower, column of ants was moving determinedly along its length—doubtless ascending from the ground outside the hut, up the palm trunk to which my hammock rope was tied, thence along the rope to the hammock, and back to the ground similarly on the other side.

"Well," Sasha said dryly as he tossed his dying third match to the ground and helpfully took Sandra, whose crying had now subsided to a softer, complaining fretfulness, "we obviously can't sleep here."

"Darn!" I muttered.

He was silent for a minute; then he must have sensed, despite the darkness, that I was trying to reach the other stinging bite between my shoulder blades, for he chuckled. "Are you in need of first aid, my dear?"

I was about to make a scathing retort, when abruptly there was a shout from outside. It was Lauro.

"Patrão!" he called anxiously. "Is something wrong?"

He had been awakened by our voices, of course, and perhaps even had seen the flare of Sasha's matches through the thin straw wall of the hut nearby in which his family and Floridad slept. Sasha bade him come on but to watch where he stepped.

"The coyapos are marching, Lauro!" he warned.

Lauro halted with a colorful curse, then shouted that he would "get some fire" and strode rapidly away.

He returned in a minute with a flaming torch—a long stick around which he had quickly wound a thick swatch of dried marsh grass. He stopped in the doorway of his own hut to shout imperiously for Floridad; then they both hurried toward us—Lauro lighting the way, and Floridad looking sleepy and frightened.

When they neared our hut Lauro held his torch close to the

ground, watching for the army ants' column. When he located it he savagely swept his fiery torch against the close ranks of hurrying ants. Sasha and I moved over to watch—Sasha outspokenly doubting that the torch would burn long enough to stop the invaders, and I feeling a little repelled by the prospect of seeing a large number of insects burned alive—while Floridad nervously took the still-whimpering Sandra from Sasha.

When I told Floridad that Sandra had been stung by one of the coyapos and that I had, too, she became extremely concerned, and tears came into her eyes when she examined the angry red swelling on the baby's hand. Little Sandra, when she saw her nursemaid crying and making a great fuss over her, started to shriek loudly again—more from the sympathy displayed, I imagine, than from the remembered sting. Though I'll have to admit my own stings still smarted and ached.

To forestall Floridad's announced intention of taking Sandra to her hut and applying some native remedy, I led the way to the oxcart and there dug out the first-aid kit and applied alcohol and salve to the baby's and my own bites. But this did virtually no good.

When we returned to Sasha and Lauro we found that Prince Olgierd had joined them after being awakened by all the shouts and the light. He was quite upset about our misfortune and wanted Sandra and me to take his hut for the night, while he helped Sasha. I thanked him and laughed and said I didn't want to miss the excitement and fun, either. So Floridad took Sandra off to sleep in her hut, amply guarded by herself and Cenaria and the children.

By this time the show had drawn a larger audience, for José and Bernardo had appeared and were offering Lauro their advice. Lauro, of course, did not tolerate this for long, and after his indignant tirade the men meekly cut themselves sticks and wound them with swamp grass. As they and Lauro held high their flaming torches, then swept them along the endless column of ants with the long crimson tongues of fire streaming out behind, they looked like ancient pagan priests at some awesome sacrificial rite.

I watched, fascinated, as the hurrying insects continued to march

(*Above*) Small anteater in tree and
(*below*) giant anteater.

in endless numbers. The torches scorched a few, but others rushed in to close the broken ranks. I could hear a faint rustling as they came through the grass toward us. With the wild flames of the flickering torches, aided at intervals by the feeble light of the cloud-swept moon, the scene was indescribably weird.

The torches burned down quickly, and the men stopped to gather more grass. I asked Sasha what he was planning to do. The problem wasn't simple. The ants weren't harming anyone now; it was merely that as long as they used our hut as a highway we couldn't return there to sleep. It was highly probable that they would continue to march through it for hours, possibly until daylight. Sasha and I, of course, could sleep elsewhere for the night, but this didn't appeal to my spouse.

"It's the principle of the thing," he explained to the prince and me with a grin. "I just don't fancy being pushed out of my bed in the middle of the night!"

He explained that the usual strategy when coyapos invaded a camp was to try to turn them by building a large grass fire in their path. However, he feared that to build such a fire now would merely direct the column toward one of the other three huts. And with so many women and children in the camp, not to mention our dogs, cows and calves, and horses, he didn't want to risk that.

There was more talk, while new torches flickered and wavered, and the ants continued their march, ignoring us completely. Several of the dogs came close to the column, stretched out their necks warily and sniffed, then backed fearfully away again.

Abruptly Sasha snapped his fingers and grinned.

"I've an idea!" he said. He turned and strode away toward the oxcart; I saw him opening his large tool chest, which he always brought along on hunts in case any of the guns or other considerable equipment might need repairs. Then he returned, smiling confidently, carrying his kerosene-fueled plumber's torch. He lit it quickly.

"Hah! This'll fix them!" He dropped to his knees.

The rest of us stared as he shot the hissing white flame at the invading insects, moving it in a slow, small arc to cover the unvarying width of the marching column. The ants shriveled and sizzled, and we actually could hear their armored little bodies pop under the searing flame.

But they continued to advance stubbornly against that certain death. Their bodies began to pile up, and still they heedlessly advanced. It was somehow dreadful. I felt, as I watched, that I was witnessing a thing almost obscenely revealing of the savage heart of the jungle—that determined march of the coyapos into the face of inevitable and horrible death, in obedience to their age-old instinct to follow their leaders no matter what the consequence.

After nearly a half-hour of watching Prince Olgierd, beside me, sighed deeply and shook his head.

"I wouldn't have believed it!" he said in an awed voice; then he turned to me and smiled wearily. "With that blind mob instinct —rushing to self-destruction—they're almost human!"

I looked at him oddly but could think of nothing to say.

The next morning, before we broke camp, the men shoveled away piles of dead ants more than several inches deep.

The rain drummed monotonously on the roof and sluiced in noisy rivulets from the palm-thatched eaves of the houseboat. It was a hot, steaming day; no breath of air came through the screened doors and windows. Though the slap and gurgle of the river underneath the floor boards sounded tantalizingly cool, I felt sticky with perspiration. When I finished what I was doing, maybe I'd cool off with another dip in our river bathtub.

December 1, 1941.

The date stood at the top of the page with gratifying blackness, for I had just put a fresh ribbon in my portable typewriter. I glanced ruefully at my still-inky fingers, then spaced down and began bucking the ancient machinery again.

DEAR MOTHER—
Thanks so much for the box of baby clothes! You wrote you'd purposely gotten things large so Sandra could grow into them, but everything fits perfectly. Which proves how slow the mails are down here, not that Sandra's big for her age.

I glanced over at Sandra sleeping in her rosewood crib and smiled to myself. She looked like a little angel in her new frilly white dress—but an earthly little angel, curled up puppy-dog fashion, with one fist still tightly clutching the striped gourd rattle Sasha had carved.

I turned back to my letter.

"She's nine months old now and has six teeth already," I typed proudly. "She creeps all over the houseboat and stands up holding onto the furniture. And she laughs and 'talks' all the time." I thought a moment and added, with honesty, "But I do wish she would get a little hair."

I sighed and stared absently out of the window.

It had been pouring steadily for three days—a torrential rain which had begun, as usual, with a violent thunderstorm, after a couple of days during which the sun had shone with blast-furnace ferocity. That was the usual pattern for our jungle summer or rainy season: The sun blazed savagely for a day or two, until the overheated atmosphere produced a noisy electric storm and an outpouring from the heavens that was like the bursting of a million dams—a downpour that sometimes lasted several weeks—and then the sun reappeared for a short time and the cycle was repeated.

I turned back to my typewriter.

I could hear Floridad moving quietly about outside at the stove, starting lunch. (As even in the rainy season it was much too hot to cook indoors, we had simply hung a tarpaulin over part of the deck.) Floridad was helpful in a lot of ways. Almost too helpful, sometimes, for she was so devoted to the baby that I often wondered whose child Sandra was; if I hadn't protested, Floridad would have taken over completely. The only thing she had ever willingly let me do for Sandra was nurse her—and I was sure she permitted me to do that merely because she herself, quite naturally, couldn't.

I resumed my letter.

Floridad still needs to be watched. She's afraid Sandra isn't getting enough to eat and tries to feed her all sorts of indigestible things, from dried meat to fried fish. And I dare say every time I leave the houseboat for so much as ten minutes she drags that "evil eye" cap out of hiding.

But despite all this, Sandra seems to be thriving on the "rigors" of jungle life. There are minor mishaps, of course. The other day when it stopped raining we had her outside for a sun bath. I left her alone for only a few seconds, but she managed to pull her mosquito netting loose. At this time of the year, whenever the rains let up and the sun starts shining, the mosquitoes swarm out in such clouds they blacken the screens—and, of course, the poor little kid got badly bitten before we could rescue her.

I frowned. Maybe I shouldn't have written that if I wanted to convince Mother that our housekeeping was as safe as hers in Pennsylvania. I certainly had no intention of mentioning the poisonous snake—a fer-de-lance—we'd found near the crib a week ago. Sasha had quickly killed it, but Mother would get the impression that poisonous snakes came aboard daily. She'd been shocked enough when I'd first written about poor, harmless Rupert!

Luckily there were other aspects of jungle life I could describe.

Our monkeys are just like children and therefore quite jealous of the baby. Particularly Chico. If he thinks he's being ignored he looks very doleful, then starts leaping about and doing his full repertoire of tricks, frantically trying to distract us. If I'm holding Sandra he runs up Sasha's leg, scolding furiously, and throws his arms affectionately around Sasha's neck and buries his face on his shoulder. Sandra, on the other hand, isn't a bit jealous of the monkeys. She simply loves them; in fact, I suspect she greatly prefers them to her parents!

There was a sudden small whimper from the crib. Sandra was squirming and rubbing her eyes. She sat up, with her cheeks a bright red from sleep and the heat, and began a louder protest.

At her first sound, the screen door had opened and Floridad had hurried in.

"Senhora," she announced happily—as though I couldn't possibly have heard the child—"the little one is *awake!*" She went on eagerly, "Perhaps she wants Floridad to play with her for a while!"

"She wants her lunch," I said matter-of-factly. I smiled affectionately. "But hold her for a minute, if you like."

Floridad pounced on her little charge, and I turned back to my typewriter and pounded away:

Your granddaughter just woke up, and consequently there will be the usual 11 A.M. intermission. At this point, Mother, I feel exactly like a Jersey cow!

Then I remembered and wrote:

Correction, Mother. We weaned Sandra completely to cow's milk last week. What a creature of habit I am! I suppose it'll take me months to realize I'm out of production.

Then I took Sandra on my lap so Floridad could get her milk and cereal ready, and finished my letter under the handicap of having Sandra "playing chords" on the typewriter keys.

Sounds very domestic, probably, but occasionally we do have a bit of excitement. A few days ago while Sasha was away at the ranch I heard a terrific hubbub from the animals in our zoo. And when I ran out I saw a huge puma slinking around in the underbrush—apparently drawn by the small flock of chickens which the Descalvados ranch manager recently gave us. By the time I got my rifle it had started off, so I jumped on my horse and chased it. It took to a tree soon, and I got it with the first shot.

Well, I'll really have to rush now. Lunch isn't half ready, and Sasha invariably comes in ravenous.

Lots of love,

EDIE

P.S. It was lucky this puma happened along when it did, because I'd told Sasha he'd have to take me on a hunt before I'd settle down to having another baby. And he'd have had to do it in an awful hurry.

You see, we're expecting again!!!

CHAPTER 6

T HE HEAVILY LOADED BARGE WAS JUST DISAPPEARING AROUND the bend in the river. From a half mile away it looked like some clumsy freighter being jockeyed into harbor by a cocky little tugboat, for lashed alongside it and supplying its sole motive power was one of our small eighteen-foot dugouts with its laboriously chugging five-horsepower outboard motor. Rosando was in the dugout, hunched over the motor. Lauro, who was acting as captain of the barge and pilot, stood high above him, and although dwarfed by distance he looked dramatically like a pirate captain in his crimson shirt and swaggeringly tilted black sombrero, with his feet planted wide apart atop the piled-up cargo in the barge's bow. The front of the barge was loaded with tiers of animal cages, stacked three deep: six held tigers; two, pumas; and in the nine others there were an anteater, a cuati, an ocelot, a sloth, parakeets and parrots, our pet macaws, Rainy and J. Pluvius, our chickens, and our widowed wild goose, Hedy, and her new mate, Rochefoucauld. Our team of oxen, the oxcart, two cows and their calves, six horses, and sacks of corn and hay enough to feed them all for weeks were being driven overland.

As the enormously overloaded barge with its straining little tug slowly rounded the Upper Paraguay's broad curve and disappeared behind the impenetrable screen of green jungle, the deep, coughing roar of a tiger issued from it and reverberated across the glassy-smooth, sunlit surface of the river—challenging, and yet with a sound of sadness in it.

There was a scattered burst of yells from the twenty or thirty ill-clad mestizos clustered on the riverbank, who had come early that morning from the Descalvados Estancia to see us leave—and, incidentally, to pick up anything of value we might leave behind. Now, with the barge out of sight, they all turned their eyes on us.

Sasha had let the barge shove off first, for he was positive, of course, that we could quickly catch up with it; and we were drifting slowly with the current into the middle of the river. From where he stood, on the roof of the houseboat, he looked down at me and nodded. I knew what he meant; he wanted us to make our getaway with éclat, to leave with a flourish! That was why he had sent the slower barge off ahead.

"All right, Edith." He grinned boyishly. "Start the motor and give her the gun! Let's give them a good show!"

I smiled up at him from the steering wheel of our new seventy-two-horsepower motorboat, which was tightly lashed to the side of the houseboat, then turned on the ignition and stepped on the starter. There was a faint whir and then the deep rumble of the powerful motor's exhaust. From the corner of my eye I could see the faces of our party on the deck, some avidly eager, others frightened. There were Cenaria and her seven children, Antonia and her four, and the five extra men Sasha had hired to help us on our hegira. I glanced quickly at Floridad in the center of the group; she stood watching me with shining, intent eyes, holding tightly in one arm our sleeping six-week-old Dora, while with her other hand she grasped the hand of tiny, wide-eyed Sandra, standing solemnly beside her. With a hurried smile for them I put the motor in gear, and then—feeling the anticipatory thrill of command over surging power—I enthusiastically pushed the quadrant-type accelerator on the steering wheel.

I was shoved solidly against the back of the seat with the suddenness of the start, and the floor of the motorboat vibrated under me; above the motor and the sudden turbulent splashing of the propeller's wake I heard the half-excited, half-frightened shrieks and cries of the women and children directly above me on my right as the heavy houseboat started to heave and move. Distantly I could hear shouts and cheers from the natives on the shore who had come down to see us off. And their plaudits were like wine, for, deciding I was succeeding in putting the proper flourish into our "getaway," I smiled to myself and pressed still harder on the accelerator.

But at that moment there were more outcries from the houseboat, this time in tones of amazement and surprise. And then, as I realized what was wrong and wrenched the steering wheel violently in the other direction, the cries, to my disconcertment, changed to good-humored laughter. For the powerful motorboat, which Sasha and I had been confident could not only easily tow the houseboat but would, in fact, even be able to *race* off with it at a high speed, instead seemed completely unable to budge the houseboat—and seemed to be anchored by it as firmly as if it had been tied to a tree on the bank. Although I was frantically pulling the steering wheel to the left, the motorboat was lunging through the water toward the right—turning the big, heavily loaded houseboat around and around like a carousel—but moving not one inch ahead!

Sasha, precariously keeping his footing atop its roof, from which vantage point he was to have piloted us down the river channel, managed finally to make himself heard above the amused cries from the houseboat's passengers.

"Take it easy, Edith!" he shouted. "Slow down! Try it slowly!"

I tried that—but without any effect; the motorboat still kept revolving *The River Gypsy* as if it were on some gigantic turntable. I looked up anxiously at Sasha, my face streaming with perspiration; I attempted a nervous smile.

The few men, the women, and the half-grown children were now all offering respectful advice in laughing, eager tones.

"All right, Edith, give it the gun once more!" Sasha boomed as he knelt to look down on me from the roof. "Warp your steering wheel harder!"

I did as he directed, and the sleek-lined speedboat throbbed and lunged forward in the water and the splashing of the propeller's wash drove a thin spray over everyone, while I warped the steering wheel hard to the left and hung onto it with the full weight of my body. But the result was only that the motorboat pushed the houseboat around and around at a faster rate—and still toward the right!

By this time the shouts and laughter from the natives on shore, as well as those from both our half-grown and adult passengers, were beginning to annoy Sasha considerably, as I could tell from his tense expression. They flustered me, too, for this was such a ridiculous anticlimax, and there seemed to be no reason for it.

Sasha met my eyes with an exasperated look, then dropped his hand in a weary signal to end the attempt.

"Cut the motor, Edith!" he called out in a discouraged voice. I could see his big frame slump as he added disappointedly, "I guess it's no use!"

"Okay." I nodded, giving him a lame smile as I turned off the ignition; I felt as disappointed and heartsick as he. Did this mean that our entire plan of moving was wrecked? Did it mean that we would have to go ashore and begin the mammoth job of unloading all our possessions? It had taken us days of hard work to load up. Did it mean that this long trip down-river which we had all so looked forward to, even though we knew it was going to entail many hardships, must now be postponed indefinitely or canceled outright? As all these depressing thoughts raced through my mind each one plunged my spirits lower.

I kept my eyes apprehensively on Sasha as the launch, its engine now dead, coasted to a stop in its whirligig route, and the houseboat, still moving slightly, slowly settled to immobility on the broad river's calm surface. The continuing laughter and shouts from the shore now came across the water distinctly, since the engine was silent. But the crowd aboard the houseboat, though they were talking and making humorous comments about the speedy ride whose end had left them exactly where they had started, apparently noticed that Sasha and I were far from amused by the debacle of our plans. A hushed quietness gradually settled over even the children as Sasha descended from the houseboat roof and morosely made his way through them and toward our captive motorboat. He began grimly untying the heavy rope that lashed it to the side of the houseboat, while everyone watched silently.

"We'd better catch the barge before it gets too far away," he said brusquely.

"Well—we ought to be able to do that easily enough," I murmured, wanting to say something encouraging to ease the rather awkward situation. I added, against my will, "Then what?"

"Well," Sasha replied sourly as he tossed the rope onto the houseboat deck and climbed into the launch beside me, "we can't use this beauty to tow the houseboat, that's certain! I guess it was made only for speed."

As we drifted slowly away from *The River Gypsy* he called to Bernardo, one of the five extra men aboard it—three others, like Bernardo, were Descalvados vaqueiros—and asked him to drop the houseboat's anchors. Bernardo grinned widely and agreeably moved off to do so. The fifth man, who was a veteran riverman and had been hired as pilot because he knew the river's channel, spoke up to ask Sasha what he was planning to use for a tow, now that the motorboat had proved impractical.

I sensed from the hushed manner of everyone aboard *The River Gypsy,* as they awaited Sasha's reply, that they feared the abysmally ineffectual performance of the motorboat had ended the long-anticipated trip. I had momentarily feared so, too, of course, until I remembered that Sasha was not easily defeated. Sasha also was aware of their disappointment, and he swept his eyes over them before answering the pilot. Then he smiled faintly.

"I'm going to catch a couple of tapirs"—his face was completely dead-pan—"and have *them* pull the houseboat!"

For a moment the faces lined up at the houseboat rail reflected a blank puzzlement. Then here and there a smile appeared. The patrão, of course, was joking! That must mean that he, himself, was no longer so downhearted! Everyone broke into wide grins of relief.

At a nod from Sasha I turned on the ignition and started the motorboat, then moved over to let him take the wheel. I discreetly said nothing, and he remained morosely silent as he put the engine in gear and bore down on the accelerator. We described a half circle, then tore off straight down-river toward the broad bend around which Lauro and Rosando and our barge had vanished; the deep roar of the big motor and the noisy splash of our wash testified to our speed.

Sasha, I knew, was deeply hurt at the failure of his prized new motorboat to perform as a tug. I could tell it in the way he almost angrily wrenched the steering wheel around and viciously jabbed at the accelerator until we fairly lunged through the smooth, sunlit water.

I could understand his heavy disappointment and his almost small-boy's way of reacting to it. Sasha had long ago wanted a speedboat, wanting it almost with the intensity that a boy wants his first shiny new bicycle. And unquestionably it would have been useful in many ways. But in our financial circumstances, as we had so often reluctantly reminded ourselves when we had considered the idea, buying an expensive motorboat had to be regarded as a foolhardy extravagance. For, after all, we *did* have our two reliable old five-horsepower outboard motors and, attached to a dugout, they always eventually got us where we wanted to go—though, admittedly, neither fast nor with a flourish. And then a perfectly legitimate reason had arisen for the immediate purchase of the motorboat—a reason which, to Sasha's enormous gratification, transformed it from a luxury into a necessity.

We had finally decided, after considerable discussion, to move to a different section of the jungle. It would be a big trip, for we were planning to go six hundred miles down the Upper Paraguay River, past Corumbá, and then one hundred and fifty miles up the Miranda River, which flows into the Upper Paraguay. We planned to make our new home on the Miranda River, within the boundaries of the Miranda Estancia, a big ranch whose manager was a European Sasha had met some time ago.

The reason we were moving was to locate in a section of the jungle that was nearer and more accessible for sportsmen in Rio and São Paulo and even Buenos Aires. The war long ago had ended the hunting trips of sportsmen from Europe, and now that the United States was in, Sasha knew he would have to depend exclusively for a while on South American patronage. He had satisfied himself, on an earlier trip alone up the Miranda River, that the jungle in that section was equally as wild and untouched as that where we had been living, and that there were at least as many tigers in the Miranda Estancia area as around Descalvados. The 750-mile river trip was rather an appalling undertaking, but we had been preparing for it for months—long before Dora had been born.

The trip had provided Sasha with a first-class reason for finally buying the long-desired motorboat. As he very reasonably explained, faced with the necessity of moving not only the houseboat but a big barge as well, both loaded to the gunwales with our possessions, obviously something more than our two little five-horsepower outboard motors was needed to provide motive power.

So he had drawn heavily on our modest cash reserve to buy the motorboat, procuring it through the Rio agent of its American manufacturer and turning in the older of our outboard motors on the deal. We had brought the new motorboat back with us when we returned from Corumbá with the newest addition to our family. It had been shipped to Corumbá knocked down and crated, and Sasha had put it together and installed the engine only a couple of weeks ago. We had, of course, used it already in cruising about on the river, and it had proved soul-satisfyingly speedy; but today was the first time we had tried to use it to pull a heavy load.

By now we had rounded the bend in the river and were rapidly overhauling the barge, about a mile ahead of us down-river. The deep, even throbbing of our engine's six cylinders, effortless and powerful, like the purring of a big tiger, and the silvery cascading in the bright sunlight of our V-shaped wake were soothing—gratifying—and Sasha finally thawed under their spell.

"She's powerful enough, all right!" he conceded grudgingly.

I had slumped lazily down in my seat beside him, lethargically enjoying the beat of the hot sun on my face, the caressing breeze created by our speed, and the intermittent cool dashes of spray from our leaping bow. I looked up at him now and smiled but said nothing.

Sasha cleared his throat in an embarrassed way. It was as though his reference to the motorboat's power had reminded him that, for the type of power which at the moment we most needed and for the provision of which the motorboat ostensibly had been purchased, it was a dismal flop. He looked, I thought, like a youngster who has become slightly conscience-stricken about having bought a baseball bat to give to his grandmother on her birthday.

"She works so beautifully now," he said apologetically but yet with ill-concealed pride, "that I just can't understand why she's so unmanageable when we try to pull a load!" He turned to look at me and waited, as if expecting a comment.

But I still said nothing.

After a ruminative moment he cleared his throat again.

"I suppose," he added indulgently, "it's like expecting a Derby winner also to be good at pulling a plow!"

At that I almost snorted, and when I turned and saw him looking straight ahead, a half-smile of obvious pride in his "racing steed" on his bearded face, I could no longer restrain myself. As if we had need for a temperamental thoroughbred at the present time!

"And just what," I demanded with a certain bitterness, "do you propose to substitute for our 'Derby winner'?"

It could have been unintentional; maybe there actually was a piece of driftwood or a submerged alligator in front of us just at that moment, though I hadn't seen anything. But he abruptly wrenched the steering wheel toward the left, the motorboat swerved sharply—and I was doused with spray!

I sputtered and wiped off the big drops of water with the back of my hand, then turned and stared suspiciously at him. However, he was still gazing straight ahead, his chin high, apparently oblivious of what had happened.

"Well, we always have the outboard motor," he drawled with perfect equanimity. "And for six hundred miles of the way we go downstream. The current will be on our side!"

"Mmmmm—it's fortunate we can count on the river, at least," I murmured politely.

We had almost overtaken the slow-moving barge. Lauro, standing on top the high-piled animal cages, took off his sombrero and waved it in greeting, grinning broadly. Rosando, in the little dugout, hunched over the steering rod of the chugging outboard motor, turned, too, and smiled in his self-conscious, rather bashful way. Neither, apparently, thought there was anything untoward in our having cut the launch free from the houseboat. Probably they assumed we merely had some additional instructions to give them and had temporarily taken leave of our tow for that purpose.

Sasha cut our engine and we silently glided to the side of the dugout. Sasha grasped its gunwale and beckoned to Rosando, leaning forward so he could be heard above the noisy outboard motor.

"Rosando——" he started.

Just then one of the caged tigers aboard the barge (all destined eventually for Continental zoos) loosed an angry roar—followed, a split second later, by an even more wrathful bellow from another. And then another joined in, and another; and in a moment there was such a bedlam of deep, coughing roars and snarls and rattling growls from the eight big cats aboard—the six tigers and the two pumas—that I clapped my hands over my ears and winced, feeling I was being deafened! Then Lauro added to the ear-splitting uproar, trying to quiet the quarreling animals by shouting at them and stamping on their cages and shooting his revolver into the air. All of which had absolutely no effect. But after a few minutes of the fantastic hullabaloo the big cats subsided of their own volition with a few rumbling, throaty growls. Each was in a separate cage, of course, but the cages were stacked together much closer than they had ever been in our riverbank zoo, and cats are not gregarious animals.

The caged macaws, parrots, and parakeets aboard were also being noisy; however, their shrilling was a minor distraction. . . . Relative quiet having been regained, Sasha resumed his conference with the men. Lauro had quickly clambered down from his lofty perch and joined Rosando in the dugout. He was now standing with legs wide apart and his thumbs hooked in his belt, listening intently to Sasha, but not forgetting for a minute his important role as barge captain. Rosando had both hands busy: with one he continued to steer the dugout-tug; with the other he held the gunwale of our drifting motorboat, helping Sasha keep the two together.

Sasha quickly related our experience in trying to tow the houseboat with the launch and his decision that the only solution was to add the houseboat to the outboard motor's present load. As he concluded he looked calculatingly at the small motor noisily chugging away.

"It'll be an enormous load for that little outboard!" he observed dubiously.

Lauro jammed his thumbs deeper beneath his broad cartridge belt, cocked his kinky head to one side, and gazed with narrowed eyes first at the laboring outboard motor and then at the glasslike surface of the sunlit river, nearly a mile wide at that point. After a moment of studying it he turned back and gravely addressed Sasha.

"I think, patrão"—he spoke in the measured, sententious tones of one who has arrived at a weighty conclusion only after considerable cerebration—"I am certain, patrão, that the little one"—he jerked his head toward the outboard—"can do it! Sim, patrão! While we go with the river, he can do it!"

I met Sasha's eyes and forced myself to keep a straight face.

Lauro, oblivious of my amusement, added a realistic postscript to his optimistic prediction:

"But perhaps, patrão"—he spoke even more deliberately, frowning with concentration—"perhaps we will go no faster than the river! And that is not fast! Não?"

I was taken with a sudden violent fit of coughing. Sasha snorted, said something indistinctly, then brusquely directed Rosando to turn the barge and tow it back upriver, following us. He shoved our launch clear of the dugout and quickly started it, gnawing moodily on his underlip. As the deep-throated rumble of its powerful engine sounded once again he scowled through the polished windshield, then turned the launch in a tight half circle and headed it back upriver.

After virtually sitting on my tongue for several minutes I finally could no longer resist a gibe.

"Well, anyway," I said blandly, "we ought to get there by Christmas!" The date then was August tenth.

Sasha merely snorted and continued to look ahead. . . .

It was hours later and a broiling hot midday when what inevitably became known as the Siemel Ark finally was completely reorganized; and an odder floating combination was never seen, I'm certain, in the Mato Grosso jungle—or elsewhere! The forty-foot barge, with the small dugout and outboard motor lashed to its side, had been tied closely behind the houseboat, which was the same length as the barge, so that they appeared to be, and would function together as, a single eighty-foot structure—powered, God help us, by only that insignificant little five-horsepower outboard motor! The beautiful, useless motorboat was tied to one side of the houseboat, to be handy in case we might wish to run ashore or reconnoiter the channel; on the other side, two empty twenty-foot dugouts were similarly attached for emergency use as lifeboats.

The sun blazed down from a deep blue sky that lacked even the slightest shred of cloud, and the broad river glared like a mirror and shimmered with heat waves when we started again. Sasha was back on the houseboat roof with Carlos, the native who was going to act as our pilot for part of the way, and when he gave the word Rosando started the outboard motor. It began its laborious putt-putt-putting, and everyone held his breath, for it was an enormous load we were asking the little motor to push. Then, very gradually —so gradually that it was barely perceptible at first, and we couldn't be certain until one of the men tossed a stick on the water and we watched it slowly fall behind—our ark began to move. It wouldn't have been possible, of course, if we weren't going downstream. And, understandably, our total speed was only slightly faster than the river's current.

But when the mestizo ranch hands from the Descalvados Estancia, who had been scavenging about the site, finally saw us moving away, they broke into congratulatory yells and shouted their good-bys and grinned and waved their sombreros. I was standing on the houseboat deck facing them, with Sandra beside me holding tightly to my hand and looking very solemn as she stared silently at what had been our home. Floridad was on my other side, with Dora in her arms.

The riverbank was beautiful, with the piuva trees great masses of all shades of purple, and the paratudos drifts of bright yellow, and the undergrowth a freshened, rich green. For it was spring again, and all the jungle was in flower. The huge, rusty-orange tiger lilies clustered in gaudy splashes around our old houseboat site. The undergrowth was blobbed with the bluish-purple blossoms of portulaca bushes, and the ground was carpeted with patches of small blue and red blooms and the tiny white loro flowers. Several brilliantly plumed macaws winged their way vividly across the open space where we had kept our animal cages. Over the water an enormous cloud of butterflies hovered in the still air.

Looking at all this as we began slipping away, I felt a sharp
pang of regret that we were leaving. Maybe one spot of jungle was
very like another, but I remembered with a sudden breathless
poignancy all the nice things that would always be connected with
this little bit of the Mato Grosso. It was here that I had come as a
bride. It was here that we had built our houseboat home—and
brought our first-born, Sandra, when she was smaller than Dora
was now. It was here . . . My eyes misted up and I could no longer
see the riverbank, and my lips began to tremble, and I held my
chin high and pretended to be staring hard straight ahead across
the water.

And then little Sandra spoke up.

"Mamma," she said in a concerned voice, "why Mamma cwy?"

I gulped. "I—I'm not crying!" I choked with an involuntary sob.

"Yes, Mamma cwy!" Sandra nodded her head accusingly.

"Hush, *menina!*" Floridad interjected reprovingly. I felt, though
I couldn't see, that she had quickly moved behind me and had
taken Sandra's other hand and was trying to draw her away, but
Sandra refused to let go of me.

"Mamma, why——" she piped up again in a quivering voice.

At that there was a sudden booming interruption from Sasha
standing on the houseboat roof behind us.

"Sandra!" he called out jovially. "Aren't you going to wave
good-by to all those people on shore? See, they're waving to you!"

"Wave?" Sandra was silent a moment as she digested this; then
she said obediently, "Awright, Daddy! Sand'a wave! See, Daddy?"

I hastily took my handkerchief from my shirt pocket and dabbed
at my eyes.

And then we were around the broad bend in the river, and our
little part of Descalvados Estancia had vanished forever behind
the towering jungle with its riot of vibrant, exotic colors—colors
so clear and sharp in the blinding spring sunlight that they blazed
with an intensity which almost hurt the eyes. As far as one could
see the forest was solidly massed purple piuvas, and from the middle
of the river the miles upon miles of deep purple were breath-taking
—a sweep of one solid color, spangled here and there with the
lemon-yellow of paratudos and the pinks and whites of blossoming
wild fruit trees.

But I had little opportunity to feel sentimental. For one thing, our ark was far more crowded and hectic, I'm sure, even than Noah's. The big barge was fantastically loaded down with supplies and the cages of wild animals. But the houseboat was even more incredibly packed, since it held twenty-five people, including three babies less than a year old. For Lauro and Rosando both had become fathers again a short time before Dora was born.

Sasha and I and our two children and Floridad were occupying the large central room, or living room; it might have been roomy enough, even for the five of us, except that we had to share the space with all of the regular furniture, plus Sasha's photographic supplies, carpenter's tools, and guns, which he had moved out of his workshop to make room there for Lauro and his wife and seven children. Rosando and his wife and their four children occupied one of the two small storerooms back of the workshop; in the other we planned to pen Sasha's eighteen tiger-hunting dogs at night. The small room at the other end of the houseboat, which normally was Floridad's and the children's bedroom, now was turned over to the five new men, and it also held supplies. But these arrangements would be in effect only during the nights.

We hadn't been under way more than fifteen minutes when every one of the eleven native children aboard who could so much as toddle was participating in a game of tag. Even Chico, our pet capuchin, was contributing to the uproar, chattering excitedly as he vainly tried to keep his seat on the back of his own pet dog. Each time he toppled off he would scold noisily and wait until the dog came around the deck again, when he would leap on once more and frantically maintain his seat until he had again been jostled off in the general crowding and hullabaloo. The only quiet creatures aboard were Sambo, the howler monkey, who was squatting morosely under the kitchen stove on the rear deck, and Rupert, the boa constrictor, who wasn't visible at the moment but no doubt was stretched out under my bunk, as usual.

Fortunately Floridad had relieved me of both Sandra and Dora and had taken them into the living room for their afternoon naps—though how they could possibly sleep in all this racket, I couldn't imagine! A baby started wailing in the back of the houseboat, where Lauro's and Rosando's families had their quarters, and almost immediately a second baby started crying even harder. Cenaria's baby had awakened Antonia's, or Antonia's had awakened Cenaria's, whichever it was. I expected Dora to start yelling, too, of course.

I wasn't disappointed—for at that very instant she started volubly protesting in her high treble. I thought I heard Floridad's soft drawl as she attempted to pacify her, and then Sandra began fretfully complaining, as she, too, was awakened.

And at that moment one of the tigers in the barge just behind loosed an angry roar, and in another instant two more joined in, in another noisy, bad-tempered quarrel that temporarily drowned out every other sound.

"Heavens!" I sighed as I leaned grimly against the doorjamb. This was just the first day, and there would be weeks of it!

Abruptly I heard a terrified scream.

Rising even over the continued snarling of the tigers and the wailing of the babies and the barking of the dogs, there was a sudden excited childish babble of frightened incoherencies—and finally the information, repeated over and over again in a terrorized shout:

"Carlotta's in the water! Carlotta's in the water! Carlotta! Carlotta!"

I heard Sasha bellowing to Rosando—telling him to stop the outboard motor, I supposed.

I pushed the screen door open, then gasped as a man's body hurtled just past my head. There was a splash as it plunged into the river. I had ducked back when the body had dropped past me; I opened the door again and rushed to the rail in time to see the diver surface. He was now some distance behind the houseboat, alongside the barge. He half turned, and I saw the beard. It was Sasha! I might have known it was Sasha.

A cold terror fastened in the pit of my stomach as I thought of the piranhas and alligators which were always about in the wide Upper Paraguay. Especially the piranhas, though they were not nearly as numerous as they would be in a couple of months, after the rains started. Carlotta was the child who had had her toe bitten off by a piranha two years ago, when she had dangled her foot over the water. I bit my knuckles as I saw Sasha falling farther and farther behind. Then he abruptly disappeared, and I almost screamed as I visualized him dragged under by some huge alligator.

But in a minute his head and shoulders bobbed up again, and I saw that he had something in one arm. An exultant shout rose from Lauro, at his vantage point atop the animal cages on the barge.

All the while I had been dimly conscious of the steady, labored chugging of the outboard motor, and suddenly I was again on the verge of screaming because Rosando still hadn't stopped the motor, and every moment we must be getting farther away from those two in the water. Then, with a vast relief, I realized that instead we were getting closer, for Rosando was slowly turning the huge, clumsy ark in a circle. Although he couldn't drive the ark upstream against the current, by turning it he enabled the outboard motor to hold it stationary—which allowed Sasha to come down with the current toward us.

I glimpsed Lauro clambering quickly down from his perch on the cages. He crossed from the barge to the houseboat and ran to the front deck, near where I was, for now that the ark was turned, the front of the houseboat naturally was closest to Sasha. Lauro grasped the rail with one hand and leaned under it, hanging far out over the water. There were triumphant cheers from the watching men, women, and children. I saw Sasha's head and shoulders rising into view as he handed up Carlotta's limp form to Lauro. Then he climbed onto the houseboat himself.

With that I suddenly felt weak and faint.

"Sasha," I choked in a barely audible voice, looking hard at him. "Sasha," I repeated, louder this time, and even achieving a steady smile as I started toward him. "Should I—— Do you want me to get some—some cachaça?"

Then I was beside my dripping-wet spouse and Lauro, who held his unconscious, bedraggled, and pitiful-looking child. While they laid her on the deck, face down, and began using artificial respiration, I repeated the question, which Sasha hadn't heard the first time, about the cachaça. He said yes, it would be good for Carlotta when she regained consciousness, and for himself now.

I opened the screen door again, grateful to be in the dimness of our living room, where no one would notice that my knees were still trembling, and found the cachaça. Now that Sasha was safe, I wondered briefly why I had been so close to hysterics a minute before—since, after all, Sasha was in greater danger whenever he faced a charging tiger. I had heard that women were often nervous and high-strung for some time after childbirth, and at this point I believed it.

Sasha's vigorously applied artificial respiration soon opened Carlotta's eyes, and in a few minutes she was sitting up and choking and spluttering over the rum. A half-hour later Cenaria had dried her own tears—for she had been alternately weeping and praying, but mostly weeping, while Carlotta lay unconscious on the deck— and she was again berating her daughter in her normal manner.

For the remainder of the day the children all were abnormally quiet and well behaved and dutifully minded Sasha's and their mothers' stern admonitions against racing around the houseboat deck.

Shortly before sunset we tied up at a fairly open stretch of riverbank, for Sasha had no desire to travel at night and add to our hazards the risk of blindly running aground or colliding with a sunken log in the darkness. Despite the attractive shore and the crowded conditions on the houseboat, everyone spent the night aboard—as they were to do throughout the trip, for Lauro's and Rosando's wives, and even the new men, were afraid of roving tigers ashore.

Sasha, of course, scoffed at their fears. Although sometimes we did hear tigers roaring in the jungle, it was extremely unlikely that one would approach a campfire and attack a sizable party. But when Sasha tried to reassure our passengers, he met with a chorus of almost hysterical protests. It seemed that Francisco, one of the new men, had been circulating stories of man-eating tigers that had harassed a small village far down the river. He said a tiger had entered the town church and killed two padres; a third padre, investigating, had been badly mangled before his screams brought help. The panicky villagers finally had killed the tiger by climbing a wall and shooting down on it. The tigers in the vicinity were so bold, he insisted, that at night they had even boarded several small boats tied up at the dock and had killed members of the crew.

We didn't even cook dinner on the bank, for Cenaria and Antonia preferred using my big iron kitchen range on the houseboat to working over an open campfire. They were elected to do the cooking throughout the trip; I supervised and helped to some extent.

We had brought along a good supply of rice, beans, sugar, flour, and charqui, or dried meat. And of course we expected to kill wild game and catch fish along the way to supplement this.

Our needs were considerable, for with the twenty-five humans aboard, Sasha's eighteen hunting dogs, and the bargeload of caged wild animals, we had nearly a hundred stomachs to fill every day.

That night we dined on capibara, for Sasha had shot two a short time before we tied up. We had noticed a "village" or cluster of capibara houses in the shallow water and reeds on the far side of the river a half mile distant and had seen the animals, which are really enormous rodents—in fact, they're the world's largest rodents—swimming and sporting about. Sasha and I had untied the launch from alongside the houseboat, and in a minute we were speeding across the river. The ark, of course, had continued uninterruptedly at its tortoise-like speed.

As we neared the capibara houses, which are simply mounds of reeds similar to the piles muskrats make, I could see there were young in several nests. Capibaras, unlike muskrats, do not live inside their pile of trash, but in a shallow nest they build on top, out in the open like birds. There were six or eight full-grown ones squatting on as many heaps, too; they looked something like guinea pigs—but weighed at least one hundred pounds each. They made no move to dive into the water, merely turning to stare curiously at us, for the capibara is an unwary, rather stupid animal.

Sasha cut the motor, and we glided in still closer. He picked up his rifle, handed me mine, and nodding toward the two nearest full-grown animals, quietly told me to pick off the one on the right. I raised my gun, and as my victim continued to stare innocently at me I felt an instant of compunction at thus taking advantage of his ignorance of men and firearms. . . . We shot almost simultaneously.

There was a quick series of heavy splashes. . . .

When I lowered my rifle there were only two full-grown capibaras in sight—the one Sasha had shot and which he had apparently killed instantly, for it lay still on its reed heap; and, farther away, one who was either braver or more stupid than his fellows, for he sat as he had before, still absorbed in watching us. The one I had shot at had dived into the river; either he had been only wounded, or my momentary qualm at shooting the trusting dope had caused my aim to waver so that he had escaped with a whole skin.

Sasha grinned at me in an annoyingly patronizing manner.

"It must have been the wind, my dear," he said kindly.

There wasn't a breath of air stirring, of course. I made a face at him.

"Well," he said as he raised his rifle again, "we need one more."

There was a report, and the waiting capibara grunted and slumped—victim to an overdeveloped curiosity.

The dead animals each weighed close to one hundred and twenty pounds, which is about as large as capibaras get. We loaded them into the launch and then, after stopping at a third mound to admire a nestful of small capibaras, who looked like cute half-grown puppies, we set out to overtake the ark.

Rosando and Gonzaga, another of the new men, dressed the animals on the riverbank after the ark was tied up, and Cenaria and Antonia broiled steaks for everyone on our stove. The men built a fire on the bank and boiled half of the remaining meat in a big kettle we always used for that purpose; this cooked meat was fed to the dogs. What was left was given, raw, to our carnivorous zoo animals.

It wasn't a bad meal at all, our first dinner aboard the ark—even though the steaks were a little too fatty, as is always true of capibara meat. Our cooks also had prepared a big potful of that standard Brazilian caboclo dish, boiled rice and beans, and had baked cassava cakes. Lauro and Francisco had found a small copse of acuri palms and had brought back enough palm hearts to provide a salad for everyone. And, as always, we had maté.

After dinner the big job remaining was getting all the kids to bed as quickly as possible so we adults could have an hour or two of peace and quiet before we turned in also. Floridad put Sandra to bed while I nursed little Dora. Although Dora customarily fell asleep in my arms while I was feeding her, tonight she was fretful and I had to walk the floor with her for nearly a half-hour before she finally dozed off—which was unusual for Dora. In contrast to Sandra, who had demanded a lot of attention throughout her first few months, Dora so far had been unusually good and easy to take care of.

I decided that her restlessness tonight was the natural result of the noise and excitement that had been going on around her all during this first day of the trip—what with Carlotta nearly drowning, and all of Lauro's and Rosando's children racing about in their games of tag, and the dogs barking, and everything.

Even now it was far from quiet, for one of the other babies was wailing and several children were noisily quarreling in their quarters in the rear of the houseboat. Abruptly I heard Cenaria's voice raised threateningly, and a moment later the sharp report of a slap. The sounds of quarreling ceased, but the punished squabbler began bawling loudly.

Sasha, who had been talking to the men around the fire on the bank, had entered the living room in time to hear the exchange between Cenaria and her child.

I smiled ruefully and shook my head in desperation.

"I certainly hope this trip won't last as long as I know it will!" I sighed.

Sasha grinned sympathetically. "What's the matter, Edith? You're not giving up yet? Remember, the worst is probably still ahead!"

I dropped into my bunk and wearily held my hand to my forehead, for now the other small native baby was also wailing, and I was certain that after all my work Dora would be awakened and make it a trio. Instead, at that moment there was a plaintive cry from another direction.

"Mamma!" Sandra called out from her crib in the corner. "Mamma, come!"

Floridad had disappeared after she had put Sandra to bed. She was either on deck or with the crowd about the fire on the bank, talking to the new men—at least two of whom, it was quite obvious, were smitten with her. I sighed and hurried over to quiet Sandra before she woke up Dora.

"Wataw, Mamma!" she demanded with a smile; she was standing up in her crib, with sleep apparently the farthest thing from her mind. "Sand'a want wataw!"

"Sandra doesn't want a drink of water," I said firmly. "She just had her milk. Now, go to sleep, dear." I picked her up, patted her pajamaed little bottom, and laid her down tenderly. "Go to sleep, and Mamma will sit here and sing to you!"

Sandra stood up again and drew herself stiffly erect on her tiptoes, trying to look fierce.

"Sand'a want wataw!"

I sighed. Sandra was frequently difficult at bedtime, though tonight I couldn't much blame her after the upsetting day we had all had.

"All right, dear. Daddy will get you some water." I looked imploringly at Sasha. "But then Sandra must promise to go to sleep!"

Sandra nodded her head, and when Sasha returned with her drink she sipped it gravely, making it last as long as possible.

I reminded her of her agreement, and she reluctantly but obediently allowed me to lay her down and tuck her light coverlet over her again. But when I said good night she merely stared at me silently, wide-eyed and with a slightly hurt expression, as if she couldn't understand the injustice of being forced to go to bed while we stayed up.

Sasha, standing beside me, gently urged me toward the door. After a hasty peek into the bassinet at the sleeping Dora, I blew out our kerosene lamp and joined him. A baby in one of the back rooms was still wailing fretfully, but the other had stopped. I could hear Antonia crooning vigorously, though rather tunelessly, and the steady pad of bare feet as she presumably walked the floor with the baby in her arms.

We stepped out on the deck.

There was no moon, but the stars were so near and bright and thick that they looked like glittering tinsel hung within reach. Without moonlight the quiet, unrippled surface of the huge river was like black velvet, and the ragged jungle growth on the shore was notched blackly against the sky. I noticed an odd phenomenon on a slight rise to the left: a phosphorescent mound that gave off a wavering, greenish glow. It was probably a stump or an anthill covered with glowworms, but it suggested a small, eerily lit fairy castle. Closer to us on the riverbank, the fire the men had built flickered and gave an unreal look to the shadowed figures sprawled about it. I could hear the deep rumbling of lazy male voices. Sasha placed his arm affectionately around my waist, and we stood there together on the deck for a long moment, gazing silently across the river. There was a loud splash, and then I heard the bellow of an alligator nearby.

On the third day we came to a small creek, the Cara-Cara, which Carlos, our pilot, declared to be a short cut through which he could guide us. He explained the creek cut straight across a big loop in the Upper Paraguay, rejoining it after a distance which we should be able to make in three or four days. So Sasha decided to take advantage of the short cut, and we entered the inlet.

The Cara-Cara was narrow, but nevertheless we kept the ark moving through it the first day without difficulty. The next morning, however, the creek's relatively clear channel and banks disappeared into what looked like a big swamp—a wide expanse of shallow water thickly clogged with water lilies and marsh grass. We tried to negotiate it, but by ten o'clock in the morning the ark was stuck fast, to the considerable disconcertment and loss of face of Carlos, who had so confidently led us into the mess.

Carlos was a stocky, dark little man with an elegant mustache and a very dignified manner. He had consistently held himself apart from our other native helpers, apparently considering them only unsophisticated, untraveled vaqueiros—ordinary ranch hands whose knowledge of the world couldn't be compared with that of a veteran riverman who knew all the eccentricities of the Upper Paraguay and was as familiar with its ever-shifting, frequently dangerous channel as a lover is with his sweetheart's face, and who had piloted everything from tiny dugouts to small steamboats along the upper half of the huge river. As a result of his barely concealed scorn for the other men and his withdrawal from their company, he had seemed to me to be a rather lonely little man.

He had inspired a resentment among the men and, in Lauro, an attitude approaching active hostility—for Lauro was not a man who could be snubbed with impunity. Therefore, when Carlos's piloting landed the ark solidly in a thick tangle of marsh growth, the other men, Lauro especially, made no effort to conceal their gloating over Carlos's part in our predicament.

At the time, Carlos had been at his usual post on the forward roof of the houseboat (from where he guided the ark by signaling with his arms to Rosando, nearly eighty feet behind in the dugout with the outboard motor). Sasha also was on the roof, for he spent much of his time there; and I had just gone up myself, in order to talk to Sasha and at the same time have a better view of the scenery.

When the narrow creek channel had abruptly vanished and we were confronted with the broad marsh, so rankly overgrown with high green swamp grass and floating islands of thickly matted, purple-blossomed *camelote,* or water lilies, that the water was barely discernible, Carlos had signaled Rosando to a stop, while he worriedly peered ahead. Sasha had commented dubiously on our chances of getting through. And then Carlos, apparently fearing his reputation as a pilot was at stake, and hoping he could force a way through, had signaled Rosando for full speed ahead. The ark had moved jerkily a few yards into the tangled vegetation, and then, with a sudden lurch, had become lodged fast, while the little outboard motor in the dugout continued valiantly, but vainly, chugging away.

The children all rushed forward to see why we had stopped. And from Cenaria, standing on the deck with her infant in her arms, there came a worried wail: "Oh, Mother of God! We'll tip over!" Then she looked up and caught my eye. "Senhora," she called out, "are we in danger?"

The dogs all started barking madly directly below me. At that moment, first Floridad, with Dora in her arms, and then Antonia, holding her baby, came out of the living-room door and also looked worriedly up at me.

But by this time the dogs and the children were making so much noise that it would have been useless for me to try to make myself heard. So I merely shook my head and smiled reassuringly back at Cenaria.

Lauro and Gonzaga rushed forward from the barge and began

226

shouting at the barking dogs to quiet them. When they finally had succeeded, Lauro looked up at Sasha and me and grinned.

"So Senhor Carlos was whelped in a dugout and weaned on a paddle!" he shouted in a loud, bombastic voice heavy with sarcasm. He jerked his head toward the vegetation-choked water ahead of us and inquired with a blandly innocent expression: "Does he think to pilot us across this field of swamp hay? Maybe he supposes we are all tuyuyu, with wings?"

Carlos's ramrod-like back stiffened indignantly. But he made no attempt to reply to Lauro and in no way even recognized his presence; he continued scowling straight ahead. Sasha and I politely pretended not to have heard Lauro, either.

Then Gonzaga, a fat, not overly bright clown who had established himself as Lauro's chief toady, and who had guffawed raucously at his idol's comment, added one himself:

"Is it possible, Lauro"—Gonzaga slyly cocked his head and rolled his eyes with exaggerated innuendo—"is it possible that this person who calls himself a pilot has ever been on the river before? I think he just came off the back of a horse!" He laughed uproariously at his own words, waiting for Lauro's approval.

Lauro winked at him—after a quick glance up at Sasha, apparently to see if he was frowning—and retorted:

"That one a vaqueiro?" He snorted scornfully. "He can't keep this boat in the river! How could he keep his fat backside on a cavalo?"

At this final insult the pendent tips of Carlos's luxuriant mustachios quivered wrathfully, but he gave no other indication that he had heard. Sasha, to one side and behind him, raised an amused eyebrow, and I repressed a smile with difficulty.

From below, on the houseboat's forward deck, came the shouts and laughter of the children, who were again playing; the renewed barking of the dogs; the wails of Cenaria's baby.

Carlos abruptly turned to Sasha.

"Senhor Siemel"—his expression was concerned, though his dark eyes were fairly smoldering—"Senhor Siemel, I did not plan for you to become stuck fast in this miserable swamp! The last time I passed through the channel was clear. The grass and the camelote have all grown up within the past dry season, senhor, believe me!"

He looked genuinely worried, and he turned to me, too, momentarily with an expression that pleaded for belief.

Sasha grinned, and I smiled sympathetically.

"Don't worry, Carlos," Sasha said heartily; he smiled with a forgiving, almost benign expression, although I knew he must have been annoyed at our predicament. "I know how fast things grow in the jungle!"

Though Carlos was singularly reserved for a Latin, he fairly beamed at this expression of confidence. He explained that if we could only make our way through this marsh he would guarantee that the route from then on would present no difficulties, for beyond it the channel was wide and deep.

"I think perhaps, senhor," he said earnestly, "if a couple of men were sent ahead in a dugout to chop away the grass and camelote . . ."

So this was done. Gonzaga and Jorge, another new man, put out in a dugout with their machetes. First they chopped at the entangled vegetation that had brought our ark to a stop. Then they spent half an hour industriously hacking at and clearing away the grass and camelote ahead on the route we would have to travel. Then Rosando again started the outboard motor.

We moved about fifteen feet into the channel they had cleared, but then we became stuck fast again.

"And that one calls himself a pilot!" Gonzaga spat savagely. He addressed his companion in the dugout loudly and with great bitterness. "He has piloted us into a job of chopping our way across the jungle!"

"You are ungrateful, Gonzaga!" Lauro chided from the houseboat deck; he cocked his head up at the pilot to make certain he did not fail to hear. "You need never go hungry again. Our fine pilot has got you a job that will last. You can wear out many machetes between here and Corumbá!"

Sasha turned abruptly to Carlos and me and explained a new plan. In brief, we would imitate the device used by the captain of the steamboat on which Sasha and I had gone down-river with Katharine and Tom Elling two years earlier, to get married. The technique had gotten the stranded steamboat off a sand bar in record time. Carlos and I agreed it sounded practicable. Sasha summoned Lauro to his captain's bridge on the roof and explained the procedure. . . .

The sun was uncomfortably hot, despite the haze, and the men were all perspiring mightily in the still air as they worked. They had brought out Sasha's heavy carpenter's bench and had secured it, upside down, to the front deck of the houseboat. Then between the upside-down legs they had braced the chain-and-axle device that was the nub of the idea; the axle had a handle like the crank on an old-fashioned automobile, and when this was turned it would wind up the chain. The other end of the lengthy chain was attached to the anchor. They intended to take the anchor ahead in the dugout and fasten it to the matted water-lily roots; then, by turning the crank, they would wind up the chain and thus slowly drag the ark over the thick tangle of vegetation that was blocking her progress.

When the axle was fastened securely Sasha and Lauro put out in the dugout, with the anchor attached to the chain. After some minutes of leaning over the side of the dugout and fumbling about with the heavy anchor Lauro got it securely lodged among the roots below the surface. Then Sasha gave the signal to Gonzaga and Jorge, who had been given the strenuous job of turning the crank.

They began. . . . The slack chain rose from the water, swung dripping, and quickly rattled aboard as they wound it in. Then it tightened with a jerk, and the men were forced to use all their strength in cranking. The massive carpenter's bench, lashed tightly to the boat, began to creak. And finally the ark moved!

Sasha and Lauro shouted triumphantly. I gave such a loud "Hooray!" myself that I frightened little Dora, whom Floridad was holding beside me, and she started crying. But all the rest of the children, even small Sandra, yelled and shouted, and the women and men, including the reserved Carlos, were happily grinning. Jorge and Gonzaga, who took these plaudits as a personal tribute, grinned in a slightly embarrassed but pleased manner and bent their backs harder as they continued vigorously turning the crank, the sweat streaming down their dark faces and running in rivulets down their chests. And the big, clumsy ark continued moving forward, foot by foot.

Sasha and Lauro remained in the dugout out on the swamp, and when the arduous cranking finally had brought the ark tight up against the anchor, they unfastened it from among the entangling roots and carried it ahead in the dugout to the full length of the chain, where they once more secured it under water. The men on the houseboat again began bending over the crank and painfully winding in the chain.

This laborious inching along continued for four hours, while Bernardo and Francisco periodically relieved Jorge and Gonzaga at the crank. . . . And then we finally had crossed the matted islands of purple camelote and the snarled growth of marsh grass and were once again in the open creek channel.

The short-cut creek soon opened up into a series of wide lakes, which could have proved dangerous if a south wind had developed, for our houseboat and barge certainly wouldn't have lasted long in the waves, two or three feet high, which were blown up on wide bodies of water by such a wind. (Below the equator the south wind is, of course, comparable to the north wind back home.) While we were passing through these lakes we therefore traveled night and day without stopping.

After a day's travel on the majestic mile-wide river we approached the tiny settlement of Amolar. While we were still— and very fortunately—close to the opposite bank, a stiff south wind blew up, raising dangerously high waves on the broad river, forcing us to remain moored for three days opposite the settlement. Here Carlos, our pilot, left us, as he had wanted to go no farther south.

When the wind finally died down we started out again, and after several days of uneventful traveling we came to where the big river divided, for a distance of about a hundred miles, into two channels. The main channel led to Corumbá. The smaller channel, known as Paraguay Mirim, or "Little Paraguay," detoured around Corumbá. It was this channel which Sasha had decided to take— not only because it was slightly shorter than the other, but also because he didn't want to pass Corumbá with our bargeload of wild animals. Too many people in Corumbá knew him, and he was afraid that our appearance would bring out every dugout in town; that virtually the entire population would set out to intercept us and demand to come aboard to gawk at our caged tigers and

(*Above*) Oxcarts crossing lake at Corcunda and
(*below*) Miranda River at Barranco Vermelho.

other animals. To allow crowds of people to surge over our already greatly overloaded ark would not only have caused impossible confusion but would have been highly dangerous.

We picked up another pilot, who knew the Paraguay Mirim channel, at its mouth. On the afternoon of our third day on the Mirim, when we came to where the two channels of the Paraguay merged again, our new pilot left us.

That night we tied up to the bank just a quarter of a mile below the junction of the two channels; and now, for the first time since leaving Descalvados, we were careful to hang riding lights fore and aft on our ark as soon as it became dark. From that point on, down-river, there was some river traffic, and we were liable to meet boats traveling between Corumbá and Porto Esperança, the railhead two hundred miles farther down-river.

We started out unusually early the next morning, for Sasha was afraid of another south wind blowing up while we were still on the broad Upper Paraguay, and he was anxious to complete our last one-hundred-mile lap down it and get off the big river as quickly as possible. Of course we would still have to go one hundred and fifty miles up the Miranda River to reach our new homesite. But on that tributary, a smaller river, our cumbersome ark would be in much less danger from a sudden windstorm.

Late the next day, after having completed approximately six hundred miles of our trip, we reached the mouth of the Miranda River. Here we would leave the huge Upper Paraguay for good. However, though we were that close to the end of our long journey, this last stretch undoubtedly would be the most difficult. From now on we would be fighting the river current instead of being helped by it, and making any headway against it, Sasha feared, would be quite a battle.

Just how stiff a battle this would be, we quickly learned.

Sasha and I were sitting in his pilot's post atop the houseboat when we sighted the Miranda's mouth; the ark was hugging the Upper Paraguay's left bank. Sasha immediately signaled Rosando to head us into the tributary and added in a shout that he should keep us as close to the shore as possible.

I could sense Sasha's tenseness and anxiety as we approached the Miranda, for in this maneuver of rounding the corner from the Upper Paraguay into the Miranda, as Sasha earlier had pointed out to me, the eighty-foot ark necessarily would be turned broadside for a short time to the Miranda's current. This would be the critical point, for if the Miranda's current was strong, we might easily be carried back into the broad Upper Paraguay and swept on, past the Miranda's mouth. Then it would be impossible to return to the Miranda, for it already had been demonstrated, at the time Carlotta fell overboard, that our feeble little outboard motor was powerless to propel the ark upstream against the Upper Paraguay's strong current. However, we had prepared for this maneuver.

Sasha stared straight ahead with a rather grim expression as we came closer and closer to the Miranda's mouth. I, too, was silent and anxious as I gazed ahead at the brightly sunlit huge expanse of water where the two streams merged. At that point the Upper Paraguay is truly impressive—a silvery, smoothly moving picture of overwhelming size and power in which our ark seemed a puny, fragile thing. We were still some distance from the Miranda's mouth when Sasha abruptly stood up on the houseboat roof and shouted back:

"Lauro, break out the *zingas!* And post the men at once!"

Lauro, who had momentarily disappeared among the high-piled animal cages and boxes aboard the barge, poked his head out from behind one of the cages and looked up.

"It shall be done with the utmost haste, patrão!" he shouted back, a broad grin spreading over his black face. "The men are ready."

The zingas were to be our auxiliary motors—heavy, long hardwood poles which Sasha had available for just such an emergency. In the hands of strong men, and used in sufficiently shallow water, they were a reliable, though primitive, method of propulsion.

But the unexpected happened, as it invariably does in a critical moment.

What we hadn't anticipated was that the shore current in which we were traveling would suddenly quicken as it neared the junction of the two rivers. One moment we were proceeding toward the Miranda's mouth at the same leisurely speed at which we had descended six hundred miles of the big river's length, and the next instant we were being almost hurtled toward the junction at a speed several times that of before. I could see Sasha was suddenly alarmed, though he tried his best to hide it. He stood up on the houseboat roof and turned to shout again at Lauro:

"Lauro, get those zingas out before it's too late! Hurry up, man!"

I could hear the outboard motor chugging away loudly, adding to our speed, but Sasha didn't need to tell me it would have been dangerous to cut the motor, since this represented our sole means of controlling, to the slight extent we were able to control, our direction.

Lauro excitedly yelled something back in reply. Then two of the other men shouted something almost wildly and simultaneously, so that their words merged and drowned each other out. But as I stood on the roof beside Sasha, looking back, it was evident the men were having difficulty getting the long poles out from among all the cages and stores crowding the barge. I could see them struggling and fumbling and heaving at boxes, and I heard Lauro cursing and barking at them. Sasha, even more excitedly, again shouted to Lauro to hurry. And then abruptly I saw, with a sensation of shock, that the Miranda's north bank was receding behind us! We were passing its mouth!

Then all at once we seemed to come to a standstill.

I could hear our little outboard motor putt-putt-putting valiantly behind us as Rosando desperately tried to follow his earlier directions and swing the huge, unwieldly ark around to the left and head it up the Miranda.

And then, to my horror—and I found myself actually digging my heels into the houseboat's tin roof, trying to stop us—as the ark presented its eighty-foot broadside to the Miranda, that river began carrying us sideways and out of control, like a huge piece of driftwood, toward the middle of the Upper Paraguay! I was horrified because I knew that once we were swept out into the deep water the zingas would be completely useless, and without their aid the outboard motor could never get us back to the Miranda.

Then I saw the four extra men hurriedly scrambling forward along the crowded edge of the barge toward the houseboat—each trailing in the water beside him one of those heavy, long poles. They crossed to the houseboat and separated, two on each side;

then with feverish haste they thrust their zingas into the water and tried to find bottom.

It seemed hopeless to me, and I turned and stared despairingly over the water at the Miranda's receding north bank.

Abruptly there was a shout from the houseboat deck.

"Patrão, there is a bottom!" Bernardo exulted from the portside. "I have found bottom!"

Sasha and I both spun around. Bernardo looked up at us, grinning triumphantly, as he firmly grasped the end of his pole which protruded from the water. A split second later the other polemen called out that they, too, had touched bottom.

Suddenly I realized that we were no longer moving; we were no longer being carried out onto and down the broad Upper Paraguay. The men were holding us firm, with their long poles thrust against the river bottom.

The outboard motor was still chugging away bravely but ineffectually. And in the midst of the triumphant shouts and rather nervous laughter and the relieved expressions of all of us, Lauro—obviously eager to assume command over the men—called out from his high perch on a tiger's cage, like the overseer of a crew of Roman galley sweeps:

"All right, my fine *homens!*" he shouted, as he arrogantly stood, legs wide apart, with his head thrown back. "Get yourselves ready! Pronto!"

And the four zinga men—one at the port bow, one at the starboard bow, and one amidship on each side—firmly grasped their long, heavy poles and simultaneously bent over them.

"At this moment, as one!" Lauro barked. "Now—walk!"

With that, the four together gave a long, extended grunt as they walked toward the rear, half the length of the houseboat, meanwhile keeping their poles firmly jammed against the river's bottom. Their propulsion, added to that of the outboard motor, pushed the ark noticeably ahead into the Miranda. What they actually were doing, of course, was shoving the eighty-foot ark forward with their bare feet by walking rearward half the length of the forty-foot houseboat deck, while obtaining leverage by holding their long poles stationary against the river's muddy bottom.

Enthusiastic shouts again rose from our passengers.

The four straightened up and, grinning proudly, dragged their poles loosely through the water behind them and leisurely returned to their original posts. We didn't lose ground while they were doing this, for the outboard motor was able to hold the ark stationary when the men released their poles, even though it was as powerless to move the ark upstream on the Miranda as it had been on the Upper Paraguay.

Then Lauro droned out again: "Get yourselves ready!"

The four again planted their poles firmly on the river bottom, bent over them, and the walking procedure was repeated.

We had one hundred and fifty miles to go at that snail's pace! The men actually had three hundred miles to walk, counting their returns to position on the forward deck.

Sasha was philosophical about it.

"At least we have some very fine scenery to see," he explained cheerily with a wave at the luxuriantly forested riverbank on either side. "And we're not going so fast we'll miss half of it!"

"That," I interjected a trifle sarcastically, "is an understatement."

It was true that the country we were seeing, all new to me, of course, was strikingly beautiful. The brilliantly colored flowering trees that had made the region about our old home on the Upper Paraguay so lovely in the spring were equally plentiful here. And in traveling up the Miranda, since it was a much smaller river, we were able to watch the animal and bird life on both banks— impossible on the mile-wide Upper Paraguay.

But it was painfully slow traveling.

Finally, one blazingly hot afternoon as we were rounding a bend, I had my first glimpse of what would be our new home. Sasha proudly pointed out the site as we sat perched on the houseboat roof, and I had no difficulty in recognizing the spot he meant even though we were still nearly a mile distant. It dominated that flat, though tree-clad country sufficiently to well warrant the name he had already given it: *Barranco Vermelho*, or "Red Bluff."

The word quickly got around among our passengers, and the front deck was soon crowded with excited children straining to see, and quarreling over who had been first to glimpse, our new

home. Cenaria, with her baby in her arms, and Floridad, carrying
Dora, hurried out on deck and crowded past the sweating men
with their zingas.

"Senhora"—Cenaria shaded her eyes from the blinding sun as
she anxiously peered up at me—"is it true—that we soon will make
an end to this journey?"

I smiled and nodded happily.

"Yes, Cenaria. Believe it or not!" I raised my arm and pointed
to that commanding rise on the bank, now only half a mile away—
crowned with the vivid purple of piuva trees and the yellow of
paratudos and the whites and pale pinks of blossoming wild fruits
—and proudly announced: "There's our new home!"

Cenaria stared in the direction I had pointed, then again met
my eyes, and the anxiety and incredulity she had at first shown
slowly gave way to a blissful, almost beatific smile. Half closing
her eyes, she hugged her child closer and crossed herself.

"I give thanks to the Holy Mother!" she murmured reverently.

Floridad beamed; I could see her eyes filling with happy tears.
She quickly dropped her head over little Dora. Cenaria, with
Floridad close behind, stepped aside for sweating Bernardo as he
once again padded heavily forward, gripping his sturdy zinga.
Everyone not actively engaged in propelling us onward began to
drink in the details of that purple-topped, heavily foliaged high
bank of rusty red earth coming ever nearer. Even the dogs, locked
up in their room in the back of the houseboat to keep them out
of the way of the zinga crew, seemed to have heard, for they were
wildly barking and yipping, frantic to get out. . . .

A short time later we had arrived and were moored in the cool
shadow of that high red bank with the exotically colored trees and
underbrush, and the gangplanks had been let down and the men
and Cenaria and Antonia and their broods of noisy, eager children
had all gone ashore and scrambled up the bank. After a minute of
suddenly realizing that I was once more alone on *The River Gypsy*
with only Sandra and Dora and Floridad, and ruefully surveying
the Jovian job of house cleaning that lay before me when all our
human passengers, not to mention the eighteen dogs, would move
out, Floridad and I and my babies also went ashore. Sasha met us.
And after we had climbed the bank I saw that Sasha's enthusiastic

236

descriptions were borne out—that there was even a tiny stream on the site, running through a picturesque little gully.

While Lauro and Gonzaga had gone back to free the dogs and lead them all ashore, Rosando had set to immediately with the other men to knock together a stockade, as well as straw huts for his and Lauro's families. (After a few days, when this construction work was completed and they had rested a bit, the four extra men would return in a dugout to the Descalvados Estancia, where they would don their spurs and resume their vaqueiro life.) The children, meanwhile, were shouting and running about, discovering new things constantly and loudly announcing these discoveries. The dogs, almost beside themselves with glee at having finally escaped their close-cramped quarters, were barking and hysterically racing about. The tigers, sensing the excitement though their cages hadn't been unloaded yet, began their usual furious bedlam of snarls and roars, which reverberated across the water and echoed from bank to bank.

And in the midst of all this chaos and hullabaloo a horseman abruptly rode up out of the thick purple-blossomed piuva trees which surrounded us on every hand and gave the customary warning shout:

"O de casa!"

Sasha, some little distance from me, turned with a startled expression, and then a broad smile spread over his bearded face. The newcomer—who, I guessed from his rather quiet, obviously expensive clothes and the dignified manner in which he sat his horse, was the manager of the Miranda Estancia—spurred his horse nearer, smiling in return. Sasha previously had told me about Raul Nesheim, the reserved, expatriate Norwegian who long had operated the huge ranch for the foreign syndicate which owned it.

Sasha strode eagerly forward; and Senhor Nesheim, smiling, leaned from his horse to shake hands. Then he sat stiffly erect again, his sun helmet shading his somewhat florid face.

Floridad, holding Dora on one arm and with her other hand grasping Sandra, stood beside me, bashfully staring. From the sudden lull behind me I gathered that the rest of the natives were similarly gaping. I suddenly realized that I looked a wreck; my clothes and hair were disheveled, and I was sure there was a smudge of dirt on my face. But it was too late to escape being seen, though I wasn't close enough to be able to hear more than fragments of their conversation.

A Miranda Estancia vaqueiro had seen us about ten miles down the river and had quickly ridden back to the ranch house with the news. Senhor Nesheim congratulated Sasha on our safe arrival. . . . Did he need anything? . . . What kind of a trip had it been? . . .

Sasha thanked him but said easily that we lacked nothing. I could see him draw himself up rather proudly as he carelessly mentioned that we had made the trip up from the mouth of the Miranda in ten days, and that the entire 750-mile journey had taken us only exactly one month. The trip, all in all, Sasha concluded with a deprecatory shrug, had been "smooth and uneventful."

I gulped. . . . "Uneventful!"

Then Sasha turned graciously and called to me.

CHAPTER 7

G OODNESS, BUT YOU'RE SLOW, DORA! WHEN I WAS THREE
years old I could ride better'n Mother and Daddy!" Sandra,
now a little over four, rode so well she was getting insufferably cocky. She twisted about on her frisky calico pony to look back
scornfully at Dora, who sat her own plodding, dun-colored little
pony with her short legs sticking straight out on either side.

"Well, I'm not three yet, Sandra," Dora protested indignantly.
"And you do *not* ride better'n Mother and Daddy!"

"I do so!"

It was a beautiful fall day in early May. The sky was an intense
blue, and the air was so clear and sparkling that it made even the
drab browns of the grassy largo over which we were riding seem
excitingly vivid. As it was still early in the morning, the sun had
not yet become uncomfortably warm.

We had spent the night on the largo, sleeping in our ponchos
on the ground around a campfire. It wasn't as comfortable as
sleeping in a hammock, of course, and I had felt somewhat stiff
when I awoke at dawn. We had spent the previous night in hammocks which we had hung in a little copse of trees on the fringe
of the jungle, but yesterday we had found ourselves on a treeless
stretch of largo when time came to make camp. Not that either

arrangement had been any less then one-hundred-per-cent perfect in the opinion of our small daughters, especially Sandra.

Sandra regarded our little trip as being made especially for her and, of course, Dora too. In a way, it was. Sasha had been promising for some months to take the girls on a trip. And he had been promising, for about the same length of time, to take me "out of the kitchen" for a few days. So when Lauro had heard from a passing Miranda Estancia vaqueiro that a small band of Yanayguas had been captured by soldiers after having massacred a hunting party and were being held temporarily in a stockade on a neighboring ranch, Sasha had suggested that we ride over to see them. It would be a nice holiday trip for the girls, he had said, as the "neighbor's" ranch house lay about sixty miles to the southeast.

A slight breeze was blowing across the largo as we cantered easily along, and the tall, dry brown grass bowed in waves, like a sea, over the flat terrain. We rode in an almost straight southeasterly direction toward the unchanging horizon, detouring only for the numerous thick clumps of caraguata thorn bushes, which rose to as high as our heads when we sat our horses, and the obelisk-like anthills, often fifteen and twenty feet tall, with which the largo was studded.

We were riding slowly for Dora's benefit. As we had started her riding lessons when she was two and a half, only four months ago, this was her first expedition. Very often while we rode, Sasha or I took Dora up in front of us on our own horses so she could rest; and we paused frequently, of course, to let both children dismount and stretch their legs.

Dora's placid little mare had been selected for her predisposition never to exert herself. But Sandra for the last ten minutes had been impatiently urging us to go faster so she wouldn't have to hold her pony in. She was riding in short spurts back and forth, or off to one side, much like a dog casting about for trails. Now and then she returned to ride in a circle around her sister, standing up in her stirrups and flagrantly showing off. Naturally, poor Dora, busy concentrating on keeping her balance in her saddle, scarcely appreciated this.

"Daddy, let's have a race!" Sandra rode back beside us and

looked up coaxingly. "I want to show Dora how fast I can ride!" She glanced at the little girl, then added casually, "I'm pretty good, aren't I, Daddy?"

"Sandra," I said, frowning, "it's not very nice to brag!"

But nonetheless I thought to myself with a smile that I did have quite a little horsewoman for a daughter. Sandra sat her horse ramrod-straight, holding her reins loosely with her elbows in, in the best riding-school form, and she had been able to canter before she was four.

"Daddy, come on. Let's race to those trees!" Sandra pointed to a clump of several small paratudos that dominated the flat grass-land a few hundred yards away. "Come on, Daddy!"

Without waiting for her father's reply she spurred her horse and started off at a canter. She must have thought he was following her, for in a moment she called back delightedly, "I'm beating you, Daddy! *Pressa!* Hurry up!"

She leaned forward, kicking her mount in the ribs and scream-ing with excitement. But her little horse evidently resented this treatment, for he suddenly snorted, arched his neck, and changed his direction—heading, at a gallop, for a small thorn thicket off to the right.

Sasha began spurring his horse ahead.

Sandra stopped shouting and silently, gamely, hung on, throwing her arms around her pony's neck. Suddenly her horse pounded along the edge of the thicket, tossing his head and scraping his flanks against the thorny bushes—and Sandra was speedily knocked off to the ground.

"Oh, poor Sandra!" Dora turned to me, horrified. "Mamma, is she *dead?*" Tears spilled out of her eyes, and she began crying loudly.

Sandra wasn't crying at all, and consequently for a moment I was panic-stricken. Then, just as Sasha reached her, I saw her scrambling to her feet, apparently quite unhurt. She glanced around, looking not a bit disconcerted by her fall, and demanded breathlessly but with considerable poise:

"Daddy, where's my pony?"

As Dora and I rode up she spotted him about a hundred yards

away, nonchalantly grazing. He paused just then and swung his head back to eye us with an innocent expression.

I hurriedly dismounted and rushed up to Sandra to examine her scratches and hold her tightly to me for a moment. But she twisted away to stare at her pony.

"Daddy, look at him!" she said admiringly. "Isn't he—isn't he just a regular *devil!*"

"Sandra, don't you ever do that again!" Sasha said sternly. But as his eyes met mine they had a singularly proud look.

Seeing that Sandra was safe, Dora had overcome her concern for her sister with remarkable speed. As Sasha rode off after the truant pony she looked down from her horse pleasantly and said in a satisfied voice:

"See—I'm not the only one who falls off!"

Dora had had a tumble the week before. I had put her back in her saddle quickly before she had had time to become afraid of her horse, but Sandra had been maddeningly superior about the mishap.

We reached a stretch of thick jungle shortly before noon and drew up among the scattered, smaller trees on its edge for lunch and our midday siestas. By this time the sun was at its hottest.

After our naps we set out again, skirting the solid mass of thick, deep jungle which, with its towering, centuries-old forest giants and dark, impenetrable depths, bulged out in a lush, brilliantly green peninsula into that sea of dried brown marsh grass over which we were riding. As we alternately cantered and walked our horses between the scattered clumps of smaller trees and isolated single trees that made up the ragged fringe of the jungle, Sasha entertained the girls and amused himself by commenting instructively on the flora and fauna—particularly the latter, since the jungle's edge, like the huge marshes, is especially rich in wild life.

He had been noting the rarer kinds of trees that we passed—rarer, that is, only in the sense that they didn't grow on the stretch of riverbank immediately adjacent to our houseboat. On the edge of the jungle he had pointed out a stand of angico, or redwood, trees through which some monkeys were swinging, and, farther on, a good-sized grove of the commercially valuable quebracho trees, from the bark of which tannin, used in tanning leather, is extracted. Sandra, who was riding a little distance to my right and ahead, abruptly turned in her saddle as she passed beneath a rather ugly tree growing alone and rising to a height of nearly eighty feet, and called out to me:

"Mother, this tree smells awful!" She held her nose with an expression of violent distaste. "Why is that, Mother?"

"The tree, darling?" I echoed rather absently.

"Yes, Motherrr! This tree stinks!" Sandra said bluntly.

And then I, too, noticed that the air was redolent with an extremely noxious odor, overwhelmingly like that of garlic.

Sasha, riding with Dora just behind me, spoke up.

"That's not surprising, Sandra," he drawled. "It's called the stinkwood tree! It smells even worse if you cut into the bark!"

"Oh, so *that's* a stinkwood tree!" I murmured, for of course I had heard of them, though it happened I had never seen one before. I guided my horse to give it a wider berth, adding, "I must say it's aptly named!"

Sandra giggled, and Dora rather tardily pronounced with amusing emphasis: "That tree smells nasty, Mamma!"

Sandra looked at her serious-faced small sister tolerantly, then turned to me and said with a patronizing smile: "Dora is *so* observing, Mother!"

I glanced at Sasha and caught a twinkle in his eye; with difficulty I maintained a dead-pan expression.

Dora was sullenly regarding her older sister.

"Daddy"—Sandra turned in her saddle to look back at us again —"why does a stinkwood tree smell bad?"

Sasha smiled at her. "Why does a piuva blossom smell sweet?" he asked enigmatically.

Sandra puzzled over this a moment, then smiled happily.

"Oh, Da-a-a-addy," she beamed. "You're so smart!"

Sasha looked at me and solemnly winked.

We rode for a while beside a small stream flowing along the edge of the jungle and skirted a large thicket of bamboo. The girls were quite incredulous when Sasha explained that the slim, straight, jointed stalks, some of which grew to a height of thirty or forty feet before sending out horizontal branches which intermeshed to form a dense canopy overhead, really were a species of grass.

Then Sasha chanced to see and pointed out a sloth hanging by all four legs, with its back downward, from a leafy branch of a paratudo tree, about twenty feet above the ground. Although we drew up our horses and sat for some minutes watching the animal, which was about two feet long and looked something like a small bear, it did not move in all that time.

"Why doesn't it run away, Daddy?" Sandra demanded after she had shouted at the animal and it had still failed to stir. "Is it dead?"

"No, it's sleeping," Sasha replied.

He explained that a sloth is active only at night, when it climbs about in the trees and feeds on leaves, buds, and young shoots. He added that the sloth is a badly slandered creature, since it really isn't as lazy and slow-moving as the word "slothful" would cause one to suppose. It suffered from the fact that zoologists who had written about it invariably had observed it only during the daytime, when it was sleeping. At night, he said, it really is quite active and moves about in the trees in its queer upside-down fashion with surprising agility.

"Why don't you catch it, Daddy?" Sandra suggested. "And we can take it home and put it in our zoo."

Sasha chuckled.

Little Dora was craning her neck, continuing to stare up through the luxuriant foliage at the sleeping animal. With a deep sigh she turned her big blue eyes on her father.

"Daddy, catch it!" she seconded hopefully.

"We don't have a cage to put it in if I did catch it," Sasha explained patiently with a smile at both girls. "How would we carry it?"

That *was* a poser, they reluctantly admitted.

Then Sasha explained that we had once had a pet sloth he had caught near our former home on the Descalvados Estancia, but that the animal had soon died. He said that maybe in the spring he and Lauro would catch another one, a young one. He asked Dora if she would like to have a baby sloth as a pet.

A big smile lighted the little girl's face. "Oh yes!" she breathed.

Sasha said it was easy to catch a young sloth because it hung to its mother's back—like the baby opossums we had passed a little

244

while ago—until it grew up sufficiently to shift for itself. But each mother sloth had only one baby a year, he added.

Then he cleared his throat and said he thought we had better be getting on. He tightened his reins.

But Sandra, who was still staring up into the tree, protested.

"Daddy," she said dubiously, "I think it's dead!"

"You do?" Sasha smiled.

He stood up in his stirrups to break off a small branch from the tree and quickly stripped off the leaves. Then he flung it upward. It thwacked dully against the furry flank of the suspended, sleeping animal, causing it to swing gently, like a pendulum, from the limb. As the stick fell to the ground our eyes were on the sloth. For almost a minute there was no slightest hint of motion other than that lifeless, slow swinging. And then, with a deliberation that made a slow-motion movie seem lightning-fast, the sloth slowly began to stir. It lifted one forepaw from the limb from which it was suspended and with extreme sluggishness moved it a few inches forward. I thought it had fallen asleep again, but after some moments it very slowly moved another leg, rested again, and then continued. After several long minutes it finally arrived at a position only two feet farther along on that same limb, where thicker foliage almost entirely screened it from sight. There it stopped and, presumably, fell fast asleep again.

Sasha looked at Sandra and grinned.

"Do you believe me now, Sandra?" he asked. "That it's alive?"

"Well," Sandra replied defensively, "it's not very much alive!"

Sasha laughed. Then he turned and caught me in the middle of a yawn.

"Excuse me, please!" I smiled. "But if I watched that animal any longer, I'd fall asleep myself!"

About an hour later we came to another small stream flowing out of the thick jungle, and we rode along its bank, which was rather thinly grown up with wild fig, paratudo, and rough-leaved lixeira trees for several miles. It was here that Dora was badly frightened by an iguana.

We were riding single file—Sasha led, the two girls followed, and I brought up the rear. Sasha and Sandra already had ridden past the spot without noticing anything unusual. Then Dora came along on her docile little pony, her short little legs sticking out awkwardly, as usual, and her straight blond head turning from left to right as she tried hard not to miss seeing everything. Suddenly she shrieked in such a frightened manner I thought she was going to fall from her horse.

"Oh, Mommy!" she gasped, staring with fear-hypnotized eyes into the leafy wild fig tree at her left. "Mommy—look!"

I drew up beside her quickly and put a restraining hand on her pony's withers; then I gazed at where she was pointing.

Fortunately I'd seen an iguana before.

As it stared back at me, unafraid, the five-foot-long big green lizard, with its upright comb of pointed teeth extending along its back from its neck to the tip of its tail, looked exactly like a small dragon—or a midget prehistoric dinosaur. Its cold eyes gazed at us unblinkingly for a moment from its odd-shaped head, with its large pouch of loose skin at the throat. Then it abruptly turned and moved with surprising speed a few feet along the tree limb.

"He won't hurt you, baby!" I told Dora soothingly. "He's perfectly harmless."

Dora tore her alarmed eyes from the hideous creature and looked dubiously at me; then she again stared fearfully at the iguana, which was once more watching us.

Sasha and Sandra were both beside us by now. Sasha studied the iguana with the professional eye of a collector, commenting on what a fine large specimen it was. And he supplemented what I had told Dora about its harmlessness by explaining that it lived solely on leaves and fruit and insects.

"And Dora was scared of it!" Sandra said scornfully.

Dora's face crumpled up as if she were about to cry.

"Now, Sandra," I said severely, "I want you to stop that!"

Sandra stared back at me, then tossed her head defiantly, wheeled her horse about, and resumed the trail.

I took little Dora onto my own horse, and Sasha put a lead rope on her pony.

"I hope it's not much longer, Sasha," I said anxiously. As he met my eyes I looked meaningfully down at the little tousle-headed figure on the saddle before me. "We're getting pretty tired!"

It was midafternoon and still extremely hot when we finally

246

sighted our objective—the ranch house of Jorge Gomez. It was situated on a slight rise in the flat largo, before a straggling growth of trees that testified to the presence of a small stream in the depression behind it.

The ranch house and outbuildings looked run-down and completely desolate in the harsh, glaring sunlight. The low one-story house had mud walls, and its small secretive windows were barren of glass. There were no shade trees close enough to hide its naked ugliness, and the yard around it was hard-packed red clay without a blade of grass. One would never guess from Senhor Gomez's home that he owned thousands of acres of land. As with most of the smaller ranchers, all of his profits went into buying more cattle; his own living conditions were unimportant.

Despite the bleak, abandoned appearance of the establishment, as we rode nearer we could see it was far from deserted. Several vaqueiros were lounging about in the yard, and off to one side more were sprawled in the shade of the trees. A small flock of chickens was scratching industriously in the dust, and a few mangy curs wandered around, sniffing, or lay panting in the shadow of the house. A long wooden trestle table was set out in the yard, covered with half-empty platters of food and dirty dishes. And at one end three soldiers in the olive-green uniform of the Army of Brazil sat around a jug of what was undoubtedly cachaça, smoking cigars and playing cards.

A couple of dogs began barking noisily as we approached.

"O de casa!" Sasha shouted the customary greeting somewhat belatedly, but in a lusty voice.

The soldiers looked up with interest, the dogs raced forward, and a middle-aged, swarthy man came around the house, shouting heartily:

"Greetings, *meus amigos*. . . . Approach!"

As we reined up in the yard our host strode forward and shook Sasha's hand with great enthusiasm. He was a fat, baldish, jovial-looking man with a bristling black mustache and snapping black eyes. He was, of course, a mestizo, but despite his dark complexion he showed little trace of Negro blood and was probably mainly Portuguese. Sasha had told me he had been born a poor caboclo and had attained his present holdings through sheer hard work.

"Ah—Senhor Siemel!" he was saying expansively. "At first I did not know it was you, mi amigo. It has been many years since our paths have crossed! But again I say welcome, then! It is good to have guests any day, but especially on a feast day. And it is most good to have an old friend, não?"

We dismounted, and Sasha smiled and replied in kind; he introduced Senhor Gomez to me and presented the children.

While the two men were exchanging compliments I looked around more closely. We had expected, of course, that our host would be celebrating the Third of May—*O Tres de Maio*—the anniversary of the discovery of Brazil and a national holiday. This explained the number of men lounging idly about, the heavily laden dinner table, and the prominently displayed jugs of cachaça.

O Tres de Maio was the reason we hadn't taken Lauro or Floridad along with us, for all of our native helpers were celebrating it together; Sasha always let them make a big thing of their national holidays. He had provided cachaça for the men, piquy for the women, and candy from Porto Esperança for the children. And he had even let them have the use of our new phonograph and entire stock of Brazilian records.

Senhor Gomez was addressing me:

"The senhora and the little ones must be weary—and hungry as well! And we have plenty of food. So you will all have a big dinner at once, não?" He turned and bellowed in the direction of the house, "Maria! Maria, you fat, lazy good-for-nothing! Bring plates for our guests!" He turned back to Sasha and grinned. "Maria is my estimable wife. She is a fine mulher, but women must be kept in their place!"

It was true that there was plenty of food on the table, huge roasts and platters of cassava cakes, beans and rice, stews, and fruits—but everything was black with flies. I explained hastily that we had already eaten.

Dora and Sandra, who had been unnaturally silent all this while, looked ready to protest, for they were always hungry, and I wondered how I was going to get out of this awkward situation. Fortunately Sasha came to my rescue. He turned to Senhor Gomez and asked about the captive Yanayguas, mentioning how particu-

248

larly anxious we were to see them. From the presence of the soldiers, he assumed they were still on the ranch?

"Oh yes, the Yanayguas!" Senhor Gomez finally gasped. At the first mention of the Indians he had begun chuckling delightedly, laughing so hard his eyes became mere slits in his broad face, continuing until he was positively roaring with guffaws and choking for breath. "The Yanayguas!" he repeated, going off into another series of strangling chuckles. "Ah, wait until you see them, Senhor Siemel! Just wait!"

I wondered whether he hadn't had too much cachaça, for surely no Indians could be that funny.

Finally our host managed to restrain himself and his mirth, then wiped his streaming eyes on his sleeve and said to Sasha:

"Yes, mi amigo, you shall see them soon. And you, too, will laugh, believe me! But first, if you are sure you will not have dinner—não? ah, too bad!—you at least will have cachaça with me, and your wife will have maté with my daughters and Maria, here. I insist!"

Maria had come out and was waiting silently to one side. She was a plump, tired-looking woman with a mole on her chin and large, soft eyes; she had a timid, hesitant manner, and she stood rather nervously smoothing her shapeless calico dress.

When her husband thus finally noticed her she smiled shyly and echoed his invitation in a low voice. At a curt nod from him she began leading Sandra and Dora and me in the direction of the house. Out of the tail of my eye I noticed Sasha and Senhor Gomez sitting down at the trestle table with the soldiers, and Senhor Gomez reaching for the cachaça.

Then we were inside and being seated at a crude wooden table. Maria presented her daughters—three large, plump, rather sweet-looking girls who were exact replicas of their mother except that they had no moles and naturally were younger—and they began exclaiming over Dora and Sandra and bustling about, preparing fresh maté. I observed that away from the restraining presence of her husband Maria became extremely voluble.

I had expected it would be a relief to get out of the blazing sunlight, but it proved to be almost hotter indoors. The air was stifling, for the small high windows admitted no breeze—and little light. It was too dark to see the far corners distinctly, but I could tell the room was very meagerly furnished.

"Mother, will we have ice cream?" Dora squirmed uneasily on her wooden stool.

I smiled at her. "I'm afraid not, Dora. But we'll probably have something else."

"Of course we won't have ice cream," Sandra said loftily. "Just because we have an icebox now, you think everybody has!"

"Oh—I did *so* hope we would have ice cream," Dora said in a small, wistful voice. "I'm *so* hot and thirsty!"

On his last trip to Porto Esperança, Sasha had picked up a kerosene refrigerator which we had had shipped from Rio. And ever since—after years of living without refrigeration—we had been on an ice-cream binge. Making it involved additional arduous milking of our longhorn cows on the part of Lauro and Rosando, but Sandra and Dora had never tasted ice cream before, and after their first incredulous delight they demanded it daily. And I must admit that Sasha and I were just like kids about it ourselves, and equally gluttonous.

I smoothed Dora's hair back from her face. "Be patient for a little while, dear," I said gently, "and then we'll all have some maté."

"You mean—you mean Sandra and I can have it too?" Dora's eyes sparkled, and she sat up very straight. "Just like grownups?"

"Yes, dear. I don't imagine anyone drinks milk around here."

Senhora Gomez set a dish of cassava cakes on the well-scrubbed table top, then poured scalding water over the maté leaves in the large family gourd and politely offered it to me.

I waited a minute for it to cool and then handed it to Dora—rather reluctantly, for I hated to think of her drinking from the family's sole silver straw—but there was no help for it.

She raised it to her lips and gingerly took a sip of the steaming drink. Then she closed her eyes tightly and made a dreadful face.

"You don't have to drink any more, Dora, if you don't like it," I said hurriedly.

"But I *want* to drink—more," Dora spluttered. She added valiantly, "It's very good. I—I like it."

250

Then she closed her eyes again and began swallowing the unsweetened, rather bitter stuff as rapidly as possible.

Finally she had had enough and passed it on to Sandra. And Sandra, too, looked as though she could scarcely bear the unfamiliar taste but insisted on drinking a great deal, nonetheless—they had never been permitted to drink maté before, so this was a "special treat," no matter how unpleasant.

Then I had some and passed the gourd on to Maria and her daughters, and we all began munching on cassava cakes.

The three Gomez girls were bashful at first—as their mother explained, they almost never had a chance to talk to strangers; few women ever called at the ranch, and they were forbidden to talk to men—but gradually they became more at ease. They seemed quite taken with Dora and Sandra and started asking them questions about our "foreign" way of life. As I was interested in hearing about their own life on this isolated ranch, we soon were having a regular hen session.

In the midst of it Senhor Gomez strode in, followed by Sasha—and there was a dead silence.

"Have my women been treating you well, Senhora Siemel?" our host roared jovially. "If not, I shall certainly beat them!"

I hastened to assure him that we had been treated in a most excellent manner and to thank him for their hospitality.

He beamed and went on: "Then, if the senhora has finished with her maté, we will proceed to the Indian stockade. Are you ready, senhora?"

I replied that I was quite ready and stood up. We left our children behind with Maria and her children, and as I followed Sasha and Senhor Gomez I thought of what Sasha previously had told me about the Yanayguas.

The Yanayguas, I knew, were one of the most savage tribes of Indians in the Mato Grosso jungle. They originally had lived deep in the Chaco but had been driven out during the long bloody war over that territory between Brazil and Paraguay three quarters of a century earlier. Now they pursued their nomadic hunting existence over a large area of jungle and swamp in eastern Bolivia and the southern part of Brazil's Mato Grosso. They were much feared for their murderous raids on the isolated settlers in that huge region, and horrible tales were told of the way in which they first tortured their hapless victims before putting them to death.

The Yanayguas, Sasha had told me, were the most primitive of the Mato Grosso jungle tribes. They hadn't even attained a Stone Age level; as weapons they used only clubs and a crude type of bow and arrow. They did no planting, living on roots which they grubbed out with their hands and on what animals and birds they could kill with their clumsy weapons. They made no attempt to cook their meat, but ate it raw.

I was thinking of these things and imagining the scene we were about to see, when we arrived at the makeshift prison.

A short distance away, in the shallow depression between the outbuildings and the small stream which flowed behind Senhor Gomez's place was a cattle stockade about fifty yards square. Almost a dozen of Senhor Gomez's vaqueiros and at least that many soldiers, some with rifles, were standing in various lounging attitudes before it, smoking cigarettes; a few were sprawled lazily on the ground or squatting on their haunches. One of the vaqueiros was tipping a large earthen jug to his lips. Most of them were staring, with varying degrees of boredom or interest, at the prisoners within the stockade. At the sound of Senhor Gomez's voice they turned and stared curiously at us.

Senhor Gomez insisted on taking us right up to the edge of the stockade, which was built of thick upright posts, closely spaced, and had considerably obstructed my view.

Our host shouted arrogantly, and his vaqueiros and the lounging soldiers made way for us at the stockade fence. At Sasha's urging I stepped close beside him to peer between the stockade posts set a few inches apart.

About thirty Indians, both men and women, as well as two or three children, were standing idly about inside the stockade or squatting on the ground; a few were chewing on big ruddy hunks of raw meat. All were silent and looked overwhelmingly bored as they lolled about, apparently totally oblivious of their audience. At first I had a slight feeling of disappointment, for they didn't look much different from the Bororos with whom Sasha and I had become so well acquainted, though they were not nearly as impressive physically as the Bororos—being shorter and squattier, as

252

well as dirtier and more unkempt. But their bodies were all painted with the same red urucú paint the Bororos used, and their greasy black hair was cut in the same long Dutch-boy bob.

I noticed that none wore the slightest shred of clothing—not even *bas* or the tiny aprons with which the Bororo men and women, respectively, made their slight concession to modesty.

Sasha called my attention to the Yanayguas' hands, telling me to notice how much they resembled claws. He said he had observed that characteristic during previous contacts with members of the tribe—their fingernails invariably were very thick and long and curved like the claws of an animal, and the ends of their fingers were thickly callused.

I peered through the stockade and observed with some surprise that none of the Indians seemed to close their hands, which remained, when idle, half opened and clutching—exactly like a claw.

"That," Sasha explained, "undoubtedly is the result of their using their hands principally for grubbing for roots!"

As we observed them I remembered one story in particular which Sasha had told about a German cattle dealer and his son who had been attacked by a small band of Yanayguas while proceeding by oxcart into this territory to buy cattle from the isolated small ranchers. They had gouged the father's eyes out while he was still alive and then finally killed him and horribly tortured and killed the oxen while the son was forced to watch. They had been about to begin on him when he had managed to break loose, regain his horse, and escape.

The Bolivian authorities, I had heard, were ruthless in their treatment of the Yanayguas, and whenever their military sent a punitive expedition after a band as the result of a massacre, they maintained a policy of "bringing back no prisoners." The Brazilian military, however, pursued exactly the opposite policy, much to the disgust of most of the ranchers and hunters in the Mato Grosso. For they were forbidden to kill an Indian *even if attacked,* under an explicit, long-standing order from Brazil's Director of the Commission for the Protection of Indians, General Candido Mariano da Silva Rondon, who, himself, was of largely Indian ancestry. That was why, Sasha had explained, this small band of Yanayguas was being held in Senhor Gomez's stockade. A detachment of soldiers from the garrison at Corumbá had captured them after they had wiped out a hunting party in the vicinity; they were being held temporarily on Senhor Gomez's ranch until the commander received orders from Corumbá on what to do with them.

After several more minutes of observing them we returned to the ranch house. We had dinner and stayed overnight, and the next morning immediately after breakfast we set out for home again. Senhor Gomez was effusively polite when he bade us good-by, and his wife, smiling with pathetic eagerness, insisted that we come again soon.

In August of that year there was the episode of Servino Jacques.

Servino was as colorful a character as ever came out of the North American Old Wild West. He was the leader of a band of outlaws who, for years, had regularly robbed the few scattered ranchers around the Miranda Pantanal. And he was reputed to have personally killed more than sixty men.

Servino's reputation, which Sasha and I had learned shortly after moving to the Miranda Estancia, painted him as a sort of jungle Robin Hood who robbed the rich and gave to the poor, and who was ever the polite and gallant gentleman, especially with the senhoritas. And the truth, I guess, was not far from this, for Sasha told me Servino frequently made gifts to poor caboclos who were in need, and his treatment of women always was unfailingly polite. It was said he had once shot a follower just to emphasize his order that there was to be no mistreatment of women by his band.

However, Servino would have objected to the use of the word "rob" to describe his operations, for he shrank from anything so crude as a holdup. His method was to wait until some rancher had just sold a herd of cattle. Then he galloped up to the ranch house with his heavily armed henchmen. While his small army dismounted, politely turned their backs, and pretended a sudden absorption in the rancher's flower beds, let us say, Servino courteously knocked on the door. When the rancher appeared the bandit chief apologetically explained that he was suffering, unfortunately, from "a temporary financial embarrassment."

"A little loan, senhor, would be much appreciated—if you would be so kind," was his customary suave way of putting it.

Each time, Sasha said, the amount Servino suggested would, by some strange coincidence, be just slightly under the amount the rancher had received for his cattle.

Ranchers who put up any argument found out, however, that Servino could be just as tough as he had been urbane, and occasionally there were killings during his polite loan negotiations. Nor did Servino hesitate to shanghai ranch hands to replace casualties in his band.

Naturally, the cattlemen about the Miranda Pantanal long had rankled under Servino's continual "borrowing." Pleas to the government had resulted in the sending out, several times, of detachments of soldiers to wipe out the bandits. But Servino, with his intimate knowledge of the jungle, each time led the town-bred soldiers in a series of feints deeper and deeper into the swamp, until they became hopelessly mired down. Then he turned and slaughtered them. The military soon gave up.

So Servino became more and more legendary. . . .

It was a hot spring day, and the jungle was, of course, beautiful with the rioting purples of piuvas, the yellow of paratudos, the greenish-white blossoms of wild figs, and the gaudy colors of the rusty-orange tiger lilies and smaller ground flowers. As at all times of the year, the brightest splashes of color were provided by the parrots and parakeets, squawking and darting through the foliage in flashes of vivid reds and yellows, greens and blues. The sun beat down from the sky with blast-furnace heat, although the air was hazy from burning grass fires somewhere on the far reaches of the Miranda Estancia. This was August, the season when the ranchers burn off the tall, dried-up dead grass to expose the fresh green grass and provide easier grazing for their cattle.

Sasha had been away for several days on one of his tiger-hunting expeditions; he had taken only Lauro with him so Rosando could stay behind to look after the livestock and zoo animals and do whatever other chores might be necessary. But today I was alone with the women and children, for Rosando had ridden over to the Miranda ranch house to pick up some supplies for Sasha.

We were all on the riverbank. I was supervising Cenaria and Antonia in the making of soap, and we had just dissolved a quantity of caustic soda in water and had added the beef fat. They were standing beside the huge kettle, which was suspended over an open fire, and were taking turns stirring with large wooden paddles, being careful not to let any of the scalding yellowish-white stuff splatter onto their arms or in their eyes.

Floridad was sitting under a tree nearby, keeping an eye on my daughters and at the same time rather indifferently mending some of their old overalls and shorts. Sandra and Dora were romping about with Cenaria's and Antonia's children.

"Oh, look! See what I found!"

Dora had stopped suddenly in the midst of a game of tag and was squatting with her hands on her knees, peering intently at the ground.

As the other children crowded around I heard excited cries of *"Olha!* Oh, look! Dora has found a lizard!"

"Isn't it pretty!" Denizia said admiringly. "All green like the grass."

"That's so it can hide," Florenzia, who was older, explained importantly. "If we put it in the mud it would turn mud color!"

"Oh, it would not!"

"Sim, it would so!"

"Well, let's try it," Sandra suggested practically. "Let's catch it before it gets away!"

I watched, rather amused, as the children all dropped to the ground, laughing and shouting and bumping into each other as they made repeated snatches at the little lizard, which frantically darted this way and that. Suddenly Carlotta stood up triumphantly, cupping it in both hands. The other children clustered around, jockeying for position and demanding to be allowed to hold it. But Carlotta was adamant. *She* had caught it, so it was her lizard and no one else could touch it.

"Selfish thing!" Sandra said finally, turning away in disgust. "I'm never going to play with you any more, Carlotta!"

She was stalking away, when Dora, who had stood silently on the edge of the group until now, said in a pleading voice:

"Oh, Carlotta, can't I hold it for a little while, please? Because I did see it first."

"That's right, Carlotta!" Sandra spun around and hurried back.

"Dora saw it first, and so it's her lizard. You give my sister her lizard right now!"

"Não!" Carlotta shook her head stubbornly. "I caught it and it's mine!"

Dora had a very disappointed look on her face; I thought she was going to cry. "You can have it, Carlotta," she said, swallowing hard. "I didn't want to keep it. I just thought maybe I could look at it for a minute."

"You give my sister her lizard!" Sandra repeated belligerently. She put her arm around her little sister's shoulder and scowled at Carlotta.

"I won't!"

"Yes, you will!" Sandra advanced with a grim look on her small face.

I decided it was high time to interfere. "Sandra and Dora," I called out, more sharply than I had intended, "come here this minute!"

"But, Motherrr," Sandra wailed indignantly, "Carlotta stole Dora's own lizard, and I've got to make her——"

"Come here, dears," I said firmly, but with a smile to show I wasn't angry at them. "After all, Carlotta did catch the lizard all by herself. And if she isn't going to be nice enough to let you look at it, we'll find something else for you to play with."

Dora started toward me obediently, but Sandra hesitated, looking back at the smugly smiling Carlotta with frustrated rage.

"Carlotta," she said furiously, "you—you bad old—— You just *wait*, Carlotta! We'll get even with you! We'll chop you up in little pieces and throw you in the river for piranha bait!"

Then she started walking toward me reluctantly.

I smiled ruefully to myself, for this was my small daughters' original and favorite idea of revenge. Both Sandra and Dora shocked me at times with their bloodthirsty ideas. I supposed it was inevitable that their jungle upbringing would make them little barbarians, but I sometimes wondered with a shudder how they would fit into civilization. Their favorite amusement, currently, was watching Lauro and Rosando at their weekly job of slaughtering a beef steer, and commenting with a detached, precocious interest on all of the gory details.

Just then Carlotta let out a shriek of horror and threw her lizard violently to the ground. "Oh!" she screamed wildly. "Ugh! Its tail came right off in my hand!"

I didn't doubt this, because I knew that shedding part of its tail was a lizard's method of distracting its enemies.

The children began shouting and babbling and running about, some frightened and trying to get as far away as possible, others interestedly trying to recapture the lizard and see if Carlotta's statement was true.

In the midst of the confusion, while Cenaria repeated, "Senhora, the soap——" and the children continued their treble hullabaloo, a hearty masculine voice shouted suddenly from behind a clump of piuva trees:

"O de casa!"

I turned, startled.

The shout was repeated.

And then, as I automatically replied with the customary "Approach!" three riders galloped into our clearing and, with a great jangle of spurs and silver bridle trim, sharply reined up their lathered, exhausted-looking horses. The horses stamped and snorted; one neighed and reared, then dropped back, pawing the ground.

When the dust had cleared I saw before me three grim-looking vaqueiros who sat their mounts with an indolent grace, although the fine dust that covered them bespoke hours of hard riding. Two were dressed in ordinary vaqueiro fashion with cowhide leggings strapped to their belts; their enormous spurs had outsize roweled rosettes, and they were, of course, barefoot. The third, apparently their leader, was dressed similarly, but his huge black sombrero was excessively decorated with silver, his heavy red shirt looked tailor-made, he had a poncho slung dramatically over one shoulder, and, rather to my surprise, for this is unusual in the Mato Grosso, he wore elaborately tooled leather boots.

His eyes passed quickly over Cenaria and Antonia, who were still clutching their wooden spoons and gaping with their mouths open, hesitated momentarily on pretty Floridad, and then settled upon me. He spurred his horse forward a few feet, swept off his sombrero, and bowed gallantly from his saddle—all, I realized with a start, in the best Errol Flynn manner. He was a man in his forties, large and powerfully built, clean-shaven except for a day's growth of beard on his underslung jaw; and, incidentally, he was almost handsome.

When he spoke his hoarse, heavy voice sounded as though he was accustomed to roaring orders to recalcitrant vaqueiros, but he said soberly, with drawing-room politeness:

"Do I address the Senhora Siemel?"

I replied that he did, and for a minute he sat silently studying me—with such piercing black eyes that I felt a little alarmed, wondering what in the world he wanted. I was suddenly aware of how untidy I looked in my rumpled shirt and slacks and then was sharply annoyed at myself.

Evidently our visitor concluded that I met his specifications, whatever they were, for he relaxed slightly and smiled.

"Well, Senhora Siemel, my compliments!" he boomed as he climbed from his saddle. "I am fortunate in finding your establishment so easily. Is Senhor Siemel about?"

I hesitated. I was reluctant to admit that he wasn't, for despite the stranger's politeness there was something swaggering and aggressive and ruthless about him, and his air of command suggested that I, not he, was the trespasser. I felt, understandably, very uneasy, and I wished that Rosando at least were here.

"No," I said curtly. "I am alone with my women."

"Alas, how unfortunate. I had business with the senhor."

The stranger frowned thoughtfully for a moment at the ground, then looked up abruptly. "Well, senhora, if your husband is not here, I must ask a favor of you!" He paused, then added with a grin, "Do not be alarmed, senhora; I will not take advantage of you in your husband's absence. Não, I will drive as fair a bargain with you as I would with him. I have a reputation for not taking advantage of women. . . ."

He went on to explain that he had heard of Sasha's expertness in repairing guns and that he had hoped Sasha could fix the broken trigger springs in his two Smith & Wesson revolvers but that, since it was impossible for him to wait for Sasha's return, he would now exchange them for one of our guns which was in good working order.

He produced the six-shooters. As I had by now a fair knowledge of firearms and could see these were high-priced guns and in reasonably good condition, I agreed to the trade.

He had one further request, the stranger explained with an easy smile. He was on his way upriver with his vaqueiros to examine some land he had just purchased; the jungle was becoming increasingly thick and he had decided he could make much better time by dugout. Would I favor him with the loan of a dugout? He and his men would leave their horses as security.

"That," he concluded, "is an excellent bargain, for the senhora will be getting three fine horses—from which I hate to part." He glanced regretfully over his shoulder at the animals.

"Yes, senhor," I agreed, "it is indeed an excellent bargain." Then I added with a faint smile, for I had regained my composure and was rather relieved he was demanding no more, "And it is also a necessity, for it is impossible to put three men and three horses in one dugout, não?"

He looked at me sharply, then grinned. "The senhora is indeed astute!"

He turned abruptly and ordered his men to dismount and follow.

"And now," he said, smiling, "if the senhora will be so kind as to direct my men to the dugout and bring out her gun, we will be off and annoy her no longer." He glanced at the sun, which would be setting in another hour. "It grows late, and we have much distance to make upriver."

I led the way toward the houseboat, and the three men followed. Dora and Sandra trotted beside them. Floridad, with Cenaria and Antonia and their children, trailed a little distance in the rear. All had remained silent during the exchange between me and my guest. Dora and Sandra looked greatly pleased with him, I thought; the women looked equally impressed, but a little timid and nervous; and their children seemed merely curious and shy.

"You were saying, senhor," I murmured, as though I were only making idle conversation, "that you are traveling upriver?"

"Sim, to inspect some new holdings of mine," he replied, brushing off the question impatiently.

"Then," I said somewhat unwisely, "you have decided to settle down and become a rancher—Senhor Servino Jacques?"

Servino—I had been sure for some time that it was he—stopped dead in his tracks; his black eyes bored into me, and I noticed with a certain alarm that both of his men had automatically clapped their hands to their holsters and were eying me hostilely.

For a minute there was a dreadful silence, then Servino began roaring with laughter.

"Senhora," he said heartily, sounding hugely pleased, "you are even more astute than I thought!" He gave me an admiring look. "I wish that Senhor Siemel were here; I would like to congratulate him on his choice of a wife!"

Cenaria let out a piercing shriek.

"Servino Jacques it is!" she exclaimed with horror. "Oh, Mother of God, the *bandido* and his men! Now we will all be ravished!"

She glanced wildly about, rolling her eyes. Antonia looked equally terrified but was apparently tongue-tied with fright; she grabbed Floridad by the arm and started dragging her away. Taking their cue from their mothers, the children began screaming and running off in all directions. Soon no one remained near the houseboat with the men but Sandra and Dora and myself. And Sandra and Dora were beginning to look alarmed too.

Servino was scowling blackly, for I knew he prided himself on his chivalry to women; and I myself felt embarrassed and highly provoked at Cenaria's silly, hysterical reaction. If she had wanted to leave, she had been perfectly free to do so quietly; instead she had insulted the highly touchy Servino and left me in a very awkward situation as well.

"Senhor Jacques," I said hastily with as much self-possession as I could muster, "while your men are readying the dugout, would you do me the honor of taking maté with me and my children in the houseboat?"

Inside, while I prepared the drink for Servino and myself, and poured glasses of milk for Dora and Sandra, the girls suddenly found their tongues and began plying our guest with questions: Was he really a bandit, like Robin Hood? Did he have any little boys and girls of his own? Did he kill tigers, like Daddy? How did it feel to be a bandit? Why was he a bandit?

Servino obligingly supplied them with whatever information they demanded. He said he had no children, but he certainly had a way

with mine. Dora and Sandra were enchanted and hung on his
every word, and I could see any minute they were going to decide
to grow up into bandits themselves.

When the steaming gourd was ready I sat down with the three
of them in the living room. The children drank their milk, still
staring with wide eyes at Servino over the rims of their glasses,
and I sipped maté with my bandit guest, politely discussing cattle
ranching in the Mato Grosso and Sasha's tiger-hunting expeditions,
avoiding any mention of outlaw raids. We all munched the little
cakes I had made that morning. And I thought, with a sense of
shock, that I had never had "afternoon tea" under odder circumstances.

Finally Servino stood up and said regretfully that it was time
he was on his way. He thanked me courteously for my hospitality
and added after a slight pause, "Senhora Siemel, it is not only
for the refreshments I thank you. It is not often a gracious lady
receives one with a reputation such as mine." He frowned a
moment, then smiled at Sandra and Dora, who were begging him
not to leave just yet. "You have two fine little daughters, senhora;
they would do well to grow up like their mother!"

I hastily got out a gun to exchange for Servino's revolvers, and
he strode rapidly outside and climbed into the dugout beside his
men—who, at his instructions, had already driven their horses into
our stockade—and with a shout of farewell and a final grin for
Sandra and Dora, he gave the command to shove off.

We stood watching until they were out of sight around the bend.
Just as they were blotted out by the wall of jungle Floridad
appeared suddenly around a corner of the houseboat deck.

"Senhora," she said seriously, "I thought someone should stay
within hearing in case you needed us. So I came back and hid
nearby."

I was a little surprised. "Why, thank you, Floridad," I said,
feeling rather touched.

Then Cenaria and Antonia came walking toward us down the
bank, looking shame-faced and ill at ease.

"Senhora," Cenaria began, wringing her hands, "I am sorry
we left you alone with that monster. But, senhora, we were praying
for you all the while! Senhora, believe me, we are——"

(*Above*) *River Gypsy* at Barranco Vermelho and
(*below*) Christmas aboard the *River Gypsy*.

"Never mind, Cenaria, let it go," I interrupted wearily. My indignation at their behavior had worn off by now. "Do you think we can still salvage that soap?"

Just at sundown and barely half an hour after Servino had left we had more unexpected visitors. Four soldiers rode up while we were still working on the riverbank and asked whether we had seen any strange men about. I sent Cenaria and Antonia off to their huts with their children, and Dora and Sandra into the houseboat with Floridad.

The sergeant in command explained that he didn't want to alarm me, but Servino Jacques had been seen heading this way. A large detachment of soldiers had been sent out from Corumbá to capture Servino and his men, and after a skirmish with the military Servino's band had broken up into twos and threes and dispersed into the marsh. This, of course, explained why our guest had been in such haste to go farther upriver.

I acted properly shocked at the news and said that three men had indeed been here and left—but I'm afraid I said they were heading down-river. . . .

When Sasha returned the next day and I told him of Servino's visit and our transactions, and Cenaria's fright, and our tea party, he at first looked grave. But the more he thought about it, the more amused he became. He congratulated me on my presence of mind—though I thought he greatly overrated it—and when I protested that Servino had behaved very gallantly and had been a perfect gentleman, Sasha shot me a quizzical look and then re-marked with a twinkle in his eye:

"Servino's reputation for having a way with the ladies evidently hasn't been exaggerated!"

I was about to make some flippant retort when there came an interruption which shoved Servino out of our minds for some time.

We had been standing on the riverbank, where Sasha had been showing me the two tiger skins he had brought back from his hunt. Dora was with us, but Sandra had wandered off to the houseboat.

Suddenly she appeared on deck and called to us, excitedly:

"Mother! Daddy! The war's over!"

"What?" Sasha demanded incredulously.

"It's really over, all right," Sandra confirmed importantly. "Japan just sur-ren-dered!"

"Sandra, are you sure you know what you're talking about?" I asked skeptically.

"Of course!" Sandra sounded highly indignant. "The radio just now said so!"

Sasha and I, with Dora at our heels, rushed onto the houseboat and over to the radio from which issued, in a frenzied blur of static, the words, *"Hoje, em Washington, o Presidente Truman . . ."*

It had stopped pouring shortly before dawn, for when I awoke and hurried to the window rain water was still dripping desultorily from the thatched eaves of the houseboat, falling with a gentle, monotonous plashing into the river. The sun, a disk of blinding red fire, already was rimming the silhouetted jungle at the horizon, and bright sunlight danced over the water, giving promise of a day even more unbearably hot than those that had preceded it. After two weeks of continuous rains the sky was gratifyingly blue, the air was fresh and clean-smelling, and the heavy, green foliage glittered wetly in the early light. I stood for several minutes drinking it all in, especially appreciating the fact that the rains had stopped on this particular day.

Then, even as I watched, the sun's rays grew hotter and the entire rain-soaked jungle began steaming—and soon a dense white vapor hung over it, rising from the more thickly forested sections like columns of smoke, and a thin white mist started trickling out over the river and eddying around us.

It was Christmas Day.

Sasha was still asleep in his bunk, and so were the girls and Floridad in their bedroom. I began dressing leisurely.

This would be Sandra's and Dora's first Christmas celebration alone with us; we had all spent the three previous Christmases as Raul Nesheim's house guests at the Miranda Estancia, and the children were too young to remember anything before that. Consequently, this year Sasha and I had spent weeks planning for the holiday, improvising ways to make it a big day for our little daughters and as much like our own childhood Christmases as possible.

Sasha had made toys, I had made dolls and new dresses on my faithful sewing machine, and each night, of course, I had told Sandra and Dora bedtime stories of Santa Claus. It was easy enough to give Santa marsh deer instead of reindeer, but beyond that I found jungle-izing the story difficult, for when I robbed Santa of his red-tasseled stocking cap and fur-trimmed robes and put him in a tropic-weight costume I felt that he definitely lost glamour—and face.

But, nonetheless, the girls had been almost beside themselves with excitement.

And now that the long-anticipated day had arrived, even the sun was co-operating: Christmas wouldn't be just another dark, depressing rainy day! I began humming under my breath as I fastened my dress.

Thank heaven it wouldn't be another rainy day! During the past two weeks we had been driven almost frantic trying to keep Dora and Sandra amused indoors. They had been good for just about two days—and then, as usual, they had grown restless at their enforced confinement and bored with their old toys. "Helping" me with my housework had lost its novelty, and they had started spending all their time alternately demanding to be allowed to play outside in the mud and quarreling with each other.

As a distraction we had let them bring the two monkeys indoors, and the monkeys had made a shambles of the place, pulling books out of the bookcase and tearing the pages, breaking a large pottery vase, and strewing the contents of my sewing basket all over the living room. Once I had taken the girls to Lauro's hut to play with his children and had returned late in the afternoon to find them wide-eyed and frightened, for Cenaria had been telling them dreadful stories of Kuka, the jungle bogeyman. At another time Sasha had given Sandra a two-foot hunting horn made from the horn of a bull and had taught her to blow it, which was quite difficult, for it involved a special technique and plenty of wind, and she had gone around inside the houseboat from morning until night blowing great earsplitting blasts, until she could do it much better and louder than Sasha. Then, desperate for some quiet game, we had persuaded the children to concentrate on tiddlywinks, which they played with alligator teeth.

"Wake up, Dora! Wake up!" Sandra's excited voice sounded shrilly in the bedroom. She went on: "Wake up, you little dope! It's Christmas!"

"Christmas?" Dora sounded half drugged with sleep, but in a moment she was wide awake. *Christmas!* Oh, Sandra, wait for me!"

"Well—hurry up, then!"

Sasha sat up in his bunk and swung his feet to the floor, yawning and grinning at me. "I take it, it's Christmas."

Bare feet pattered across the bedroom, and Dora and Sandra stood in the doorway. They stopped short and stared across the living room with eyes like saucers.

"Oh, Sandra," Dora breathed finally, "it's—it's a Christmas tree!"

"It is! It really is!" Sandra temporarily forgot the dignity of being an older sister and nearly five years old and began jumping up and down excitedly. "Did Santa Claus bring it? Did he, Mother?"

Sasha and I looked at each other with pleased grins, for it was very heart-warming to have our labors rewarded with such an enthusiastic reception. I felt a glow of happiness at the children's delight—and at the same time felt a lump in my throat, thinking of this makeshift jungle Christmas contrasted with my own lavish girlhood Christmases in Philadelphia.

"Yes, Santa Claus brought it," I said with a smile. "Merry Christmas, darlings!"

But the little girls hadn't waited for my answer. They had raced across the room and were standing, hand in hand, staring at the tree with shining eyes. They made no move to go nearer; apparently they were too awed to touch anything.

And the little tree really was surprisingly impressive, I thought.

Sasha had spent hours making it in his workshop after the children were safely in bed. He had taken a length of mahogany beam and turned it on his lathe to give it the proper roundness of a tree trunk, and then he had bored a number of holes in it and inserted palm fronds for branches. We had both spent several evenings cutting tinsel icicles out of the tinfoil in which some of our supplies were wrapped and making shiny ornaments from disks

266

cut out of tin cans, which we slashed and fringed with a heavy
scissors and bent into elaborate flowers and pinwheels and stars.
I had spent another evening making small beeswax candles from
wild bees' honeycomb.

What with the glittering tin ornaments and tinfoil icicles half
hiding the palm branches, and the tiny candles glowing brightly
all over—I had hastily lighted them when I heard the children
waking up—the little tree made a very brave showing.

"Well, darlings, aren't you going to open your presents?" I
asked half teasingly as I joined them. "That's what they're there
for!"

"Mother, everything's so pretty," Sandra said slowly. "Can't
we just leave them there for a while?"

"My, what unnatural children I have!" I said, laughing.

But in a moment, of course, the children had changed their
minds and were sitting on the floor, eagerly tearing off wrappings—
wrappings I had carefully saved from gifts Mother had sent us
during the past year. (Mother had mentioned she was sending
Christmas presents for her granddaughters, but these evidently had
been delayed in the mail.) They were ohing and ahing and exclaiming ecstatically over each new find.

Sasha had carved wooden toys—a monkey on a stick, a jack-in-
the-box, and alphabet blocks for Dora; and a Chinese puzzle, a
dollhouse, and miniature furniture for Sandra. I had made both
girls new red checked frocks—and, out of an old bedsheet, large
dolls with brown shell eyes, seed-pod noses, red flannel mouths,
and hair of monkey fur.

Floridad came in from the bedroom at this point, and she also
had gifts for the children—mussel-shell necklaces and bracelets
she had strung. I let Dora and Sandra present Floridad with the
bright red dress I had made her. And, although Sasha and I had
agreed not to exchange gifts, he had had a handsome pair of
Inca-style turquoise-and-silver bracelets made for me by an Indian
craftsman, and I had made a lightweight dressing gown for him.

The children proved to be far too excited to eat breakfast,
and even when we had dinner, several hours later, they could
hardly bear to tear themselves away from their new toys.

Dinner was an unusually elaborate affair, for I had decided

to make it as much like a traditional Christmas dinner as possible. We began with breasts of *arancuão*, or pheasant, and followed that with roast *mutum*, or wild turkey, and rice; but the pièce de résistance was an eighty-pound peccary, roasted whole, served on a specially constructed huge platter and surrounded by browned cassava cakes, complete with a ginipapo, looking like a large, greenish-gray peach, in its mouth! (This sounds like an appalling quantity of meat for only five people, but our eighteen hunting dogs would account for all leftovers.) We had guava-jelly relish and palm hearts. And for those who still had room for dessert, there were great stacks of fruit—ginipapo, cherrylike jaboticaba, huge papaya, *tarumá,* and the quaintly named *água pomba,* or "water of pigeons."

After dinner, understandably, no one felt like doing anything very active—particularly as under the beating, merciless sun the day had grown terrifically hot, and the air was heavy and humid. We sat around in the living room singing "Silent Night" and "Hark, the Herald Angels Sing" and "Adeste Fidelis"—which seemed so incongruous with the steaming green jungle all around us that I felt a sudden, dreadful pang of homesickness—while I provided a jangling, discordant accompaniment on the piano.

Mother finally had shipped my old upright piano from Philadelphia, and Sasha had brought it crated from Porto Esperança just the week before. It was badly out of tune after its long trip (and of course there were no piano tuners in the jungle), but as I was very much out of practice, anyway, that hardly mattered. Everyone on our place marveled at it; no one but Sasha and me ever had seen a piano before. I had spent the past week frantically teaching Sandra and Dora Christmas carols, just so we could sing them today.

When we had run through our limited repertoire and the little girls began looking tired from the unaccustomed excitement but protested indignantly when I suggested a nap, I sat them on my bunk, still tightly clutching their new toys.

I began telling them about Christmas and sleigh rides and holly and mistletoe at my mother's country home in Pennsylvania. And Sasha told of his boyhood Christmases in Latvia, and how he always went ice skating and skiing.

After the girls had made us repeat everything several times, they finally had had enough. While we sat quietly, contentedly, for a few minutes, I stared through the window out at the heat waves shimmering on the river, listening to the drowsy squawking of parrots and parakeets—thinking, once more, how unlike Christmas this was, with the temperature well above one hundred degrees.

Suddenly Dora spoke up, frowning with concentration.

"Mother—what is *snow* like?"

I had gone through this many times before.

"Well," I said glibly, "it's whiter than the sand in your sand pile —and softer than milkweed silk—and stinging cold, something like ice cream. And it falls out of the sky in beautiful flakes—and piles up like frosting on all the trees and bushes—and you make snowballs and snow men out of it. . . ." I was getting nostalgic myself as I pictured it. However, apparently I wasn't satisfying Dora.

"I know all that, Mother," she said eagerly, "but what's it *really* like?"

And for nearly half an hour Sasha and I tried in vain to describe it to her.

CHAPTER 8

IT WAS THE LAST MONTH OF WINTER AND THE DRY SEASON. IN another month, in September, all of the Mato Grosso would be in flower again. And although fall and winter were our pleasantest, least humid seasons, this year I had found myself looking forward unreasonably to the coming of spring. Perhaps it was only because of my increasing pregnancy that the miles upon miles of dried-up grassland seemed so drab and depressing, the sun so merciless in its steady beating down upon us, and the air so lifeless and stifling.

Tonight a slight breeze had sprung up, but it only stirred the thick dust on the riverbank and brought no cooling relief. The houseboat seemed unbearably hot, and although I had gone to bed early, it was a long time before I was able to get to sleep. I lay tossing in my bunk, worrying over trifling domestic problems, wondering why I hadn't heard from Mother for nearly two months, thinking about Dora's bruised knee. Sasha was already asleep, for I could hear him breathing deeply and evenly in his bunk. So were the girls and their new nursemaid, Luiza, who had taken Floridad's place after the latter's marriage, for it was never this quiet when they were awake. It was, in fact, an unnaturally still night, for even the crickets seemed subdued by the heat, and the only sound was an occasional plaintive cry from some distant bird. I decided I would begin packing tomorrow, despite the fact that Sasha and I wouldn't be leaving for Corumbá for another week. It was always a job to go over our clothes and get organized for these "baby" trips to relative civilization.

Finally I must have fallen into a restless sleep, for suddenly there was a feeling of lateness in the air, and I sensed that several hours had passed. It had grown no cooler, but quite a wind had blown up. Its hot breath was billowing the curtains inward, and it rustled with a dry, rasping sound through the palm thatch on the roof.

Something was banging back and forth out on the deck. For a minute I supposed that that was what had awakened me—and then I realized, with an unpleasant, sinking feeling, that it was something entirely different. For my back was aching dully, and I felt an abrupt wrenching pain in my abdomen.

"Sasha," I called quietly so as not to disturb the children, "Sasha—wake up!"

I needn't have bothered lowering my voice, of course, for as soon as we were certain the baby really was coming several weeks early, Sasha awoke Luiza and explained the situation. The two of them got Sandra and Dora out of bed and started dressing them hurriedly so Luiza could take them to one of the native huts and stay with them there.

It would be just as well to have sixteen-year-old Luiza out of the way, for I could see she would be of no help whatsoever; she was already half hysterical with nervousness at this unexpected turn of events, and I could hear her banging drawers and dropping things in the bedroom.

"Is it morning, Daddy? Why is it dark?" Dora repeated her question sleepily, but no one took the time to answer her.

"O Mary Mother of God, where are your socks, Sandra?" Luiza mumbled vaguely.

"Daddy, is Mother sick? Why is she in bed?" Sandra was standing barefoot in the doorway, regarding me with a grown-up frown. She held her shoes in one hand, and her hair was rumpled.

Somehow Sasha had herded the three of them out onto the deck and lowered the gangplank, which was always hauled aboard at night, and had given Luiza, whose teeth were chattering with excitement, explicit instructions to send both Cenaria and Antonia over at once and then to try to get Dora and Sandra to sleep. He had cut short the children's innumerable questions and had started them all off. . . . Finally he and I were alone in the suddenly silent houseboat, and I was again conscious of the wind in the palm fronds above us.

Sasha came over to my bunk and looked down at me with an almost comically alarmed expression. So far he had handled the situation with admirable poise and dispatch, but now that there was momentarily nothing for him to do I could see he was almost as nervous as Luiza.

"Edith, my dear, how do you feel?" he asked after a minute of peering at me.

Until now I had had almost no chance to think about what a fix I was in. But suddenly I realized, full force, all the disadvantages of living so far from a doctor. Sasha, I knew, would try his best to be helpful, but he naturally had had no experience with this sort of thing, and I would have to rely heavily on Cenaria and Antonia. They, of course, had had plenty of experience, but with their defiantly medieval ideas they had little else to recommend them. True, native women frequently had babies completely unattended, and I supposed I should be thankful to have two husky matrons to assist me. But I would have given anything to be in Corumbá with our faithful doctor on call. If things went smoothly, all would doubtless be well—but supposing something should go wrong? Supposing this would be a breech baby or I should start hemorrhaging? What could anyone do? I began to be dreadfully frightened. . . .

I smiled up at Sasha.

"Why, I feel fine, darling. Aren't we lucky Cenaria and Antonia have had so darned many babies! They're probably the best experts at it in the Mato Grosso!"

Sasha's smile looked forced. He began pacing the floor and after a minute asked me again how I felt. When I reassured him once more, he suddenly looked absurdly hopeful.

"Then maybe you're mistaken. Maybe you can wait a while!"

His eyes lit up, and he went on rapidly: "I'll get out the launch and bundle you in, and we'll start right away. . . ."

His voice trailed off.

Another pain began abruptly, and I bit my lip hard.

Sasha ran his hand through his hair. "What's keeping those damned women, anyway?" he said impatiently.

He began striding up and down again in a kind of impotent rage, glancing frantically from me to the door, and finally I could stand it no longer.

"Sasha," I suggested, smiling a little, "why don't you start boiling some water? It's always done in the best circles, in books!"

Sasha looked pathetically grateful at finally having something to do.

"Of course!" he muttered. "Why didn't I think of that? I'll boil gallons and gallons of water. Now, where's a big kettle? Somewhere near the stove, I suppose."

He rushed back through the houseboat, and then I could hear a great clatter of pots and pans on the rear deck. It was quite some time before he returned, and when he did he was grinning with self-satisfaction.

"I've got the top of the stove covered with kettles of water!" he announced triumphantly. "And I have four extra kettles of water on the floor, just in case!" He paused, then asked, as though the thought had just occurred to him: "By the way, what do we use this water for, anyway?"

I began laughing. "Well, I understand it's for sterilizing and for washing things, like your hands, in. But then again, maybe it's just a simple way to keep relatives, such as expectant fathers, busy and out of the way."

Sasha grinned rather sheepishly, then changed the subject.

"A scissors!" he exclaimed abruptly. "We'll have to have a scissors! Now where's that big shears? I know I saw it a few days ago." He strode over to the mahogany cabinet and began opening drawers.

"You're really getting into stride, dear," I teased. "Look in my sewing basket. I think——"

Bare feet pounded suddenly up the gangplank and padded across the deck.

274

"Patrão, patrão!" Cenaria called as she opened the screen door and came in, panting. "Are we in time?"

She was followed closely by Antonia, who was equally breathless. They stood still a moment, blinking in the light, and then their eyes fell upon me and they bustled over to the bed—looking, I thought, like a couple of anxious, fussy, fat hens. And they began cackling at once, which increased the similarity considerably.

"Senhora—senhora, is it very bad?" Cenaria asked with deep concern. Without waiting for my reply she went on rapidly, "Alas that it has to be, but this is what comes of having a husband; but no matter, it is very nice afterward to have a fine baby, não, senhora? That is worth much pain, senhora—não?"

Since this was going to be my third child, I wondered why the sales talk at this late date.

Antonia was clucking sympathetically, over and over, "Oh, the poor senhora! The poor, poor senhora! And her with no extra fat on her bones!"

What that had to do with it, I couldn't quite see; fat or thin, I'd still be having labor pains.

Cenaria ignored Antonia's comments and went on briskly: "Senhora, we delayed not because we were not anxious to come. It was because we stopped to prepare the things which are necessary. The senhora understands?" She gave me a pleading look.

I nodded and said that, on the contrary, I thought they had arrived remarkably fast; but I didn't understand at all what she meant, for she and Antonia both had come empty-handed.

Cenaria grinned broadly with relief, then thrust her hand into her ample bosom, fumbled around, and proudly drew forth an almost indescribable object: a small leather bag to which were attached some dangling seed pods, feathers, and bones. As she held it out for me to see, whatever was inside rattled noisily, and I was aware that the whole thing gave off an extremely offensive odor.

After granting me a minute to admire this contrivance properly, Cenaria squatted and placed it carefully under my bed; then she arose and beamed at me.

"So, senhora, it is done! I was a little worried for fear we would not arrive in time, but now all will be well. The birth charm will draw the pain down under the bed. It is of the most powerful!"

I didn't have quite as much faith as she did in the potency of
the charm, for she had barely stopped speaking when another and
more violent pain wrenched through me, but I knew it was useless
to protest; and from then on I was unpleasantly aware of the
odoriferous little bag beneath me.

"Now," Cenaria said decisively, "it is merely a matter of time!
But we had better see how this thing progresses, não?" She took
hold of the bedsheet that covered me and said firmly, "So, if the
senhor will leave . . ." She turned to Sasha, who stood helplessly
to one side, and added pointedly, "This, senhor, is a matter for
women!"

I felt panicky at the thought of being left alone with them.

"Sasha," I said desperately, "don't you dare go out of this
room!"

I wondered how I could tactfully insist that Cenaria and Antonia
wash their hands before we went any farther, and I decided to
leave that up to Sasha. Any minute he would surely remember his
kettles of boiling water.

"Of course I won't leave you, dear!" Sasha's voice was tender
and reassuring as he came toward the bed. "And the women
aren't going to do anything you don't want them to."

"But, senhor"—Cenaria wasn't going to give up easily—"senhor,
the homen never remains with his *espôsa* when she——"

"That's quite enough, Cenaria!" Sasha said curtly. "I'm staying!
And now you can get some water off the stove and bring it in here,
where I can see you and Antonia scrub your hands to my satisfaction. We're going to start at once having some decent sanitation
around here!"

"Sim, senhor." Cenaria's tone was meek, but as she stalked out
to get the water she was stiff with indignation at this affront to the
proprieties.

Antonia hesitated, uncertain as to whether or not she was expected to follow. She looked a little green at Sasha's displeasure;
she tried to say something, but for a minute no sound would come.
Finally she spoke, addressing me with a pathetic quaver in her
voice.

"Senhora," she gulped, "I am sure Cenaria did not mean anything!"

276

I smiled at her, and then another pain gripped me violently. After it had passed Antonia took courage and said in a low voice:

"Senhora, I, too, have made a charm for you."

"Why, Antonia, how nice!" I said encouragingly, though I hardly cared to see what it was, if it smelled like Cenaria's.

Antonia reached down into her dress and drew forth a small object. I saw, to my relief, that it was only a doll-like figure made of straw.

Antonia turned a rather frightened sideways glance upon Sasha and said: "Have I the senhor's permission? If this amulet is tied around his wife's neck, it will bring the patrão a fine son!"

Sasha nodded with a rather amused look, and Antonia groped further for a piece of string and then attached her creation to me.

While the women were obediently soaping and scrubbing their hands in the almost scalding water for a full ten minutes, as commanded, Sasha wandered to the bookcase and stood scanning the titles. Finally he flipped out one of the books and said with satisfaction, "Ah—*The Expectant Mother!* I knew it was still around somewhere!"

He dropped into a chair and began leafing through the pages.

"You know," he mused, "this might prove very helpful."

He glanced up once to eye me thoughtfully—but at the moment I was feeling quite comfortable, between pains—and, apparently reassured, he left me to the ministrations of the women and lost himself in the text.

Some little time passed. . . .

I was aware of the loud ticking of the clock on the bookcase, the wind rattling through the palm fronds on the eaves, an alligator bellowing in the river, the sound of pages being turned; and then all of this would be blotted out abruptly, and nothing existed for me but the tremendous searing pain.

Each time when the pain receded and I came back to the room I was surprised, and somewhat resentful, at how normal everything looked in the lamplight. The women stood waiting at the foot of my bunk, for at this point there was little they could do. The curtains continued blowing about in the wind in an everyday manner, and Sasha was still absorbed in his book. Darn him! He had seemed so concerned about me earlier. . . . And then the dreadful pain would come tearing at me again.

Suddenly I realized that Sasha was speaking.

"—really extremely interesting, Edith," he was saying. He glanced up absently for a moment and turned back to the book. "Listen to this: 'How to prepare for childbirth at home.' " He began reading excerpts aloud, half to himself:

" 'Have several freshly ironed bedsheets ready, a dozen ironed towels, rubber sheeting, several delivery pads, one pound of absorbent cotton, box of sterile gauze, two enamel basins ten inches in diameter, one skein of sterile bobbin, boric acid, disinfectant, two dozen safety pins size four, two nail brushes, three nightgowns, one pair white stockings.' Hmmm . . ." He looked up and grinned off into space. "Now, who do you suppose the white stockings are for? The patient—or the nurse?"

He returned to the book and after a moment resumed reading aloud:

" 'Remove every unnecessary object from bedroom and cover furniture with sheets.' Too bad we don't have more extra sheets, Edith. 'Previously have prepared a crib for the newborn baby: a clothesbasket lined with freshly ironed blankets will do. Have a good supply of flannel wrappings, olive oil, and three hot-water bottles.' Good lord, it would take the full nine months to get these things ready! 'How to sterilize articles: Place towels, pads, and sponges in packages of six each into pillowcase, and suspend pillowcase over six inches of water in a large——' "

"Sasha!" I half screamed through clenched teeth. "Sasha, if you don't stop reading that damned silly nonsense—— If you can't contribute anything useful—— You might at least come here and let me hang onto your hand!"

Sasha's jaw dropped and he tossed the book aside and hurried over to the bed. I grabbed his hand and hung on hard, with all my strength. The pain this time was unspeakably severe, a white-hot, searing thing that climbed and climbed until I felt that I was being torn in two from head to foot, and when it left me I was soaked with perspiration and so was the sheet beneath me—and to my surprise and horror, the baby still wasn't born, and I would have it to go through all over again!

At times I realized dimly that Cenaria—or was it Antonia?—was pressing with both hands on my stomach, trying to force the baby down. At times I was conscious only of a life-and-death necessity for holding harder and harder, with more and more strength, to Sasha's hand.

Finally I was too exhausted to wrench at Sasha's hand any longer; my arm had gone numb and I felt my hand relaxing nervelessly on his. But the pain still continued without lessening, and I suddenly realized Cenaria and Antonia were praying loudly and wailing—and, close to my ear, Sasha was saying something over and over. . . .

Then the light went out, and everything was pitch-black.

"My God—the kerosene ran out! What a hell of a thing!"

It was unmistakably Sasha's voice, loud and earthy and raging, and so I concluded reluctantly that I wasn't dead, that the light really had gone out.

A roving tiger roared distantly in the jungle. . . .

Sasha struck a match, and in its glare I saw Cenaria and Antonia clearly for the first time in hours. The sudden darkness had shocked them into silence, and I found it a welcome relief. It must have shocked me, too, for I felt a momentary respite from pain.

"I'll have to get more kerosene from the rear deck!" Sasha groaned. "No, wait—there's a capibara-oil lamp in the cabinet, I think." He strode rapidly across the room and struck another match. I could hear him fumbling around, and then he gave an exclamation of satisfaction and strode back and banged the lamp onto the table beside me.

In a moment he had this old lamp lit, and while the wick smoked and the light was decidedly dimmer than kerosene and the flame flickered wildly in the wind and the oil smelled like an old shoe burning—still it was a light much brighter than a match.

Then Cenaria screamed.

"The criança!" she gasped. "The criança has arrived!"

The baby had been born while the light was out!

"Well—*do* something!" Sasha shouted in a frenzy of excitement.

The tiger roared again, sounding closer. . . .

Antonia joined Cenaria beside me, and they began rapid, deft manipulations at the foot of the bed. Sasha looked wildly about, raced across the room, and stumbled back carrying the scissors and a ball of twine.

"I congratulate the senhor!" Cenaria said suddenly. "It is a little menino—a fine boy!"

"But of course," Antonia murmured calmly. "My birth charm was for a boy!"

A thin but decidedly lusty wailing began. . . . And, close at hand on the riverbank, the rattling roar of the tiger sounded so loud that it seemed to shake the houseboat. . . .

Dawn was breaking, and the grayness in the eastern sky was taking on delicate mother-of-pearl tints when Sasha and I finally were alone with the newest addition to our family. Cenaria and Antonia had just left for their huts after getting me settled comfortably and straightening up the room.

"I told them to send Dora and Sandra back with Luiza if they were awake," Sasha said absently. He was standing beside my bed, but concentrating all his attention on his tiny, sleeping son bedded down temporarily in a cabinet drawer and nearly invisible in a nest of blankets.

I felt very drowsy and contented, and my eyes also were on the baby.

"Hello, little Sasha," I murmured fondly. "You really are little Sasha, aren't you? You took a long time coming!"

"Over five years!" Sasha added with a smile.

He bent forward to adjust a blanket a trifle. "Did you notice, Edith," he said in a pleased voice, "how much hair he's got?" He fingered his beard and mused, "This one's a regular chip off the old block."

"Now, Sasha," I protested halfheartedly, "just because both of your daughters were bald . . ." I closed my eyes for a minute and luxuriated in the simple pleasure of freedom from pain. Then I opened them suddenly to study my spouse.

"You know," I said thoughtfully, "I hardly dare have another baby. These births get progressively worse. I barely got to the hospital before Sandra was born, and Dora arrived right in the hotel—and now this! Next time I'll undoubtedly be alone and out in the jungle somewhere, astride my horse!"

Sasha chuckled. Just then the screen door opened and Sandra and Dora came in very quietly, followed by Luiza.

"Daddy, is it true?" Sandra whispered eagerly. "Do we really have a little baby brother?"

"Come here and see!" Sasha suggested with a proud smile. As if, I thought wryly, he had had the baby entirely by himself.

The girls tiptoed across the room and bent over the bundle of blankets, literally holding their breath. After a long moment they backed away and looked up with wide, shining eyes.

"Ohhhhh—he's so little!" Dora sighed ecstatically.

"He doesn't look much like any of us, though," Sandra said critically. "Does he, Daddy?"

"Now, give him time!" Sasha said indulgently. He turned to me. "How do you feel, dear? Are the children tiring you?"

"Oh, I'm enjoying this!" I said truthfully, though I did feel rather exhausted.

Seeing that neither Sasha nor I was whispering, the girls began talking in more normal tones. Apparently Luiza had spent a good part of the night telling them of tuyuyu, the big white stork who wades about in the streams and marshes, fishing, but occasionally takes time out to bring new babies. Dora had been greatly intrigued by this news and insisted on repeating the whole story to me.

"Isn't that nice?" she concluded happily. "But, Mommy, how does the tuyuyu know when the baby is ready?"

Sandra, who had been listening rather impatiently, evidently could bear it no longer, for she broke in scornfully:

"Oh, Dora, you're so dumb! That's just a fairy tale! Don't you even know that much?" She drew herself up with all the maturity of her five years, and explained with exaggerated patience:

"Dora, don't you remember how fat Queenie got before she had her puppies? Well, one night while she was asleep, they crawled right out of her stomach!"

I was somewhat dumfounded at this precocious piece of information.

Sandra regarded her puzzled little sister in a superior, exasperated way for a minute, frowned, then turned to me and concluded tolerantly:

"Mother—I guess Dora's just awfully *young!*"

CHAPTER 9

SASHA AND I WERE SAUNTERING ABOUT ON THE RIVERBANK, reveling in the beautiful countryside.

It was September, and the middle of spring, and the jungle for miles around was a carnival of brilliant color: almost a solid purple with the blooming piuva trees—a deep purple, shot here and there with the molten yellow of blossoming paratudos and the piquant white and pink of wild fruit blossoms.

Suddenly we heard a terrorized cry:

"Daddy, *help!* Daddy, it's pulling us in!"

I looked at Sasha with alarm. "It's Sandra! What in heaven's name——"

"Hurry! They're down this way, fishing!" Sasha took my arm, and we started running toward the river. We hastily descended the steep bank—and there, just below where the houseboat was moored, stood Sandra and Dora. They were both hanging grimly onto one of Sasha's heavy fishing poles, digging their heels frantically into the ground; but even as we rushed toward them they were being dragged rapidly toward the water by whatever it was they had hooked.

"Daddy! Daddy, quick help us!" Sandra shouted again as she saw us racing toward her.

283

"Oh, my! Oh, my! Oh, my!" Dora was repeating over and over.

Sasha looked relieved, seeing that their predicament was no worse than this. He quickly seized the heavy fishing pole from the children and started to give it a sharp yank. Then a surprised expression crossed his face, for the pole was nearly knocked out of his hands, and he hastily dug his own heels into the ground, bracing himself. He paused a moment then to fling a few words of advice to our daughters.

"When you catch such a big fish that it's pulling you in," he said with an amused half-smile, "the thing to do, you know, is just let go of the pole!"

"Why, Daddy, I never thought of that!" Dora looked dumfounded but pleased at the solution.

But Sandra frowned. "Oh, Daddy!" she said indignantly. "Why, then the fish would get away!"

"Sandra," I interjected with barely controlled exasperation, "would you rather get drowned?"

"Good lord!" Sasha exclaimed at that moment. "You girls must have a real monster on this line!"

And then I saw that the fishing pole was jerking about violently as whatever was hooked on the heavy line began making energetic efforts to escape. Sasha, however, started to back up the bank slowly, leaning backward and digging his heels into the sandy clay, obviously straining hard to pull ashore the girls' catch. Gradually—very gradually—he was gaining on it, dragging it in.

Both little girls were jumping up and down with excitement.

"Oh, Daddy, Daddy! We're winning!" Sandra exclaimed, her eyes shining; then, impulsively, she ran over and grasped the fishing pole too. "Here, let me do it, Daddy! Let me help, anyway!"

"Me, too, Daddy!" Dora said quickly, not to be outdone by her older sister. She scurried over and placed her little hands back of Sandra's, around the heavy butt end of the pole protruding behind Sasha.

Sasha smiled over their heads at me, amused, as both girls, with earnest, deeply intent expressions, tugged manfully at the butt of the pole, bracing themselves with their heels in the sandy ground and grunting loudly with the ostensible intensity of their exertions, as they had often heard Lauro and Rosando do.

"Watch out! Don't get hurt now," I admonished.

"Of course not! Do you think we're babies, Mother?" Sandra scoffed indignantly. She added in a slightly malicious tone, looking pointedly at Dora, "At least I'm not!"

A moment later the pole tipped up with a sudden lurch as Sasha's underwater opponent made a more violent move to escape, and the surprised Sandra and Dora were raised off the ground. Then the pole as suddenly straightened again, and Dora lost her hold and fell flat, and Sandra stumbled, and in her effort to avoid stepping on her prostrate sister she tripped and fell over her.

"Dora, why don't you leave the pole alone!" Sandra exclaimed angrily, quickly scrambling to her feet. "You're not helping Daddy! You're just getting in the way!"

"Oh, I am so helping Daddy!" Dora insisted as she continued to sit where she had fallen; tears shone under her dark eyelashes as she looked up at Sasha. "Aren't I, Daddy?"

Sasha continued backing up, pulling at the swaying, jerking pole, but he smiled at Dora.

"You were a big help, Dora," he assured her; then he looked meaningfully at me. "But I think you'd both better stand back now. I'm going to land your catch in a couple of minutes!"

Taking the hint, I moved forward and scooped little Dora up off the ground. And Sandra, with an expression of resentment, moved reluctantly back, out of Sasha's way. She looked superciliously at Dora, now standing beside me holding my hand.

"Dora's an awful nuisance at times, isn't she, Mother?" she observed.

Dora started to screw up her face, again on the verge of tears.

"Sandra!" I said reproachfully.

Just then Sasha called out elatedly: "Here he comes! We'll see him in a minute!"

I looked toward the river. For the first time since the lengthy tug of war had started the surface a short distance from shore was disturbed, but it was an odd sort of disturbance—a sort of shallow, frothless heaving of the water over a relatively large area—and yet nothing was visible of the thing that was causing it.

"That certainly doesn't act much like a fish," I observed, puzzled. "You'd think he'd be breaking the surface now, at least—if not long before!"

"Maybe it's 'n alligator!" Dora spoke up hopefully.

"You're so stupid, Dora!" Sandra scoffed out of her vastly superior knowledge. "You can see an alligator's eyes on the top of the water!"

"Stand back!" Sasha shouted abruptly from halfway up the riverbank as he continued, more rapidly now, to pull in the line.

But he spoke a moment too late.

Suddenly it seemed as though a large section of the river's surface erupted, and an ugly black, oddly flattened-out creature, larger than a man and shaped like a huge circle, was dragged, resisting, up out of the water and for a moment hung poised on the brink of the bank like an extremely hideous gargoyle. Then Sasha, as surprised as we, must have inadvertently slackened his line, for the monster abruptly dropped back flat on the river, spanking the surface with a sound like a cannon shot, splashing water all over us in bucketfuls.

Completely drenched, I gasped and grabbed the shrieking Dora. Before I could move out of range Sasha had again dragged the monstrous thing out of the water. But an instant later he stumbled, the line again slackened, and once more the huge, ugly creature flopped broadside on the river's surface with a deafening report, and more water showered us. Then Sasha shouted excitedly, "Get back, Edith! Girls, get back!" I heard Sandra shrieking, eagerly and not a bit scared, "Daddy! What is it? What is it?" And Dora was burying her face in my skirt and clutching my legs with such a terrorized grasp that I was unable to move.

Sasha finally succeeded in dragging his catch out onto the bank; and as he did so, through some muscular contraction, the horrible creature raised itself slightly off the ground and then came down again with a thumping, splatting sound, and immediately it jumped up again, tossing up a small shower of sand and pebbles as it did so. It continued jumping up and coming down hard—each leap carrying it only an inch or so above the ground—looking like some enormous, frenzied bat.

I finally managed to drag Dora out of range of the showering sand. Then I saw Sasha striding rapidly toward the monster with his spear in his hand. He stabbed several times in quick succession.

The huge thing took some time to die, alternately contracting and relaxing its wide, flat, muscular body in spasmodic convulsions, which failed, however, to lift it from the ground.

We all stood around it, staring at the horribly ugly, repulsive creature after it had finally quieted. It was about five feet across from tip to tip of its circular-shaped body, and it had what looked like two nostrils on its ugly, flattened-out head, as well as—at the other end, of course—a short pointed and barbed bony tail which, Sasha explained, it used as a stinger.

"It looks just like the pictures I've seen of devilfish!" I commented after a moment.

"A devil!" Dora, standing close beside me with her arm about my legs, looked timidly at the ugly creature and shivered expressively. "It looks just like a devil!" she gasped with awed conviction.

Sandra, who was squatting as close as possible to the creature's carcass, examining it with an ichthyologist's eye for details, looked up at her sister and laughed merrily.

"When did you ever see a devil, Dora?" she demanded.

I met Sasha's eyes, and he smiled with amusement.

"It's a close relative of the ocean devilfish," he put in hastily to forestall another squabble, "the fresh-water species. It's known as a sting ray!" He mused thoughtfully, "But I never expected to find one in our front yard!"

Soon after, Lauro and Rosando appeared, and Sasha had them drag the carcass higher up on the riverbank to a scale which he had set up there. It weighed 220 pounds. And then Sasha sliced off a portion of what he considered was edible flesh, and after giving Lauro and Rosando each a good quantity for their families he brought a smaller amount to the houseboat. The men fed the remainder of the carcass to our wild animal pets. An hour later we ate sting-ray steaks for lunch. And the meat, though coarse-grained, was surprisingly good.

After lunch it was siesta time.

During this hottest part of the day—when even the jungle itself seems to slow down, sprawling out enervated under the glaring sun—not only humans, but animals, birds, and even insects, wel-

come the chance to drowse off for a couple of hours and escape
the blistering heat. Every living thing in the jungle, I thought
ruefully, except Dora and Sandra.

I had early acquired the siesta habit from Sasha, who himself
had adopted the universal native custom when he first came to the
jungle twenty-odd years ago. As far as I was concerned, it was one
of the things that made life in the jungle endurable. And tiny
Sashinho, who was not yet three months old, still slept most of the
time. Although a nap during the heat of the day was almost a
physiological necessity, our vitality-packed Sandra and Dora never
willingly went to bed.

Today, when siesta time came, it was the same old story.

"Mother," Sandra said wheedlingly as I was herding the girls
into their bedroom, "why don't you and Daddy take your siestas,
if you want to, and Dora and I'll go out and play with the baby
ostriches for a while? We're not the slightest bit sleepy!"

"Oh yes, Mommy!" Dora caught the idea up eagerly.

The week before, Sasha had found an ostrich nest while he was
riding over the largos, and with considerable difficulty he had
caught and trussed up and brought back eight small ostriches. He
said there had been at least seventeen in the nest, but even if they
had been less lively and evasive, there would have been no point in
capturing that many.

"No indeed! The ostriches can wait until later," I said firmly.

"Oh, Moth-errr!" Sandra protested indignantly. *"Why* can't——"

"Now, Sandra," I said hastily, "you're not going to start that
again! You know very well why we all take siestas down here." I
sighed. "I'm sure none of Lauro's and Rosando's children argue
like this! They're probably all asleep already."

"Then they're little dopes," Sandra said flatly.

"They're nice, obedient children," I corrected. "Now, girls, let's
be quiet so we don't wake Sashinho." I glanced at the bassinet (a
large bread basket) and then smiled at Luiza, who had just got the
baby to sleep with some little trouble.

"He's a little dope too!" Sandra muttered resentfully, half
under her breath.

I wished heartily that Sandra had never heard the word "dope,"
for it had become her favorite expression. However, I didn't dare

288

say much, because she could have picked it up from no one but me—even though I didn't remember ever having used the word in front of her.

I decided to change tactics. "Hop into bed now, girls! Remember, poor Luiza's been working hard all morning and needs her sleep too. And when you wake up we'll all have some ice cream."

"We will?" Sandra looked somewhat mollified at this obvious bribe but still hesitated a bit sullenly beside her bed.

"Yes, we will. That's a promise!" I gave her a smile, ruffled Dora's hair, and walked out quickly, before Sandra could think up some new argument.

When I, too, was in my bunk in the living room I congratulated myself, for absolute quiet prevailed in the bedroom. I should have been suspicious, I suppose, but I wasn't.

When I awoke a couple of hours later, it was still extremely hot and I felt uncomfortable and groggy, as though I had had no rest at all. The baby was wailing fretfully. I sighed and pulled on my sandals, envying Sasha, who was still peacefully asleep; then I stood up and hurried into the bedroom.

Apparently Luiza had just gotten up, for she was standing by the bassinet, yawning and stretching. When she saw me she hastily scooped Sashinho up and cradled him in her arms, murmuring, "There, there, little one!" in a most attentive manner. Dora and Sandra were nowhere to be seen.

They often awoke before we did, and they were allowed to get up and play anywhere they pleased on the houseboat or in their little stockade; they had strict orders, of course, not to go anywhere else without our permission. So it wasn't until after Sasha had awakened and gone down-river and I had nursed the baby and then remembered my ice-cream promise that I sent Luiza after them.

She was away for some time, and when she came sauntering back from the play stockade she was alone. She strolled up the gangplank with her nose buried in a large piuva blossom and came over to me, where I sat on the shady side of the houseboat deck holding Sashinho.

"Senhora," she said blankly, "the children are not there." She extended her purple flower for me to admire and went on: "Senhora, is it not lovely? Shall I pick a large bunch and——"

"Oh, dear," I said, frowning, "I suppose they went down to the
zoo to look at the ostriches. I forgot they'd been wanting—— Luiza,
run down and get them right away, will you?"

Luiza was gone even longer this time. And she was walking a
little faster when she came back.

"Senhora," she said pleasantly, "they are not there either."

"Are you sure, Luiza?" I asked somewhat skeptically. "Did you
look all around?"

"Sim, senhora," she said placidly. "I even looked inside all the
cages. But"—she spread her hands, pink palms upward—"alas, they
were not there." She paused thoughtfully. "Senhora, what is that
small spotted animal in the far cage, the one that looks like a
tiger?"

"Luiza," I said impatiently, "where do you suppose the girls
can be? They know very well they're supposed to tell us where
they go!"

"Perhaps, senhora," Luiza suggested helpfully after a pause,
"perhaps the little girls have gone to the huts to play with the other
children." She smiled, obviously pleased at the idea, and her dark
face lit up. "Sim, I am certain they have gone to the huts. I will get
them, senhora!"

"Well, perhaps they are there," I agreed with a slight smile.
"But if they've gone without letting anyone know, I should spank
their little bottoms. . . . Yes, go ahead, Luiza; see if they're there!"

Luiza was halfway down the gangplank before I remembered
to add:

"If they are there, bring them back at once, Luiza! Be sure not
to stop and gossip with Cenaria and Antonia!"

Luiza's face fell; she turned with a rather petulant expression and
walked off stiffly.

I was beginning to be very annoyed with Sandra and Dora.
They had never been disobedient in this respect before, for Sasha
and I had many times stressed the fact that it could be dangerous
for them to wander off alone, even near the houseboat.

When Luiza once more returned without them, actually hurrying this time, I was not only annoyed but considerably alarmed.
I sent her off to get Sasha, who was a little distance down-river

with Lauro and Rosando, building a new double cage for two half-grown tiger cubs which he wanted to mate.

While she was gone I began pacing up and down on the deck, still holding Sashinho, trying to imagine where the girls could possibly be, and trying not to think of the dreadful things that could have happened to them—remembering how they had looked that morning when they were struggling with the sting ray: Dora with her blue eyes wide and intent, her sturdy legs planted well apart, and the sunlight glinting on her tangled golden hair; and Sandra with her eyes flashing and her small chin squared with boyish determination as she pulled on the fishing pole with all her strength —even wondering whether I hadn't possibly been rather harsh with Sandra about taking her siesta.

I stopped my aimless pacing often to glance anxiously about for some sign of the children, and even more often to listen for Sasha's approach. Never in all my life had I felt more wretched than I did then, alone with the baby in the harsh afternoon sunlight, on the dreadfully empty houseboat.

Abruptly Sasha arrived with Lauro and Rosando at his heels and Luiza trailing far behind them, now apparently as alarmed as I and weeping loudly, with fright or hysteria, or possibly just a desire to dramatize the situation.

With Sasha back, I felt somewhat better, for he immediately began organizing a searching party. Although I knew he himself must be equally worried, he took time out to reassure me: Sandra and Dora were self-reliant, sensible children; even if they were lost they would keep their heads; but probably they were just playing somewhere nearby, as they couldn't have gone far on foot.

To explore this last possibility first, Sasha sent Lauro, Rosando, Cenaria, Antonia, and even a few of their older children off in different directions—beyond the zoo, to the livestock stockade, into the groves of trees behind Lauro's and Rosando's huts—to look everywhere and shout the children's names. I hurriedly gave the baby to Luiza, who had instructions to remain on the houseboat in case the children should return by themselves, and myself began wildly searching in all the near-at-hand places, even in their play hut and on the houseboat. I saw Sasha peering into the dugouts and the launch, and I thought with horror of how easily the children might have fallen into the river.

Then Lauro raced up to Sasha, shouting that the little donkey was gone from the livestock stockade.

So Dora and Sandra *hadn't* gone on foot; they might be miles away by now, as they had been gone for hours! I had a dreadful, sinking feeling.

Some time ago, when Sasha had taken the children with him one day to the Miranda Estancia, they had seen, and been given rides on, a small, gentle burro. Despite the fact that they had their own riding horses, they were so taken with the absurd little donkey that Raul Nesheim, the Miranda manager, had promptly presented them with it. I had whimsically christened it Pegasus. From then on Pegasus was the girls' favorite mount, and they vied hotly with each other for the privilege of riding him.

At Sasha's orders, Lauro and Rosando brought out our horses and we saddled them hurriedly. And then, just as we were mounting, Rosando gave a sudden exclamation of dismay.

"Look, patrão! Look!" He pointed off to the right. "Patrão— I am sorry. . . ." His heavy face wore a sympathetic, almost heartbroken expression; in his shy, inarticulate way he was extremely fond of Sandra and Dora.

We all turned.

Pegasus was trotting toward us from the direction of the jungle. His short, fat body drooped with exhaustion and his reins trailed behind him. As he came nearer I could see he was lathered and streaked with sweat and covered with long red scratches. He was riderless.

"My God, Sasha!" I exclaimed, sick with horror. "Oh, my poor babies!"

"Now, Edith," Sasha said, trying to reassure me, "don't jump to conclusions. This undoubtedly looks much worse than it is! Pegasus probably——"

"Oh—stop it, Sasha!" I half screamed; then I caught my lip sharply between my teeth and after a moment forced myself to say calmly, "I'm sorry, Sasha. I'm all right. But let's get started!"

Sasha may have been as cool and unworried as he looked, but I noticed that he ground his spurs cruelly into his horse's flanks;

and the startled animal rolled back its eyes, reared, and then bounded off in great leaps. The rest of us spurred our mounts, too, and raced after him.

When we reached the edge of the jungle the four of us spread out in a fan-shaped formation and began shouting the children's names over and over. The sun was already low in the west, and the sky above the trees was blood-red. The jungle seemed strangely quiet except for our own frantic voices.

"Dora and Sandra! Dora! Sandra!" echoed back and forth mockingly among the trees. The still air was orange in the slanting sunset light, and long dark shadows stretched out from the jungle. I found myself thinking how peaceful and beautiful everything looked.

"Dora and Sandra!" "Dora . . . Sandra . . ."

Sasha began shooting his revolver into the air, hoping that the sound might guide our little daughters. Suddenly I realized I was crying—and had been for some time.

As the sun dropped lower behind the trees on the horizon, and the dark shadows shot out longer behind us, and the tropic night gathered swiftly, with all of its terrors for lost children, we began riding deep into the tangled jungle.

As we later learned, when the girls had slipped out of their bedroom after we were asleep, they had gone immediately to the zoo to see the ostriches. And from the incoherent details they told us and the knowledge we had of their individual characters, we pieced together what had happened afterward.

When they had arrived at the ostrich pen they had pressed their noses against the bars and watched the gawky little birds for a while.

"Sandra," Dora said finally, "do you think we could let them out and play with them?"

"We could," Sandra said thoughtfully, "but I don't think we'd better. Mother might not like it. Especially since we're not supposed to be here at all right now."

Dora began scuffing her foot at a pebble.

"Sandra," she said after a pause, "do you feel naughty about not being in bed?"

"No, of course not. Why should we have to go to bed in the daytime?" She shot a suspicious look at Dora. "But I suppose *you* want to go back already!"

Dora gulped and said stoutly, "No, I don't, Sandra! This—this is lots of fun."

There was a silence for a minute.

"You know, Dora," Sandra said abruptly, "I'm kind of tired of these old ostriches."

"Well, so'm I," Dora agreed gladly. "What'll we do now, Sandra?"

"You think up something," Sandra ordered. "I did it last time!"

"Well," Dora began quickly, "let's play with our bows and arrows."

"No," Sandra interrupted. "We did that yesterday! Hurry up, Dora, think of something!"

"Uh—then—let's play vaqueiros and bandits!"

"No, you dope! That's no fun with just two of us."

"Well"—Dora cast about desperately for inspiration—"let's get Pegasus and go for a ride!"

"Oh yes—let's!" Sandra agreed. "Why didn't you say that in the first place?" She added kindly, "Sometimes you get good ideas, Dora, for your age."

Dora smiled happily.

Together they managed to bridle the little donkey and get him out of the stockade. When they had both scrambled onto his bare back—while he obligingly stood still and looked back over his shoulder, eying them tolerantly—they gave him his head. And he trotted off toward the cool shade of the jungle.

The sky was blue, the sun was shining brightly, and although it was blazingly hot, the girls had never minded the heat. Pegasus jogged along slowly enough so that they could drink in the rainbow colors that flashed on every side: the purple piuvas, the yellow paratudos, the pink and blue and white ground flowers, the iridescent red, yellow, and blue plumage of the quick-darting birds in the heavy green foliage, the colorful mosaics of lazily drifting clouds of butterflies. Altogether it promised to be a lovely ride.

When they had approached the ragged edge of the jungle and

(*Above*) Edith and Sasha Siemel with their daughter Sandra in front of their hut in Descalvados and (*below*) Mrs. Siemel, with Dora and Sandra, on Pegasus.

were trotting along between scattered clumps of piuvas Dora said suddenly:

"Sandra, look over there, up in the sky, at those tiny little birds!"

Sandra shaded her eyes against the sun and squinted up, and after a moment she said scornfully, "Those aren't any tiny little birds—they're big vultures! They're just so high up they look small."

As the children watched, the vultures, the huge ungainly *urubús,* began descending rapidly.

"I bet you don't know what that means!" Sandra said importantly.

"Well—no." Dora admitted her ignorance with reluctance. "What does it mean, Sandra? Are they tired from flying so high?"

"Of course not! That just shows how little you know, Dora. They're coming down because they saw a kill. A tiger's kill!"

"Oooooh! How do you know, Sandra?" Dora asked admiringly.

"Oh," Sandra said casually, "I've heard Daddy say so lots of times." She paused as the descending vultures disappeared behind a large grove of trees about a half mile away. "You know what let's do, Dora?"

"What, Sandra?"

"Let's ride over and see if we can find them!"

Without further words Sandra began kicking her heels against the little donkey's barrel-shaped sides and slapping him with the reins.

"Come on, Pegasus! Come on!" she called excitedly. "We're going to see a real tiger's kill!"

Pegasus laid back his ears indignantly at this treatment and shot his big brown eyes reproachfully back at Sandra, but he obliged by jogging along somewhat faster. As the girls jounced up and down on his back Dora tightened her arms around Sandra's waist and hung on grimly, and Sandra drummed a tattoo with her heels on the donkey's sleek hide and began slapping still harder with the reins and shouting delightedly. And at this awkward gait they entered the grove behind which the vultures had vanished, and trotted between the close-growing trees until they finally arrived at the edge of a little clearing.

Pegasus suddenly halted and froze—trembling with fear.

And then, a hundred yards ahead in the center of the grassy little clearing, the girls again saw the vultures—big, coal-black urubús—coming down to within a few feet of the ground, avidly waiting to pounce—then hastily rising again with a clumsy flapping of their wings. And they saw the object of the vulture's attention—a dead longhorn cow. Standing over it was a tiger, gorging himself.

The girls stared, horrified.

For the sight of the tiger, in the open, feeding, was considerably different from what they had imagined it would be when they had followed the vultures to the kill. It wasn't at all like looking at the caged tigers in the zoo at home. There were no reassuring stout bars between this tiger and them. They had never before seen a live tiger outside of a cage. Even when they had gone along on hunts, their experience had been limited to seeing the skin of the dead animal after it had been brought back to camp.

The tiger raised his head and stared back at them for a moment, then returned to his feeding.

Dora uttered a choked, heartbroken cry: "That's our cow! It's Lily! He's eating Lily!"

Sandra gulped, then nodded silently.

The cow which the tiger was eating was of a solid brown color. Lily, who was unusually gentle for a longhorn cow and therefore something of a pet with the children, had been missing since yesterday; we had assumed she had strayed from her usual grazing area and wandered off toward the nearby jungle. And Lily was a solid brown color.

The vultures were still wheeling above the little clearing, hovering over the tiger and his kill, impatient for the tiger to finish his feeding and go, so they could feast on the remains. At that moment two of the big birds, apparently so driven by their voracious appetites that they momentarily threw caution to the winds, again dropped to within a few feet of the cow's carcass, their bald heads with their hooked beaks and ugly long necks thrust out hungrily. But the tiger bared his teeth in a snarl and slapped at one of them, and both of the birds hastily flapped their wings and rose into the air again.

The trembling Pegasus, as if the tiger's snarl had abruptly released him from his fear paralysis, immediately wheeled—so sud-

296

denly the girls almost tumbled from his back—and in a clumsy lope dashed back into the trees and toward the thicker jungle. The girls swung precariously on the fat little animal's back. Dora had her arms tightly about Sandra's waist, and she was crying in a quiet, frightened, uncontrollable manner. Sandra was determinedly gnawing on her lips to keep back her own tears.

"Sandra," Dora sobbed, "I'm—I'm scared!"

Sandra started to answer, but choked.

The little burro continued to lope hurriedly among the clumps of trees on the fringe of the jungle, still heading toward the deeper jungle.

A little later Dora halted her quiet sobbing long enough to ask: "Sandra"—her voice was fearful, and she tightened her arms convulsively around her older sister—"do you think the tiger is—is running after us?"

Sandra didn't answer immediately; she seemed to be having trouble with her throat.

"Course not, Dora!" she said finally. "Why would he want to eat us when he's got—Lily?"

Dora started to cry again—a low, helpless sobbing.

The fat little burro, apparently driven by the same fear that the tiger was following, had been gradually but steadily increasing the speed of his awkward lope as he progressed deeper into the jungle. Now he abruptly became panicky and plunged recklessly through the rank jungle undergrowth and ran headlong under the heavy loops of the vines hanging so thickly in the deep shadows among the trees.

The girls rocked dangerously on his back, and Sandra pulled tight on the little animal's short reins and shouted at him: "Stop! Stop it, Pegasus! *Stop!*" in as commanding a voice as she could. But the burro only became more panicky and ran even faster, plunging even more blindly among the huge, crowding trees, crashing heedlessly through clumps of giant ferns, driving ever deeper into the dark jungle. . . . And then there was that terrible moment when he plunged under a low-hanging limb, and the girls were both scraped from his back and tumbled into the underbrush!

Sandra frantically called out, "Pegasus! Pegasus, come back!" She scrambled to her feet and tried, for a few stumbling steps, to run after him, and called again, "Pegasus! Please, Pegasus, come back!" But all that answered her was the quickly fading echo of the vanished little burro's hoofbeats, smothered almost instantly in the hush of the dark, vast jungle forest.

A sob rose in Sandra's throat, and then she turned and saw that Dora was crumpled up on the ground, her face buried and her shoulders shaking with sobs. Sandra swallowed hard and quickly made her way back to her little sister.

The next four hours were a hell for the children.

Scratched by the thorn bushes through which the burro had plunged them, frightened first by the tiger and then by Pegasus's desertion, the girls were already worn out. But they stumbled on through the thick, choking vegetation beneath the enormous trees.

Sandra held Dora's hand tightly as they made their way through the undergrowth—undergrowth which seemed to reach out eagerly to clutch at them, and trip them, and scratch them, and which blocked their way, no matter in what direction they turned, as if it were alive and evil and bent on holding them there, perpetually entombed in that huge green prison.

Sandra called out repeatedly, "Pegasus . . ." and "Daddy and Mother . . ." in a strained, thin voice that traveled no more than a few feet and was quickly swallowed up in the forest's deep silence.

Dora had stopped crying, but she recurrently shook in choking, dry paroxysms of grief. She kept looking behind, to see if the tiger was following, and kept asking Sandra again and again if she honestly didn't think the tiger would come and eat them too. Sandra patiently reassured her each time, in a voice that was none too steady, that of course the tiger wouldn't eat them—because after he had eaten Lily he wouldn't be hungry any more.

Then Dora asked Sandra if they were lost, and Sandra hesitated and then replied that of course they weren't lost—that they'd just keep on walking for a while, and pretty soon Daddy and Mother would come riding into the jungle on their horses and would meet them, and then Mother and Daddy would put them up on their horses to ride in front of them, and then they would all go home together and have dinner.

For some time after that, as they continued to trudge along,

298

Sandra was silent. She apparently realized by then that they really were lost, and no doubt she remembered how many times she had heard her father say that becoming lost is the worst thing that can happen to you in the jungle.

And then both girls were startled by a sudden hoarse bellowing from a thick tangle of undergrowth nearby. When Dora started to cry fearfully again, Sandra told her it was just a little alligator, although, as a matter of fact, she wasn't sure what it had been; whatever it was remained hidden.

Some time later they heard a shrill, catlike scream not very far from them. This time Sandra, too, was frightened, for it had sounded like a puma. But she told Dora it must be a gray forest cat, because it was in the forest; and of course a gray forest cat is no bigger than a tame pussy cat.

By now Dora was stumbling and falling more and more often, even though Sandra kept holding her hand tightly; and she said she was getting awfully tired and wanted to lie down and sleep. But Sandra insisted they must keep on walking, for otherwise how could Daddy and Mother see them and find them? Then Dora began to cry again, softly, and without tears, for evidently her tears had all been used up. It was about this time, when they were both almost too exhausted to keep on their feet any longer— and Sandra, determined, nevertheless, that they shouldn't give in to their exhaustion, was half leading, half carrying her weary sister —that their most terrifying experience occurred.

They were staggering and stumbling along, so slowly and so painfully that they were just barely making progress, among huge trees from which the parasitic vines and creepers hung low in rankly leaved loops, many as thick as a small tree and some with smaller creepers entwined around them. Abruptly Sandra saw, hanging among the massive vines and blended with the foliage directly blocking their path, one naked vine trunk, immense and tapering, which even in the half darkness of the deep shadows was obviously different from the rest.

She stopped and stared. . . .

At that moment it moved—in a very unvinelike manner. As her fascinated gaze followed its dangling, dull-colored, mottled length up to a tree limb about fifteen feet above the ground, she saw, coiled around the limb, the remaining length of an enormous constrictor, as thick through its middle as a man's waist! The snake's flat, ugly head was lowered over the limb, and its cruel eyes were fixed unblinkingly, almost calculatingly, on r. Sandra stared, paralyzed with horror. And then Dora, who adn't seen the boa and who stood swaying beside her, wearily ibbing her eyes and hanging her head, began whimpering again, oftly and piteously. At the sound Sandra abruptly tore her eyes rom the monster snake and, with a firm hold on Dora's hand, wheeled and began running frantically off in the direction from which they had just come, dragging her weeping small sister behind her. She staggered and tripped over the rank underbrush and creepers, and several times fell flat with Dora, scrambling up only to fall again, until she was so exhausted and breathless, and Dora had become such a helpless dead weight from her overpowering weariness, that she couldn't move another step.

Sandra stopped unwillingly at the gnarled base of a huge tree. Dora, already only half conscious from fatigue, immediately fell into a deep sleep. But even then her little body was shaken spasmodically with shuddering sobs, and she recurrently mumbled, "Mamma." Sandra remained sitting up very straight—dry-eyed but taut and frightened—feverishly and fixedly staring into the jungle, with her little sister's head pillowed in her lap. . . .

And that was the way we found them, Sasha and I, when we plunged on foot through that last rankly growing, tangled mass of undergrowth, and Sasha swung the beam from his pocket flashlight slowly across the night-blackened forest floor. . . .

CHAPTER 10

HOLDING A STACK OF CLEAN DIAPERS ON MY ARM, I GLANCED distractedly about the cluttered hotel room, made nearly impassable by open steamer trunks, suitcases, and the boxes and bundles that were the result of our three days of hurried shopping in Rio.

Sasha was speaking over the telephone, as he had been doing almost continuously all morning. His many old friends in Rio had started calling as soon as they had heard we were in town, wishing us bon voyage and wanting to entertain us with farewell parties, though we had had to beg off on all invitations because of lack of time. Sasha was talking to Jerry Dill now—and he was practically shouting to make himself heard over the shrill chattering of Chico and Sambo and the squeals and laughter of Sandra and Dora as they raced tirelessly up and down the long hall and in and out of our room.

"—and I'll certainly appreciate it, Jerry," he bellowed resoundingly, "if you'll forward all our mail there! Yes, at least six months. Possibly a year. . . ."

I halted before one of the trunks with my armload of extra diapers and shifted Sandra's and Dora's new winter coats to make more room inside. I paused a moment to admire my handiwork, for the little coats really were handsome. I had made them of bright red wool, warmly lined, and they had hoods and cuffs of ocelot skin. In addition, I had made two little muffs of the same tawny, black-rosetted fur. The girls had been delighted; they had wanted to start wearing their new outfits right in the jungle with the thermometer at a hundred degrees.

I had turned from the trunk and was making my way through our closely piled luggage back to the bed, where Sashinho lay chortling and kicking his legs, when Sandra and Dora raced into the room again with a burst of clamorous shouts.

"Mother, you know what?" Sandra cried proudly as she stopped short with her eyes sparkling. "That man just let me run the elevator! He let me run it way up to the top of the hotel and down again!"

"Really?" I smiled with amusement at her enthusiasm. Then I added in a mildly reproving tone, "Did you ask him to let you run it, Sandra?"

"But of course, Mother!" she replied with considerable surprise. "How else would he know I wanted to?" She looked at her sister and added derisively, "Dora was afraid to!"

I shook my head at her, smiling slightly.

"I was not *so*, either!" Dora protested with hurt dignity. She tossed her head and sniffed. "I just didn't want to!"

Sandra gave a short, disbelieving laugh. But then she turned back to me, her face again alight, and quickly drew something from the pocket of her dress.

"And look, Mother"—she eagerly showed me a half dozen packages of chewing gum—"I got these in a wonderful machine downstairs! A lady showed me how to work it. All you do is put some money in it and pull a little lever, and the gum comes right out!"

I shook my head wonderingly and smiled. I was a little touched at the enormous pleasure my jungle-bred youngsters were finding in the ordinary appurtenances of civilization—things which I, at their age, and millions of other children who grew up as I did accepted so matter-of-factly. During the three days we had been in Rio they had both been awed and almost overwhelmed with the wealth of new things they were seeing for the first time—

trolley cars, tall buildings, automobiles, neon lights, and, of course, elevators and vending machines.

Sandra started for the door again, eagerly.

"I'm going down to the lobby again, Mother," she explained with a quick smile. "I want to watch all the people!"

"All right, dear," I said agreeably. "But be good, and don't go out of the hotel!"

"We won't, Mother," she said over her shoulder as she hurried out with Dora trotting closely behind. And the next moment I could hear them scampering down the hall toward the elevators.

It was *time,* I told myself, that I took my daughters to the States and let them have a taste of life outside the jungle! And we were doing just that, for in less than three hours we were sailing for New York.

In addition to its being a vacation for all of us, we had several good reasons for making the trip. It was now January 1947, and I hadn't been home for more than seven years. Naturally, I could hardly wait to see Mother and my sisters in Philadelphia again, and I was particularly anxious to have Mother get acquainted with the three grandchildren she had never seen. And Sasha thought this would be a good time to make contacts with sportsmen in the United States.

I glanced at my watch and decided I had better hurry with my packing; I could see Sasha would be of no help, as he was still on the phone.

I began rapidly gathering up pajamas and toothbrushes and stray odds and ends, and I thought that it certainly would be a relief when we were settled on our ship and safely outward-bound, for I really hadn't had one peaceful, unhurried moment since we had suddenly decided, a month ago, to make this trip.

First it had been quite a problem agreeing on what to take and what to leave behind, weeding out the non-essentials and then packing the truly mountainous array of things that were left.

Sasha had insisted on taking several of his spears and bows and arrows and machetes; dozens of tiger skins (some of which he planned on selling) and the skins of an ocelot, a capibara, a red wolf, and a puma; a tapir head; stuffed piranhas; some skulls of longhorn steers with their five-foot spread of horns; vaqueiro items such as huge roweled spurs, braided leather lariats, a brace of long-barreled antique silver-mounted pistols, and silver-trimmed saddles; several ponchos, his own deerskin leggings, and a hand-woven native hammock; a Bororo feather cloak; and our hundreds and hundreds of animal photographs and several reels of moving-picture film, as well as the cameras—all of this so that he would have a representative collection of Mato Grosso trophies to show to prospective sportsmen clients. He also had assembled some pickled specimens of rare tropic fish which he intended to present to the American Museum of Natural History in New York. All in all—and it was hardly surprising—these items, when packed, filled up twenty-nine trunks!

Dora and Sandra had lined up an almost equally impressive accumulation of their own small "treasures"—from birds' nests, odd stones and shells, to a dead armadillo and their extensive insect collection that included a tiny cage of large, lively beetles—all of which they could hardly be dissuaded from packing. There were very bitter tears when we finally convinced the children that their zoo pets would have to be left behind. Because of this we finally compromised on taking Chico and Sambo.

And so, with that crucial point settled to their satisfaction, there had been nothing to mar the girls' wild delight at the prospect of the trip, and they had run around from morning until night asking innumerable questions, planning what they would do "on the ocean" and "at Gramma's house," and relating, in a rather superior, tantalizing way, their own queer ideas of the travels and scenes and various other marvels in store for them to Lauro's and Rosando's frankly envious children.

I had gone over our clothes and reluctantly concluded that what had served admirably in the jungle would be useless in Philadelphia in the winter—and in the midst of packing I had taken time out to make the girls winter coats and some new dresses to replace the old ones that were mostly outgrown or too shabby.

Sasha, of course, had had to go on one last tiger hunt before he returned to civilization—and when he had returned had hurriedly supervised the boarding up of the screen doors and windows of the houseboat and the adding of locks before we left.

We were closing up *The River Gypsy,* in which we had stored all of the supplies and equipment we weren't taking with us. Our furniture had been covered with heavy tarpaulins to protect it from dampness while it was unused.

Rosando and his family would be staying on at our place to look after things generally and take care of our livestock and zoo animals. However, the restless Lauro, who would have been unable to endure such inactivity, was resuming his old vaqueiro life until we returned, and he was moving his family to a hut in the vaqueiros' quarters on the Miranda Estancia's grounds.

We had finally been ready to start out at dawn on a gray, drizzling day. Needless to say, the gloomy weather had hardly dampened our spirits.

Sasha and I and the three children were in the launch; Lauro was on the barge, which was piled high with Sasha's twenty-nine trunks and all of our luggage, as well as camping equipment and food for the two-day trip down-river to Porto Esperança; Rosando was at the outboard motor in the dugout, which was lashed to the barge to supply motive power.

On the bank, Cenaria and Antonia and all their children were gathered in a tight little cluster to see us off. Luiza stood a little to one side, regarding us somberly. Floridad was there, too, for she had come over from her hut at the Miranda Ranch to see us off. She stood smiling happily but with tears in her eyes, and in her arms she held her own little baby.

"Senhora," she called, "my blessings go with you! And may the Holy Mother see you back safely again before too long! I hope you will have a fine trip, with much happiness." She glanced at Dora and Sandra and added fondly, "I do not need to wish the little ones happiness, for I know they will be happy wherever they go. Good-by, Dora and Sandra—and think of your Floridad sometimes!"

"Oh, we will, we will!" they chorused back. "Oh, Floridad, why can't you come with us?"

Then Cenaria had called, "Senhora and meninas, please do not forget to wear the good-luck charms!"

And then everyone had choked up, and there was a hasty chorus of good-bys and wishes for good fortune and happiness, and the children on the bank had jumped up and down, waving and shouting to Sandra and Dora, who were jumping up and down excitedly themselves in the launch beside me; Sasha had started the motor, and the scene had blurred a little before my eyes as I thought of how long we would be gone from this spot which would always be "home"—and then we had roared off, speeding through the water in a shower of spray.

The trip down-river to Porto Esperança had been uneventful, and we had said good-by to Lauro and Rosando, who started back immediately with the launch and barge to return to the Miranda Estancia.

And there, at the railhead, we had boarded an old-fashioned, cindery, chugging little train and had ridden in a rickety, wooden-seated, electric-lighted car for three days and four nights until we reached São Paulo—where we had transferred to another train and traveled, for a day, to Rio. This second train had a water cooler, to the children's delight, and they had spent most of their time running up and down the aisle for "a drink in a *paper* cup!"

Our last few minutes in Rio were every bit as hectic as I had feared they would be.

We had sent all our trunks on ahead, of course, and they would be already aboard ship when we arrived at the pier. But we still had all of our hand luggage to carry. So much, in fact, that it took the two bellboys and Sasha and me, as well, to get everything down to the lobby.

The doorman procured an ancient rattletrap taxicab for us. 'And by the time we had packed in our suitcases, the two monkeys in their traveling cases, Sasha's cameras, several bundles representing our most recent purchases in Rio clothing stores, and the large, dressy French dolls each of the girls received as a going-away present from one of Sasha's old friends, we had difficulty wedging ourselves in too. But the wheezing old vehicle made it all right.

When we set foot on the pier the girls became practically beside themselves with excitement at the enormous number of new things to see. And while Sasha was arranging to have our luggage taken aboard, their heads turned from side to side as if they were on swivels, as they stared, goggle-eyed, at the bustling, raucous water front with the dozens of big ships from all over the world being loaded or unloaded at the wharves stretching far to our right and left.

Big eight-wheeled trucks lumbered up and down over the cobblestones past our pier, piled high with cargo; a little donkey loading engine on a railroad spur nearby chugged back and forth, tooting imperiously with its high-pitched little whistle, while from first one side of the big harbor, and then the other, came the deafening baying and braying and blatting of the huge passenger liners and freighters and tankers. At the pier's entrance, more taxis, handsome open touring cars, and impressive big black limousines rolled up with a beeping of horns and stopped to disgorge their passengers, merry and noisy with holiday spirits.

Then Sasha rejoined us and we started hurrying down the pier in the wake of our porters toward our ship. Chico and Sambo, as they were carried in the traveling cases just ahead of us, looked back through their small barred windows and scolded us volubly for being thus imprisoned. Sandra and Dora, subdued to an awed silence and with starry eyes, walked hand in hand, all personal rivalries forgotten, as they continued to stare at squads of husky stevedores wrestling baggage trunks, midget electric trucks racing up and down the pier, and the throngs of people, all dressed in their traveling best, who streamed alongside us toward the ship, laughing, gaily calling to each other, effervescent and ebullient with the prospects of the trip.

And finally there was the freighter itself towering above us, its sharp bow rising proudly, its fat smokestacks and funnels shining with fresh paint, and its rail lined with passengers smiling, waving, laughing, and calling down gaily to those on the pier below who had come to see them off. And there was a gay band on the pier just below, playing fast, happy music. . . .

As we neared the gangplank, for a moment we had a clear glimpse of the magnificent huge harbor, with its brightly sunlit water, and in the distance was Sugerloaf Mountain, awesome and beautiful as it stood outlined against the deep blue and cloudless sky, high above the sprawling big city.

A pair of cocky little tugs, waiting to warp the freighter away from the pier, tootled impatiently.

And then, with the band blaring brassily, and the men and

women at the rail noisy with their shouts and laughter, and our own ship sounding its huge-voiced horn in a couple of anticipatory, throbbing, deep bass blasts, we reached the gangplank.

At each stage of the trip our little daughters had had only one thought uppermost in their minds—one indescribably wonderful, magic thing that lay ahead. And as we started up the gangplank Dora turned to me and once more asked breathlessly:

"Mother—oh, Mother—NOW will we see the snow?"